Hurricane Katrina was a d in history – for pets as well as people

Frightened animals standing on rooftops, staring out second-story windows, swimming through floodwaters, and foraging for food in the muddy streets are images seared in our memory. Now, for the first time, you'll read about this tragedy, and stories of triumph, from the pets' perspective...thanks to Terri Steuben, a gifted animal communicator and trained disaster responder for The Humane Society of the United States.

Thousands upon thousands of cats, dogs, birds, rabbits, and other animals were left behind as their tearful, desperate owners had to leave New Orleans and other cities on the Gulf Coast. Only a fraction were reunited with their owners, and most went to new homes.

Too many of those pets died, but others survived the storm and the flooding. They endured days and nights of heat, humidity, fear, and loneliness—often without food and water—until they could be rescued and taken to safety.

Terri was one of those rescuers. She went into what many described as a "war zone" and searched through the streets and houses for animals that had lived through the worst.

Terri's ability to talk telepathically to animals and her experience working with aggressive dogs made her a valuable asset to the response team. She served with firefighters, National Guard troops, veterinarians, animal control officers, and volunteers from all over the U.S. to locate and help the pets. She could connect with the traumatized animals quickly, calm them, and reassure them that they were going to be okay.

That's because Terri heard what the animals were saying: *"I'm over here behind the refrigerator!" "Is it safe to go with you?" "My head hurts." "Do you have food?" "Mom said to stay here until she gets back." "Fresh air!" "I made it!"*

It took Terri almost a decade to get to a point where she could re-live the devastation and share what the animals told her. But, as she says, "Some things are just too important to let pass."

What Animal Experts Say about Terri Steuben

"The destruction and loss along the Gulf Coast after Hurricane Katrina was overwhelming. The pets brought to our staging facility in Gonzales, Louisiana, had been through a lot emotionally, and Terri's unique skills helped calm them down. Her training and special way with animals made Terri a valuable member of our HSUS response team."
Melissa Rubin, The Humane Society of the United States

"Terri is one of the most competent responders I have worked with in more than 30 years of animal rescue. She has helped me with aggressive dogs, wild geese, and upset horses."
Brynne Van Putten, Critter Catchers

"Working at the Lamar-Dixon shelter was an unnerving and exhausting experience, but rewarding beyond belief. During our Katrina deployment, Terri was a calm, thoughtful, and rational presence. The animals' words come through her head--she has told me many details through the years about pets that she otherwise wouldn't have had any way of knowing."
Mindy Miller, Miss Kitty's Rescue

"Terri has a unique way of sensing and explaining why animals behave the way they do."
Julie Johnson, Society for the Prevention of Cruelty to Animals / City of Bakersfield Animal Care Center

"I was skeptical when I first met Terri, but I have seen her set up a dialog with animals. She's not an entertainer or carnival-type communicator, she's the real deal. In a crisis, she uses her shorthand and gets the pets to respond right away. Terri can calm dogs that others can't. Her visualization ability allows her to see a better outcome, and they immediately drop their stress."
Joy Falk, City of Laguna Beach Animal Control

"Terri is a natural leader and the person to look to in an emergency situation. I took her course in animal disaster preparedness and response, then worked with her on hoarding cases and wildfire evacuations. She is one of the most knowledgeable people I know."
Kim Tillinghast, HSUS Disaster Animal Response Team

OTHER BOOKS BY TERRI STEUBEN

Secrets of a Pet Whisperer:
Stop Telling Your Animals to Misbehave

TAILS OF TRIUMPH
ANIMALS TELL THEIR KATRINA STORIES

A PET WHISPERER'S DIARY OF **COURAGE & SURVIVAL**

BY **Terri Steuben**
ANIMAL COMMUNICATOR

WITH **DIANA B. EASTMAN**

FOREWORD BY | THE HUMANE SOCIETY
ERIC L. SAKACH | OF THE UNITED STATES

McCOURY
PUBLISHING

Printed in the United States of America
Designed by Adrienne Sweetser

Publisher's Cataloging-in-Publication
Steuben, Terri.
  Tails of triumph : animals tell their Katrina stories :
a pet whisperer's diary of courage and survival / by
Terri Steuben, animal communicator ; with Diana B.
Eastman ; foreword by Eric L. Sakach, The Humane Society
of the United States. -- First edition.
  pages cm
  LCCN 2015908125
  ISBN-13: 978-0-9839297-1-0
  ISBN-10: 0-9839297-1-8
  ISBN-13: 978-0-9839297-2-7
  ISBN-10: 0-9839297-2-6

  1. Hurricane Katrina, 2005. 2. Animal rescue--
Louisiana--New Orleans. 3. Human-animal communication--
Louisiana--New Orleans--Anecdotes. I. Eastman, Diana
B. II. Title.

HV636 2005 .N4S74 2015   976.3'064
                                                QBI15-600113

First Edition 2015
10 9 8 7 6 5 4 3 2 1

This book is dedicated to the people and animals of Louisiana, Mississippi, and the other Gulf states, who endured great hardship when Hurricane Katrina entered their lives—and to the courageous individuals who came to their aid and did their best to help them through that terrible tragedy.

FOREWORD

By Eric L. Sakach
Senior Law Enforcement Specialist
Animal Cruelty, Rescue and Response Team
The Humane Society of the United States (HSUS)

I met Terri Steuben during an investigation into a large cockfighting ring in California. She was at an operational pre-briefing being conducted at a local sheriff's station, shortly before the execution of a search warrant by sheriff's deputies.

Because of the large number of fighting cocks present on the suspect's property, I had put in a request to our headquarters for assistance from volunteers with the HSUS National Disaster Animal Response Team (DART). The team members are people who come not only with the dedication and willingness to put in the long hours necessary to complete an assigned task, but also the knowledge, skills, and training to accomplish the job safely and humanely.

One of these people is Terri Steuben. And while all of our team members exhibit a variety of talents, Terri possesses something more—the ability to communicate with animals.

In my world, rescuing and handling animals is a regular part of the job description. We try to utilize our training and experience to communicate with all types of animals. When we first encounter animals, we're mindful of our methods of approach, our posture and body language, and our level and tone of voice. We want to gauge how the animals will react to our presence, taking into account the environment they're living in and whether they may be scared or suffering due to injuries or illness. We look for any signals conveyed by the animals, their body language, and any cautionary sounds they might (or might not) make.

When this is done correctly, the animals can be captured and handled safely and humanely with a minimum of stress all around. Our DART team members are good at that.

Early on, I noticed Terri's ability to communicate with the other responders and establish fast friendships. I also saw she had a similar way with the animals she encountered—a way of communicating that seemed to put them at ease, making capture and subsequent handling go even more smoothly.

Terri was also happy to share what she knew with others. She was someone I would welcome having on my team for any future deployments.

I had that chance in Louisiana in September 2005.

On August 25, 2005, tropical storm Katrina attained status as a Category 1 hurricane and arrived near Miami, Florida. More than a million people lost their electricity. Nine people died.

After weakening briefly, Katrina gained power over the Gulf of Mexico and was upgraded to a Category 2 hurricane. On August 26, the National Hurricane Center warned that Katrina would probably become a Category 4 once it made landfall, and that it would probably hit the highly populated Gulf Coast region near New Orleans. The HSUS alerted its National Disaster Animal Response Team.

On August 27, President George W. Bush declared a state of emergency in Louisiana and on the next day in Mississippi. In advance of Hurricane Katrina, the Louisiana Society for the Prevention of Cruelty to Animals (LASPCA) in New Orleans was able to evacuate 263 shelter animals to safety in Baton Rouge and Houston, Texas.

On August 28, Katrina was upgraded to a Category 5 hurricane. About 80 percent of the population remained in New Orleans. As residents evacuated, more and more heartbreaking stories emerged about people being forced to leave without their pets—animals were not being allowed on buses or in mass care shelters. While approximately 10,000 people took refuge in the Superdome downtown, an estimated 104,000 animals remained in New Orleans and the surrounding areas when Katrina made landfall early on the morning of August 29 as a Category 4 hurricane.

The storm didn't hit New Orleans directly, but floodwaters poured into neighborhoods after two flood-control levees were breached, and part of the Superdome's roof was torn away by the winds.

On August 30, the situation was becoming increasingly dire. Much of the city had been flooded. There was no power, no drinking water, and food supplies were scarce.

Evacuations from the Superdome to the Houston Astrodome began on August 31. It was expected that about 20,000 people would be moved and the Houston SPCA was set up to receive animals at the Astrodome. In the days that followed, there was increasing violence in New Orleans.

While the events in New Orleans received the bulk of the Katrina news coverage, the storm also devastated the Gulf Coast and parts of inland Mississippi, where I was first deployed. HSUS teams moved into that state on August 30, and animal search-and-rescue efforts there continued throughout September and into October.

On September 2, the U.S. Army Corps of Engineers estimated it could take up to 80 days to drain the floodwater from New Orleans. The Louisiana SPCA found a temporary sheltering site at the Lamar-Dixon Expo Center, an immense equestrian facility in Gonzales, 60 miles west of New Orleans.

Louisiana State University also established an animal-friendly shelter at Parker Coliseum in nearby Baton Rouge.

By September 4, rescue teams under the Louisiana SPCA were at last allowed back into New Orleans to pick up the animals left at the Superdome. About 40 animals were rescued there.

The HSUS was requested by federal and state officials to assist with animal rescues on September 6. The Louisiana SPCA transferred control of the rescue operations to HSUS teams on September 7. More than 1,000 animals were sheltered at the Lamar-Dixon facility by September 8. The Petfinder Foundation launched its Animal Emergency Response Network, sending thousands of evacuated pet owners to the Web in hopes of finding their pets at Lamar-Dixon and elsewhere.

By this time, there were more than twenty rescue teams working in New Orleans, fifteen of them in boats. On September 10, rescue teams delivered more than 700 animals to Lamar-Dixon in a single day. The facility was overwhelmed by the influx of animals—and the State of Louisiana and the owner of Lamar-Dixon threatened to close it unless animals could be moved and limits met.

On September 11, the Louisiana state veterinarian allowed transfers of pets to other states, and daily exports of animals began. An airplane flight, the first of several arranged by Madeleine Pickens, took more than 120 animals to the Marin Humane Society in California. In the days that followed, many more animals would be shipped to cooperating shelters and rescue groups in California, Florida, Texas, Ohio, and Missouri, with the proviso they be held for an agreed-upon period to allow displaced people time to reunite with their pets.

Lamar-Dixon reached its mandated limit on September 16. As a result, rescue teams were advised that, as long as an animal was confined and out of immediate danger and was not sick or injured, they should simply provide food and water, make a report on the location, and leave the animals where they were until shelter space became available.

On September 18, I was redeployed from Mississippi to Louisiana to assist then-HSUS Field Services Director Melissa Rubin, who was serving as incident commander at Lamar-Dixon. She brought me up to speed on the command structure, personnel and volunteers, facility layout, cages and pens available, veterinary services, and other operational matters. On September 22, I was assigned to take over as incident commander for Lamar-Dixon.

It was during one of my morning briefings that I noticed a familiar face among the rescue team volunteers. I'd seen Terri Steuben's name on the list of responders who had been deployed to Louisiana and was glad I had an opportunity to work with her again.

Over the next few days, it was a continuing challenge to make sure that the number of incoming animals didn't exceed the number of outgoing animals. The numbers came down. But then, we were faced with another problem. Her name was Rita. She was a hurricane too.

In anticipation of Hurricane Rita, many animals and most of the staff and volunteers had to be evacuated from Lamar-Dixon. After a meeting with emergency officials and drivers, we decided to have all of the tractor trucks and their trailers park tightly between the animal barns so they would help provide protection for the remaining animals from flying debris in the event of high winds or tornados. Personnel remaining at the facility were instructed where to take shelter should tornado sirens sound. We were reduced to a skeleton crew to take care of the remaining animals.

Rita degenerated from a Category 5 to a Category 3 hurricane and made landfall in southwestern Louisiana on September 24. While Rita caused widespread damage and more flooding across low-lying coastal communities, including New Orleans, the Lamar-Dixon facility was spared. Many of our volunteers were able to return to caring for the animals and resume rescue operations once the danger had passed.

On September 26, I briefed Dave Pauli, the incoming incident commander for Lamar-Dixon, and I returned to my work in Sacramento, California. The last animals were exported from Lamar-Dixon on October 10, and it was cleaned and closed on October 15.

Overall, more than 10,000 animals were rescued and cared for at emergency shelters set up by the HSUS, Louisiana SPCA and other groups. Reunion efforts for displaced animals continued until January 1, 2006 at the HSUS, other national organizations, and local agencies around the country that had received animals.

Katrina resulted in the largest animal rescue operation in U.S. history. What happened in Louisiana and the other Gulf states would not only have a profound effect on the survivors and responders like Terri, but it would forever change the way local, state, and federal emergency managers thought about planning for animals in future disaster events.

Katrina's silver lining was the passage of the HSUS-backed Pet Evacuation and Transportation Standards (PETS) Act in Congress and new state laws requiring attention to animals in disaster response.

Since Katrina, Terri Steuben has been deployed to assist us on several major animal fighting cases in California. I'm also happy to see my good friend at conferences and speaking engagements where we have a chance to catch up.

My wife and I were delighted to read Terri's first book, *Secrets of a Pet Whisperer: Stop Telling Your Animals to Misbehave*, and we use many of the communication tips she shared with the animals who are part of our family. After all, when it comes to communicating with animals, we can all use some help.

PREFACE

One week after Hurricane Katrina's storm surge breached the levees and flooded 80 percent of New Orleans, I received a phone call from The Humane Society of the United States, asking if I could come to Louisiana to help save the animals.

It was a call I was prepared for, thanks to a premonition I had four years earlier.

What if "The Big One" struck where I live in Southern California? What would I do after a major earthquake? How would I care for my animals? Where would we go to sleep? What would we eat and drink? These thoughts hit me out of the blue one day in 2001—and it dawned on me that I didn't have any answers.

At that moment, I decided to learn all I could about disaster preparedness and response for animals. If something happened, I wanted to be ready. I wasn't planning to go anywhere, though. Truth be told, I just hoped that being properly trained and owning the right gear would make me less afraid of earthquakes.

I lost count of the number of courses I took. I was trained and certified by the Federal Emergency Management Agency and became part of the Community Emergency Response Team (CERT) in California. I completed training with The Humane Society of the United States and started volunteering with its National Disaster Animal Response Team. I also became certified as a responder with the American Humane Association Red Star Team.

As a founding board member of the Surf City Animal Response Team, I trained others in disaster preparedness and response and developed classes in search and rescue of small pets and how to set up a temporary animal shelter. In addition, my training made me eligible to work with law enforcement officials on animal cruelty cases.

When the call to action came on September 5, 2005, I froze. "This is it. They need you at Katrina," I thought. My blood started pumping and my excitement began to build, as I talked to Christine Wolf from HSUS and made arrangements for my two-week deployment.

It wasn't until I got off the phone that I had a moment of hesitation. Would they let me use my skills as an animal communicator? Would they believe me? Or would I just be another volunteer?

I have what people call psychic gifts. I am able to talk telepathically to animals and hear what they say. I was born with this ability and it is completely natural for me. I have spent my life communicating with all kinds of creatures, great and small. For more than two decades, I have worked as a professional animal communicator, giving animals a voice and helping owners better understand the needs and wants of their pets.

Another one of my gifts is medical intuition—I can feel when and where an animal is experiencing pain. Pet owners often come to me for information they can relay to their veterinarians so their animals can get the most appropriate treatment. And an increasing number of vets contact me directly when they want another point of view.

I am also a trained Reiki master. Known as "energy therapy" or "palm healing," Reiki is a complementary and alternative medicine that originated in Japan and is designed to realign and balance the body. I use Reiki with animals to relax them, relieve their discomfort, and promote their healing.

My clients around the world know me as "The Pet Whisperer" and they respect my abilities, knowledge, and experience. Of course, I am used to skeptics. But standing there with the phone in my hand, I wondered what the other disaster responders in New Orleans would think.

I shook off any more negative thoughts. I knew that being recruited was a good sign—and I felt deep inside me that this was something I was meant to do.

When I got to Louisiana a week later, I became part a massive and heroic effort to find and rescue tens of thousands of pets and try to reunite them with their owners.

I worked alongside many talented and dedicated volunteers from all over the U.S. and Canada, as well as military personnel, firefighters, and other emergency responders. The people I describe in this book are all real, although I have changed some of the names to protect their privacy. Today, ten years later, I remain in awe of their commitment and sacrifice.

My special handling skills and experience with abused and aggressive animals only partially prepared me for what I encountered in New Orleans.

While Louisiana had a 1984 law on the books against dog fighting, enforcement generally had been lax. However, in the spring of 2005, Louisiana state police, working the Louisiana Society for the Prevention of Cruelty to Animals, broke up three major dog-fighting operations, including one of the largest pit bull breeding and training operations in the country. These raids sent shock waves through the dog-fighting world, so that when Hurricane Katrina hit in August, owners just abandoned many of the fighting dogs and their training, or bait, dogs and left them to the elements.

You will read the stories of these fighting dogs' fight for life, as well as the stories of beloved pets that almost drowned in the floodwaters, then endured weeks with little or no food and water, waiting for their families to come back home.

In this book, the animals finally speak. They describe their heroic ordeals, in their own words. I have done my best to relay exactly what they said to me and how they said it. You will notice that some pets use different words and have bigger vocabularies than others—oftentimes this mirrors how their owners speak. To make for easier reading, *"My telepathic conversations with dogs, cats, horses, and other animals are written in italics and set off by quotation marks."*

I have also included a photo gallery at the end of the book. While we didn't have time to take many pictures of our work in the field and at the shelter, I have been able to assemble some snapshots to give you an idea of how things looked. They show the condition of the streets and homes as well as some of pets we saved and some of the responders who rescued and cared for them.

I am proud to be able to share the animals' stories of determination and survival. I only wish I could have done more for more of them. I witnessed their joy and triumph, but I also witnessed much pain and suffering. For a long time, I was unable to write about my experiences in Louisiana.

But some things are just too important to let pass.

CHAPTER ONE

Tuesday, September 13, 2005

At 5:30 a.m., I was at the Los Angeles International Airport, waiting to take off on Delta Flight 744. My bags were stowed in the luggage compartment and my boots were on. I was ready to go to Katrina. I had a connection through Atlanta to Baton Rouge, the closest airport to the Lamar-Dixon Expo Center, a 103-acre equestrian facility an hour away from New Orleans, where The Humane Society of the United States had a command post and animal shelter.

As I sat on the plane, I wondered if the other passengers guessed where I was headed. I hadn't thought about how dangerous this trip could be until that moment. I had some fear of the unknown while I was packing, but now I remembered the Katrina coverage I'd seen on TV. I tried to picture what it would really be like in the disaster area.

Little did I know all that would happen to me during the next two weeks!

When I arrived in Atlanta, I asked for directions to my departure gate. The man at the Delta information booth looked at me a little funny and said, "You sure you know where you're going, miss? Most people are flying out, unless they are going there to help."

I told him I was deploying with The Humane Society of the United States.

"There's been several of you coming through here the last couple of weeks," he said. "You people are the best in the world. May God be with you. Thank you for your help."

I thanked him and went to my departure gate. Most of the other people there had on boots like mine and looked like they were headed for some kind of deployment. No one was very chatty, and I could feel the air had changed. I got a strong sense of determination from those around me.

The flight to Baton Rouge was an hour and a half. It must have been interesting for people to see my 5-foot, 4-inch frame carrying two big duffle bags on my back as I headed for the taxi stand. One man offered to help me at the luggage drop-off and realized he couldn't lift my bag. The taxi driver put my bags in the trunk and couldn't believe I had carried them.

When I told him my destination, he said, "Really?"

"Yes, HSUS. Can you take me there?"

"I know where it is, but it's about a 45-minute drive."

"The only way I'm going to get there is if you take me."

About 6:00 p.m., we arrived in Gonzales, the small town where the Lamar-Dixon equestrian center is located. The driver told me there was a human side and an animal side at the center. The human side was for people who had to evacuate from New Orleans, and HSUS was running the other side.

There was a large entrance to what looked like a fairgrounds, where you would expect to see horses. At the gate there was a table with a woman wearing an HSUS t-shirt, and I knew I was in the right place.

I walked up and saw it was Inga Gibson from HSUS in Seattle, who I had met during disaster training sessions the year before. Recognizing me, she said, "Terri, I'm so glad you're here! Let's get you settled, and then you can start later tonight. They come back with the animals for intake at around eight o'clock, and we have about an hour and a half to get them all checked in before it gets dark."

I put my bags in her spay/neuter van, a large two-seat cargo van with side and rear doors, and Inga drove me through the site. I saw the large arena buildings that were serving as staging areas for law enforcement and the power company and eight huge horse barns in a long row. As we passed them, she explained HSUS was renting six of the barns for its shelter operation—an area that would hold 2,000 animals of all sizes and species.

I learned the veterinarians were in Barn One, along with the cats, some snakes, and other small animals. The dogs were housed in Barns Two, Four, and Five. There were horses in Barn Three as well as Barn Six, which also had goats, pigs, and the larger animals. The birds and rabbits were in the ladies restroom across from Barn Three, where it was quiet and had air conditioning—they will die if they have too much stress.

Inga said the donated supplies were kept along the sides of Barns Two and Three, and if I needed anything to help myself. Check-in for new animals was set up at the front of Barn Five, and the bathing station was in the back of that barn.

As we went by the last barn, we had driven at least a quarter mile. Inga said, "You'll definitely get your exercise while you're here."

Next she pointed out the showers and said, "I recommend taking them at night—warmer water."

We continued on. I saw a few motorhomes and fifth-wheels on our left, and then a few tents.

"You can put up your tent here if you like, or I can show you where it's quiet," she said. She took me all the way to the far end of the complex, where there was one dome tent near a water tower. "This is my tent. You can set up your stuff next to mine. Some of those motorhomes have generators and are a little noisy for sleeping."

"I know you're busy at the front," I said. "So I'll set up. Should I head back your way?"

"Yes. Walk the way we came. There's no short cut. It's about three-quarters of a mile back. Welcome to Lamar-Dixon, and thanks for coming. As you can see, we really need the help."

My pup tent had just enough room for me and my bags. It

took me about an hour to get set up. The ground was moist, so I was glad I had brought a tarp to put under my tent and another over the top to keep the dew from soaking through at night. I laid my bags end-to-end like a second person on one side and had enough room for my sleeping bag on the other. I thought it was actually quite nice when I lay down to try out what would be my home for the next two weeks.

I walked back to the front table to meet Inga, and began to see some SUVs and trucks headed our way.

"Here they come," she said. "Sign in and you can work at intake right across the way in Barn Five. Help Chad check in animals to make sure they're ok. The vet sees them first. If they're ok, you can take them for a bath at the back—there are people back there to do that—and then they will set up a kennel and give them food and water. Make sure that whenever you move an animal, you take the paperwork with them so we don't lose who they are and where they were found."

Unfortunately, in the days to come, I heard about a few instances when the paperwork didn't get moved with the pets. There were also cases of bored dogs eating their paperwork or ripping it into small pieces in their kennels. Changes were always being made in our procedures to adapt to these issues.

Inga yelled at Chad, "This is Terri. She can do anything you need. You might find out some interesting things about the animals as they come in. I would keep her close—you will be amazed."

Chad looked at me and said, "Hi. Glad you're here. Inga speaks highly of you. That isn't something she does often. What kind of animals do you work with?"

"All kinds. I'll do whatever you need me to do."

"What do you do?"

"I'm an animal communicator."

He smiled again and his eyebrows went up. I thought, "Ok, here we go."

"What do you mean, animal communicator?"

"I can hear what the animals say and I can feel their pain in my body. So if something is wrong with one that comes in, I can tell you."

He looked at me like I was nuts. He was reacting the way most vets did back then. So I added, "I can also handle aggressive dogs."

Chad said, "Good. Why don't you hang out with me, because I have to examine every animal that comes in. If they need medical attention, they'll have to be taken to the vets in Barn One."

Vehicles had begun to line up in the area, waiting for the pets to be unloaded. It was a slow process because there was only one vet at intake. All of the animals that came in that night were dogs, most of them pit bulls in kennels, and a lot of them had no paperwork. Inga went down the line, handing out forms to be completed with information on where the animal was found, either a house address or intersection, which would be used to help identify and reunite it with its owners.

Each animal had to be taken out of the kennel so the vet could give it an exam. The people who brought the pets to us were asked to stay so they could tell us which ones might be aggressive and whether they had seen any health issues when they picked them up. Some dogs were outright vicious, frothing at the mouth and totally pissed to be in the kennels. Others were sweet, like, "Thank God, someone cares."

As the animals were unloaded, I could tell how to handle them. I let the others know that "we need to be careful with this one" or "he looks mean, but he's fine." The vet looked at me like, "Who are you? How do you know? I must really have a nut here with me."

But time after time, the animals were exactly how I said they would be: calm, pissed off, needing to pee or poop, or just a holy terror.

Chad heard me say, "Careful with this one, he's sneaky. I would watch your face. He appears to be quick."

He gave me the "I'm the vet" look and probably thought, "I'll show you. You're a nut."

Chad ended up with a small nibble taken out of his cheek and a torn scrub shirt—not a bad tear, just enough to wake him up. The dog was smiling. He didn't like his temperature taken in the butt and had never had anyone do that to him before. Fortunately, the vet moved just at the right time or it would have been worse.

I chuckled to myself and decided to walk this dog to his bath. I thought it would be a good idea to let him know what was coming, so he would be nice to the bathers. On my way to the back of Barn Five, I had a nice chat with my new friend. I told him what they would do and how good he would feel afterward, when they put him in a new kennel and got him some water and food. He relaxed as we walked.

By the time we got to the back, he was acting like a sweet boy. The bathers wanted to make sure his paperwork was correct, because he was listed as "aggressive" and they didn't see that at all. He was even giving everyone kisses on the face!

When he saw what was going on, Chad asked me, "Is that the one you walked back?"

"Yes."

"You did that 'thing' you said you'd do, didn't you?"

"Yes, I did."

"Well, we need to keep 'aggressive' on his paperwork just in case."

"Well, maybe he just doesn't like men."

"And maybe he just doesn't like vets."

We both laughed! I think I was beginning to break the ice.

As time passed, Chad asked me what I thought about each pet that came out of a kennel. I said, "Oh, now you believe me?"

He smiled and said, "Whatever you're doing seems to work—and I only have a few shirts."

I can't begin to tell you how many aggressive animals we handled that night. They just kept coming. I talked to them while they were being seen by the vet, told them what was happening, and explained what was going to happen next: a bath, some food and water, and then rest in a clean kennel.

Some of the dogs I walked a little way down the barn, and when they calmed down, I handed them off to other volunteers. One redheaded woman said to me, "They seem so much calmer when you walk them than when others do."

I explained to her what I do, and she asked if I would talk to a black pit bull who had been here for a couple of days. I followed her to a cage with three "VERY AGGRESSIVE!" signs on it. As I approached, the dog jumped at his door, like he was coming at me. I stopped in my tracks, knowing he was stressed. I was about 4 feet from him, and I just sat down on the ground and crossed my legs. I asked the redhead to walk away and give me a few minutes with our friend.

She had told me no one was able to take him out of his kennel to go potty, give him food, or bathe him. They could only get close, toss the food in, and walk away. I could see he had pooped a couple of times in the kennel and it was smeared all around.

I sat quietly looking at the ground in front of me and said nothing for a couple of minutes. He charged his front door a couple of times, but when the redhead was out of sight, he stopped. He stood in the kennel, looking at me ignoring him. After a couple of minutes, I glanced up at him and back to the ground. He continued to look at me.

I spoke to him telepathically, just in case someone would think I was nuts. I said, *"Wow! Look how handsome you are! Are you ok?"*

I waited about a minute, looking at the ground and occasionally looking up. I said, *"Aren't you tired? Do you want to sit like me? I feel better sitting."*

Then I looked him in the eyes, smiled, and said, *"You are so brave. Can I chat with you for a bit? I know you must have been afraid in the storm. I would have been. Yet, look at you. You are so brave. You are here now, where it's safe. I know you have seen all these people walk by and take the other dogs. They take them to the back to get all that dirt and poop washed off. They walk them to a place where they can pee and poop, and then bring them back. I'm sure you have seen people clean their kennels and put in a new water dish and some food. I know you had a tough time before. But look around you, see what is here now. See what people are trying to do to make you feel better."*

He let out a big sigh, took a big breath, and sat down, looking into my eyes.

I said, *"I see you have some white on your chest. I bet that is really pretty when you're all clean."*

He smiled like only dogs can, with teeth showing and tongue wagging. His eyes even lit up. I looked him over to see if there were any cuts, because I knew no vet had seen him. I spotted something everyone had missed. *"Oh,"* I said, *"You're a beautiful girl, aren't you?"*

She looked at me as if to say, "You see me, you actually see me."

"Would you like to tell me what happened to you?"

The dog said, *"I was swimming for days and floating on things that went by. I lost my house and my people. My brother floated away on a boat with some people and I was all alone. Then the water started to go down and I could touch the muddy ground again. Then a man and a woman put me in this kennel that had food in it. They put me in the back of a truck and we drove a long way. Now here I am. How am I going to find my family? And my brother?"*

I saw her eyes tearing up and the sadness cross her face. I waited to see if she had more to tell me. She said, *"I got mad and decided that I would bite anyone who tried to touch me, so they would leave me alone and I could go home."*

"I'm so sorry all of that happened to you. Did anyone tell you what they were doing with you?"

"No! They just put me in here and drove off with me."

"Wow. Well, I just got here myself. But I can tell you what I know. I know that your home has been flooded, and the people have been moved away to get them to safety. Other people are coming back to help animals like you get to safety too. That is why they brought you here, so you could rest, sleep, get a bath, eat, and get good water. I hear the water where you live is all bad, and bad to drink."

"It wasn't good."

The redhead came slowly around the corner, stopped a good distance from me, and asked, "How is it going?"

"I think we are doing pretty well. Let me chat a little longer. I think you should let the girls at the bathing section know our friend here might want a bath. And we need to change the paperwork, because he is a she."

"I'll see who is willing to give her a bath," she said.

I turned back to my new friend and asked, *"What is your name?"*

"My name is Star—after my chest."

I saw the outline of what might be a star shape in the white patch on her chest. I asked if I could move closer to look at her and she said, *"I think that's ok. You're the first person to ask me anything."*

I moved slowly to the front of her kennel. *"How do you feel? Do you have any cuts? Or pain? Feels to me like your back is sore."*

"My back is tired from swimming for days and hanging on the floating things."

"It feels like muscle pain. But everything else feels ok to me. What do you think?"

"I feel ok, just very tired. I have been afraid to sleep, not knowing why I'm here and what's going to happen to me next."

"The best I can tell you is that you're here to be safe. This is the place where your mom and dad can come look for you. Hopefully, your brother is here somewhere too."

Star sighed again. I could feel her relief from knowing what was happening—and the thought that her brother might be nearby. She looked at me and said, *"Do you suppose you could take me to that place where I can pee?"*

My face lit up as I said, *"Sure! Let me get a leash and let people know, so we can get your kennel cleaned while you're out stretching."*

"Maybe I could take that bath too?"

"I think I can arrange that too."

"New food?"

"Yep."

"New water?"

"Absolutely! And I think we will also put your name on your paperwork."

"Really? Then people can talk to me. It's Star. Make sure you put Star."

"I will tell them."

The redhead came back from the bathing section and said only one of the bathers would do it. "Good," I said, "Star only needs one bather. Right, Star?"

The dog smiled. I told the redhead I was going to take her to go potty and that we would head to the baths. She said she would get Star a new kennel and set up the food and water.

Near her kennel was a catch pole, a long pole with a loop at one end that can snare an animal around the neck, be tightened, and then released as needed. I decided to use it, since Star didn't have a collar to hook a leash on to. I said to her, *"I have to use this as a leash. It's all I have, but I will make sure it's just tight enough so we can stay together. I want you to stay safe while we go pee and get a bath."*

She looked at the catch pole for a minute and decided she had to pee. I unlatched her kennel with my foot in front of the door, so there was no way for her to get loose. I pushed the loop end of the catch pole through the crack in the door. I said, *"You have to put your head in the loop. I will make the loop smaller so it will stay on. Then I can open the door and we can go for a walk."*

She ducked her head and put it in the loop herself. I slowly tightened it so as not to scare her. I asked, *"How's that?"*

"Let's go!"

I opened the kennel door and Star and I headed together toward the back of the barn. I talked about all the doggies she could see who had already had baths and were actually sleeping and resting peacefully. I could feel Star relax with every step. Our pace quickened as we neared the open back of the barn.

Star found the grass and her relief at releasing was evident as she relaxed even more. She took a couple of steps and sniffed the ground. It was dark now, and she was hard to see in the night.

"Star, look up at those dots in the sky. That is what you're named after, isn't it?"

"Yes. My mommy named me because she said she always felt so free when she looked at the sky."

"Your doggie mommy?"

"Yes, my real mom. She said she hoped our lives would be better than hers. She lived under the people's house and just kept having babies. She wasn't let out much. Our food was pretty bad, but we ate it because that's all there was."

We stood there for a bit, taking everything in and breathing the fresh air—humid but fresh. I could hear crickets and I said, *"Do you hear that?"*

"Yes. Mom said whenever you hear that, you are safe."

"That's right, Star. Good for you! So do you think you're safe now?"

Star thought for a moment and said, *"My mom would be glad I met you and glad I'm here and glad that the crickets say I'm safe."*

"Yes, Star, I think your mom would be very happy you made it out. Now you can even pick a new home, I imagine. What

do you think?"

"I think I'd like that bath now. But first, let me go over here. I got to poop."

I smiled as she did her business. We looked back at the lights in the barn and stopped for a few more moments to take it all in. Then I asked, *"How about that bath now?"*

"Yes, I need to look clean so mom will be proud."

"I know your mom would be proud of you. Star, you're a beautiful little girl—and smart too."

We walked to the back of the barn, where a blonde, short-haired woman had been watching us in the grass. She asked, "She ready for her bath?"

"I think so," I said. "Star, you ready?"

Star smiled. I told her I would hand her off to this lovely lady and that the redhead would come back and get her and take her to her new kennel. I said I would come by later and see that she was settled before I went to bed.

The bather said, "So you're the communicator. We need one. I was watching you two chat. Star is it? I guess she told you her name?"

I nodded.

"She has been in that kennel two days. No one has been able to get her out until now. I'm glad you did. She ok?"

"Yes, I think Star will be ok now," I replied.

"Star, you ok?" I asked the pit bull aloud. Star actually nodded her head so the bather could see her answer.

Star headed for her bath and I started walking to the front of the barn. Halfway there, I found the redhead setting up a new, clean kennel for Star. She already had the dog's name and female status on her paperwork, but mentioned that at least one "VERY AGGRESSIVE" sign had to stay on her kennel, until they saw how she would act over time.

On the way to the front gate, I come across a gal who was having a tough time with a brown pit mix. He kept spinning around in circles, going this way and that. She could hardly hold on. I said, "Can I take him for you?"

She quickly handed him off to me and walked away. I figured this guy was more than she could handle.

I stopped him in the middle of the aisle and said, *"Sit down!"* He looked at me and sat down.

"Do you know why you're here?" I asked.

"No!"

"You're here because it's safe and you can take a nap, get food and water, and be taken for a walk to potty."

"Oh! No one said that. A man just poked me in the butt."

"Really rude, I know! But he is a doctor, and he was making sure your temperature was ok."

"Well no one told me that, so I bit him."

"Oh! Do you think you can be good, now that you know what's going on?"

"Yes."

"Let me get someone to help you, and you will get a bath too, ok?"

"Ok!"

A woman came around the corner who looked like she could handle this guy. I told her to tell him what she's doing and what is going to happen to him, and she'd be ok. She said, "You're the communicator, aren't you?"

"Yes. If someone put you in a kennel, drove for an hour, and you arrived here, then someone else poked you in the butt, what would you think?"

"I see your point. Makes perfect sense. So we should just talk to them, tell them what's going on, and they will know what we are talking about?"

"Yes, pretty much. Just make sure you stay away from negative words and phrases, and you'll be fine."

As I watched them walk away I thought, "Boy, I need to talk to these people so they all don't get bit."

I rounded the corner to the front where I had left Chad a while ago. He looked up at me and said, "I thought you had called it a night."

"No, I was just helping a dog get settled."

I noticed his hand was now bandaged. He gestured to it. "This is your fault. You weren't here to warn me."

I smiled. "It would really be a good idea if you just told them you are a doctor and you need to check their temperature to make sure they're healthy."

"Really?"

"Do you want to get bit again?"

"Can't hurt."

The redhead came back to let me know that Star is really beautiful and was back in her spot, all clean and settling in for the night. I smiled and thanked her for her help. She asked if I could chat with the other volunteers and give them some pointers. She'd heard that I gave a couple of tips to a woman and it had made a big difference.

I told Chad I'd be back in a few minutes.

Waiting for me in the middle of Barn Five was a group of about ten women, smiling and curious. I told them that animals can understand the words they say. Then I grabbed one of them by her shoulders to demonstrate.

"I came up, grabbed you, and started to walk off with you. And see what you did? You stopped dead in your tracks and looked at me like, 'Who are you?' Well, that is exactly what we are doing with the dogs and other animals here.

"But instead, if I come up to you and say, 'I want to take you to show you where the restroom is' or 'I want to take you to get something to eat,' you might go with me. Right?"

The woman smiled and said, "Probably."

"Tell the animals what you are doing and what you want them to do before you do it. Tell them what you want them to do when you're doing it. Then always thank them when you are finished and tell them how good they were. Let them know the truth as you know it now—and if that changes, tell them the truth as you know it then. That's it in a nutshell."

I saw a lot of smiles and nodding heads.

Later I heard back from the redhead that things were working well for most all of those volunteers, and they were glad to know I was here with them.

I continued processing animals with Chad. I think we checked in ninety-eight—this one vicious, that one not. The last pet we saw that night was a small black poodle everyone called Snuggles because she liked being held. There was not a dry face in the area after she had kissed them all. She was so relieved to be safe and have adoring fans holding her.

It was 11:00 p.m. when Chad thanked me for my help and asked me to come back the next night at 7:00 p.m. Inga had already left, so I had no ride back to my tent. I checked on Star, who was sleeping. I whispered to her that I would come back tomorrow to see her.

It was peaceful walking past the barns. The night air was pleasant—I liked the heat, so I was actually comfortable. As I walked near Barn One, I heard a woman scream, "Hello! Hello! Can someone hand me the cotton pads and gauze? Hello! Can I have the cotton pads and gauze? Hello! Hello! Anyone out there?"

At the front of the barn was a truck-like ambulance for humans with its back doors partially open. There was a folding table set up nearby, and I saw something white on the table that looked like rolls of gauze and cotton pads. No one else was around, so I grabbed the gauze and cotton pads, thinking I could at least hand them to whoever the voice was attached to.

As I opened the doors, I saw three people standing in the back of the truck, which had been converted into a surgery unit. Around the operating table, there were two men and a petite blonde woman who said to me, "Thank God. Get up here and bring that stuff with you."

I climbed up on her side of the truck and she said, "Put the gauze and cotton pads over there. Then come around me to the other side. I need you to hold the light. I can't see. The truck light has gone out and we're in the middle of surgery."

I saw one man holding up a bag of fluids going into a black Labrador retriever. The other man appeared to be assisting the woman doing the surgery.

She said to me, "Just behind you on the bench is a flashlight. I need you to hold it up here so we can finish."

I turned around and made out in the dark what appeared to be a large, handheld flashlight about 6 inches in diameter and 10 inches long. I picked it up and turned it on, trying not to flash and blind everyone in the truck.

"Hold it above me so I can see what I'm doing," said the vet. As I turned the light upside down to face the table, I had to put my arms in the air above her. "Good thing she's shorter than I am," I thought.

As my eyes began to focus, I saw that the black Lab had a huge slice in his armpit, like someone was carving a leg off of a turkey. "Wow!" I said. "What happened to him?"

The vet explained, "He came in this way two days ago, and no one wanted to do the surgery to fix him. They were going to put him down. So I decided, since he had been through the flood and the hurricane, the least I can do is patch him up and give him a fighting chance."

She continued, "Hold the light right there so I can see. Good. That's good. Can you believe people? They wouldn't help this poor guy. I have to scrape away the edge that's started to heal so we can make a good seal. That way, when we put the two ends together, it will heal without giving him a flap of skin. Look at this—it all has to come off."

I saw she was using what looked like a small scalpel to try to peel off an edge that had grown crusty. She said, "We are going to have to make three lines of sutures to get this to close. This poor dog."

I could tell the Lab was under some kind of anesthesia or drug and was resting peacefully. The vet said, "Look at him.

This is the most peace he has probably had in a while. Poor boy, we are going to fix you up. F**k those other vets who wanted to put you down just because it was easier. F**k them."

(The f-word and other curses are favorites among many disaster responders. And I admit that, toward the end of my deployment, I used the f-bomb a few times myself.)

As I stood there holding the flashlight, the vet said, "Do we have any sharp scalpels?"

The assistant opened a package and handed one to her. I saw they were trying to keep the area sanitary and had placed a white sterile cloth over the dog. There was a hole cut in it, so all they could see was the area they were working on.

Just then a breeze started to blow and the cloth began floating in the air, constantly moving. The vet said, "Can you believe it? Finally we get a breeze to cool us off and it's screwing up our surgery! Damn these blasted scalpels. Get me something sharp. This poor dog will be waking up soon."

As she said that, I heard the Lab talking in my head and I said, "He's waking up."

The man holding the fluids said, "No, he's not."

The black Lab started to move. Everyone stopped to help hold him on the table so he wouldn't fall off. The vet asked for some more sedative. The other assistant left to get the drugs as the vet's voice followed him out the door, "And get me some sharp scalpels!"

I asked the vet, "Does this dog have a name that we know?"

"Not yet," she said, taking off the cloth to let the dog know we were all there with him.

I said aloud to the Lab, "We are all fine. We are here with you, and this nice lady is going to fix your arm. We need to give you something to let you sleep so we can finish fixing your arm. Is that ok with you?"

The black Lab actually smiled and breathed deeply, letting out a sigh of relief that we could all feel.

The vet said, "I think he understands you. Tell him we are

going to make him all better."

"We are all working to make you heal and feel better. I need you to lie still while we wait for the medication that will let you sleep. Then we will get you all fixed."

As the dog relaxed on the table, the vet suggested I turn off the flashlight to save the battery. Soon she began to yell again, "Hello. Hello. Are you out there? Where are my scalpels and meds? Hello. Hello."

For the next five minutes I kept talking to the Lab and sharing information with him. When the assistant returned with the sedative and some new, smaller scalpels, I told the dog that we were going to give him a shot so he could go to sleep while we fixed his arm. I said to him that he would be ok. He relaxed. Soon I could tell he was sedated.

"It's ok now. He's asleep," I said.

The vet looked at me and said, "Who's the doctor here?"

Smiling, I said, "You are. I can just tell when they're out."

"Well, I happen to agree. Let's start."

I repositioned my flashlight and the vet placed her cloth over the Lab. She continued to separate the dead skin so she could begin the process of suturing.

However, the breeze once again became a problem. The drape kept floating up in the air and there was no one to hold it down. The vet stopped working, grabbed the cloth, and threw it out the truck doors.

The new scalpels were working well, but they dulled quickly. She had to use three of them to get the entire edge of the wound cleared with fresh tissue so it would seal properly.

Once that was done, the vet began to use the suture gun, which also wasn't working correctly. The sutures wouldn't hold the skin together.

She ordered the assistant to get her a needle and some thread, and off he went again. And again, I turned off the light to save the battery.

The assistant returned quickly, this time before the vet

started to yell. We went right back to work and she got the first layer of stitches to hold on the whole length of the wound, which was about 12 inches long. Once she saw it was holding, she said, "Now we're cooking!"

Just a few moments passed when the flashlight started to dim and then went dark. Fortunately, I had a small flashlight in my side pocket. I pulled it out and held it in place. The vet smiled at me and said, "That's what I like to see: someone who is prepared."

She continued to stitch the second layer, closing the gaping wound even more. She stopped for a moment and said, "Do we have a bigger light?"

The guy holding the fluids remembered there was a large one in the front of the truck. He handed the bags to the assistant, went for the light, and gave it to me. All of a sudden I got a feeling and said, "He's waking up again."

The vet waited a second and our Lab started to stir. I started talking telepathically to the dog, while the vet told the assistant to go get more meds.

The assistant was gone for a little while and the vet started yelling, "Hello. Hello. Did you find my meds?"

The assistant popped his head around the door, stepped back up in the truck, and administered the shot. I told the Lab we just have a little more to go and he would be all stitched up and on his way to healing.

He went to sleep again and I held up the flashlight. The vet smiled in my direction and went back to stitching up the Lab. When she got the last layer together, she said to the assistant, "Go get me another staple gun. The outside stitch needs to be a staple to hold."

The assistant left and returned pretty quickly. The vet said to him, "You knew where the gun was. Why didn't you bring that before?"

"The lights for the barn are turned on now, so I can see."

We all smiled and she said, "Let's see if this gun works," as she held it toward the door and fired one staple out of the truck.

Ping! Out it shot.

Immediately we heard a man's voice from outside the truck. "Hey what are you doing?"

"Hello. Hello. Who are you?"

"Don't shoot! Don't shoot! I'm a vet tech. I just got here and I'm supposed to meet others," he said as he popped his head around the door.

"I'm doing surgery in here. Don't bother us and go check on the dogs in the kennels. There hasn't been anyone here for a while. The charts should be on the kennels. Check for meds first. Then food and water."

"Yes ma'am." He was off and running.

"And I'm not a ma'am. I'm the doctor." She smiled and said to us, "A newbie. This is going to be fun."

She positioned the staple gun, pulled the two ends of skin together, and stapled the whole side. She said, "Let me see the flashlight."

She took it and said, "Wow, this is heavy. You must be pretty strong to hold this up all night."

She looked at her handiwork to make sure she had the dog's wound all back together. She handed me the flashlight and said, "Almost there. Can you hang in a little longer?"

"Yes, I can."

She looked at the assistant and said, "We need the cotton pads and the gauze now."

When she finished bandaging, she sent the assistant out to look for a kennel where the dog could rest for the night. "Make sure it's a big kennel. I'll need to get in there with him in the morning."

Next she looked at me and said, "You're the best vet tech I have ever seen."

I smiled and shook my head. "No, not a tech. I'm an animal communicator."

She gave me a big hug and held on to me. "You are working

with me all the time."

"Deal."

"No wonder you knew when he was waking up. What's your name?"

"Terri Steuben."

"I'm Debra Campbell. This is Rod (the fluid holder) and Jake is the guy outside."

"Nice to meet all of you."

"Can you tell our boy we are going to carry him to his kennel so he can relax and sleep."

Jake said he had the kennel ready. Debra stepped out of the truck and asked if I could watch the Lab for a minute while she got everything ready.

I held the dog and did some Reiki so he could heal more quickly. He was still lying on a blanket that they used to stretcher him into the truck. When Debra got back, we used the blanket to take the dog to his kennel.

Debra said she would take the front end so she could watch him. We carefully lifted the dog out of the truck, and I realized that Debra was pretty strong herself.

We walked the Lab to the front of a large kennel. Debra got close to the door and decided the best way to get him in was for her to go backwards inside the kennel. Next thing I knew, she was sitting with the Lab, petting him softly, and telling him how well he did and how he would be just fine.

"Do you want any help?" I asked her.

"I think I'll just sit here for a bit and hold our boy."

I smiled. "Debra, you're a great vet!"

She laughed and said, "Tell that to the people here who think I'm a bitch. I will see you here tomorrow morning around eleven, ok?"

I laughed too. "Yes ma'am."

"There is a separate sign-in sheet here at the desk, so you don't have to go all the way to Barn Five."

"Debra, you just made my night!"

"Morning. It is morning. It's 2:00 a.m."

"Well then, good morning. What is the name of our new friend?"

"I think we should call him Lucky."

Up walked a young woman who was checking in for the night shift. She told us she had just had a really good bowl of chili made by some people who were cooking at the food tent near the back of Barn One. She said it was free for the volunteers.

I said goodbye to Debra and, as I headed off, I realized how hungry I was. The last time I had eaten was a sandwich on the airplane. At the back of Barn One, I saw a small campfire and canopy tent. A man and woman welcomed me. She stirred a big pot of chili, handed me a large bowlful, and pointed to a sling chair so I could take a load off. After I sat down, we exchanged information.

The couple, Jack and Shirley, were in their early 50s. They had arrived a week ago and were cooking for everyone. When I tasted that chili, I thought it was the best I had ever eaten. They offered another bowl and I went for it.

It was nice chatting with them, but I was tired and knew that I still had a long walk in the dark to my tent. I also knew I needed to be back at work at 11:00 a.m. So I thanked the couple and set out.

The walk was peaceful and quiet. When I got to my tent, I unzipped the front, got in, and put on my headlamp. I laid out my clothes for the next day, and took off the clothes I had on (something I had to do lying down).

I started to drift off, then I shot awake. I suddenly remembered I needed to write in my journal. I had never kept a journal before, but I thought this adventure would be a good thing to document. So I made a few notes, put my paper down, and out I went.

CHAPTER TWO

Wednesday, September 14, 2005

I woke up to the sound of birds chirping and could tell the sun was out. I looked around, pleased with myself for having gotten this small, easy-to-carry pup tent. I saw my two bags lying alongside me like another person, and knew I would have privacy in my tent.

I stretched my legs and arms. I was feeling pretty good—there was no soreness in my muscles. I looked at my watch and saw it was 9:00 a.m. "Oh my! I've slept in," I thought. Then I remembered how late I had been up and decided I was probably fine, since it was now only 7:00 a.m. in California.

I crawled out of my tent, stood up, and stretched. It was a beautiful day. I could smell the moisture in the air and it was already beginning to heat up. I grabbed my clothes and headed for the showers.

I was glad to find them empty. The building was the size of a typical campsite restroom, made of brick and painted white. I was surprised at how nice and clean it was. There were three shower stalls on the right and a row of six toilets to the left.

The showers had a little dressing area with a wooden bench for my clothes and a hook for my towel. When I turned on the water, I was delighted that it was warm, even hot. I was also surprised to see electricity by the sinks so I could use my hair dryer.

My outfit for the day—and the next two weeks—was a green t-shirt and camouflage, military-type pants with pockets on the front, back, and on the sides of the legs. I also wore a military belt that can adjust to any size and be used as a tourniquet for bleeding legs or arms, if necessary. I had brought good knee socks to wear with my black mid-calf, military lace-up boots. (I always blouse my pants in my boots. This keeps my pant legs from getting caught in anything and keeps bugs and other crawlies out of my pants.) I finished it all off with a blue baseball cap and a black-and-white Swatch watch. (I have learned to never take jewelry or items you want to keep to a disaster, because you never know what might be stolen or destroyed if you have to jump in water, walk in mud and debris, or get exposed to toxic chemicals.) I looked in the mirror above the sink and decided I was ready to go, and also that I was a bit hungry.

As I arrived back at my tent, Inga pulled up in the van. She said, "I was wondering where you were."

"I was up until three in the morning helping with surgery on a black Lab."

She asked if I wanted a ride. I told her I needed to grab a couple of things first. I picked up two turkey burgers that I had brought along from home—they would be breakfast. Then I filled my pockets with a note pad and pen, rawhide blue gloves, three pairs of latex gloves, a pocket knife, ID card, my axe (which has an extra knife concealed in the handle), ChapStick, and a small dog leash. My belt had a pocket knife, multi-tool, and flashlight satchel. My hydration backpack was already filled with water—in this heat, I wanted to make sure I'd have water. I knew it was going to be a hot day.

I hopped in the van with Inga and we drove to Barn One. I told her Debra the vet wanted me to work with her today.

"This is a great place for you. They have their own signup sheet at the front of the barn. I'll drop you off here. You know where I'll be if you need anything. Don't forget to sign out at the end of the day. We're trying to keep track of everyone and the hours they're putting in."

"I did sign out last night about 2:00 a.m. at the vet's station."
I ate my turkey burgers as I walked over to the sign-up desk. I mentioned to a man in scrubs that Debra wanted me to help out again today with the animals.

"Great, sign in here. What do you do?"

"I'm an animal communicator. My name is Terri."

"I don't believe I've met one of those before. My name is Joe. Pleased to meet you. Did Debra say when she was coming back today? I think she was here into the wee hours of the morning."

"Yes, I was with her until two. When I left, she was still here. She said she would be back about eleven o'clock. Do you know anything about the black Lab we sewed up last night?"

"Oh yeah. There's all kinds of talk about it. Between you and me, I think it was a great save. He's over there, but no one wants to touch him because he's Debra's client. So you might want to feed him and check on him. After that, if you don't mind, I have a couple of dogs and a cat I'm caring for, and I'd like you to ask them some questions."

I was surprised that Joe was open to someone like me, unlike most vets back then. So I said to him, "You seem to be ok with what I do. Why is that? The others here have walked away as soon as I introduce myself."

Joe laughed. "That's because there are only vets here right now. They are all looking for vet techs, so they can go back to being bosses instead of doing their own work. They thought you were a tech they could steal. I work with Debra back home. If she says you're ok, then you're ok. Some people here are afraid of Debra. She's a spitfire, so they tend to clear out when she arrives."

It was now about 10:00 a.m. I thanked Joe and headed over to Lucky. I asked him if I could come in his kennel and he said, *"Yes."*

As I opened the door and sat down beside him to hold him and give him a well-deserved hug, he said, *"I remember you. You talked to me last night and you told me what those people were doing to me.*"

He sighed and continued, "*Thank you! I thought they were going to kill me. All the green people* (vets wearing scrubs) *were talking about me. They said I was 'past help.' They didn't think I would make the surgery. Then the lady in the blue* (Debra) *comes up yelling at all the green people, wanting to know about me and why I hadn't been helped yet. When she found out I had been here two days and no one helped me, she started throwing things and yelling at the green people. She told them to get out of her sight and go find something to do with the vet techs—that is where they belong.*

"*She talked to me nice. She lifted my arm and saw how bad it looked. Then she got the people who had this truck and they put me in there. They were talking about taking me to some hospital. But she stopped them. She said she was going to help me because that was what kind of work she does—helps dogs like me.*"

Lucky looked up at me and gave me a kiss on the nose. As our eyes met, I just had to smile.

He kept telling me about his ordeal. "*They lifted me in the truck. It was almost dark. Then she left me there with the two men. I was lying on a table. She was gone for a long time, but I could hear her talking, and sometimes yelling. I figured she might be just going to leave me in this truck with these two men. Then one of the men goes to look for her, and I don't remember him ever coming back. So I took a nap. I was tired and my arm hurt.*

"*It seemed like I was asleep for a long time. Then the door opened on the back of the truck. It was really dark out. The woman...*"

I said, "*Her name is Debra.*"

"*Debra. I like that name. She was the one who opened the door. I think she scared the man who was with me, because he almost jumped. He told her he didn't think it was right to leave me alone up on the table. She liked that.*"

I told Lucky the man who sat with him all that time was named Rod. Lucky smiled and continued, *"He is a nice man. Debra sat with me for a while too. She talks nice to me. She said she was going to fix me up and she was sorry that the other people had made me wait so long. Then Rod came back with that other man. Next thing I knew, the three of them were in the truck. The other man poked my arm with this thing that is still in there."*

I said, *"His name is Jake, and he was trying to help keep you hydrated by giving you fluids. You see the bag up there? That's empty now. I'm sure we will get you another one very soon. The fluids will make you feel better and more hydrated."*

Lucky looked up at the empty bag and then at me. He had beautiful dark eyes. I could see that he now had real hope of being able to stay alive. We looked at each other for a long moment. Then he kissed me on the nose again and went on with his story.

"They poked me again and I fell asleep. When I woke up that time, you were right there looking at me. You told me that they were helping me and everything would be ok. I was so relieved. The way you said it, I knew I could trust you. You just feel right. I felt like I could relax. You told me what they were going to do and how they were going to do it. Then I fell asleep again (the vet gave him another shot).

"You were right there when I woke up, telling me what they were doing and that there was a little more to go. I fell asleep again—I remember I was looking in your eyes when I went to sleep. You were smiling at me. Then I woke up in this cage, and Debra was sitting here with me. She was holding me, telling me it would be all right. I didn't see you then."

I said, *"I went to get some sleep, so I could come now. I'm sorry I didn't get a chance to say good night."*

"It's ok. You're here now. Debra told me to sleep and she would check on me in the morning. She even put a lock on my kennel to keep everyone out."

I looked up at the kennel door. There was a padlock that was open on the side of the kennel. I smiled and said to Lucky, *"She wanted to make sure that you were going to be ok until she came back."*

"The man over there opened the lock this morning and gave me some water. He told me Debra would be here later to check on me."

Lucky was looking at Joe, who was now headed my way with some kibble in a dish.

"Is that for our boy?"

"Yes, it is—and I see why you and Doc Debra get along so well. You both do the same things with the dogs, crawl in their kennels and chat with them right to their faces."

"That's the best way, I've found. My friend Lucky tells me Debra locked his kennel last night. To keep him safe?"

"Yes. She woke me up at four o'clock and gave me the key. She was concerned the other vets might take him away while she was gone. We have vets from a few different states. Some of them have different ideas about what should be saved and what shouldn't."

He paused. "Debra just called me. She is on her way and she's glad you came back. Some people aren't returning. They get their fill in a day and head home."

"I guess that just means there is more for us to do."

Joe smiled. "So Lucky told you he was locked in?"

"Yes. He has quite a story about last night—all good."

"Why don't you sit with Lucky until the doc gets here. Then I'd like you to help with some other patients."

"Sure, be happy to."

"Lucky, do you think you could eat for us?" Joe asked. The Lab was smiling as he handed the bowl of kibble to me and I placed it in front of him.

"Yes. I'm very hungry."

I told Joe what Lucky told me and he said, "That's a good sign. I can bring him a little more in a couple of hours—not too fast, we want to keep it in."

As Joe walked away, I smiled to myself. To be honest, I was relieved. It appeared that I had found a place where the vets were going to accept me and what I do.

True to her word, Debra arrived at 11:00 a.m. It was obvious she had been up for a while, because she and her assistant Jake looked like they had raided a local pharmacy.

I could hear Debra coming. "Jake, put that stuff over in our section. I have to check on a few guys."

She walked to the kennel where Lucky and I were sitting. "Well, now don't you two look comfy. Don't get too comfy—I have a lot of work for you to do today!"

I smiled. "As soon as my friend finishes eating, I'm all yours."

"You just sit in there until I get back. I want to check his vitals. He needs to pee, I'm sure, and maybe more—that would be good. I don't want him out of his kennel—that's why the pee pads are in there. You might want to let him know that's what they are for, and that we can clean them while we're here so his home will stay clean. I have to check in and see some of the other dogs, then I'll be back."

"Not a problem. I'll be here."

"Ok. When you do leave the kennel, here's the lock. I want him locked in at all times, just in case someone has any ideas. This kennel is way too big, but he's not—if you know what I mean."

"Lucky told me about the lock. I'm with you."

"Ok, we're good. Be back."

When she returned a little while later, she told me to go with Joe. "He wants you to talk to a few of his clients. But don't be gone too long. I have a lot for you to do."

I went with Joe from pet to pet—dogs, cats, and a couple of birds. He asked me how they felt, if they had pain, and if there was something he might have missed. We chatted with twenty animals, and as we went, he documented the file attached to each kennel.

Some of the animals were hungry. Others just needed to understand where they were and why, and where they were going next. I told them the truth as we knew it at the time, *"These people are going to help you feel better. This place is like an open-air vet's office."*

All of the pets liked it when I said that. One dog seized the moment and exclaimed, *"About time!"*

Joe and I both laughed when I told him what the dog said.

A short time later, Joe said, "That's all we need to chat with for now."

I looked around at the other kennels in Barn One. There must have been one hundred kennels with injured pets in them. "What about the rest?"

"The ones you've talked to are the pets we have under Debra's care. The rest are under other vets, and actually are small issues. The ones that are tough are being put down, if the doc doesn't take them."

"Do you think they want me to talk to their clients?"

"We can ask, but they aren't as open minded. Besides, I think Doc Debra is going to hog you. She said she wants you back up front when we finish. So why don't you go and I'll finish up here. Thanks for your help."

When I got to the front, I saw that Debra had a pit bull on a table. It looked like she was trying to get the dog calmed down, so I quickened my pace. I walked up to the opposite side of the table. She looked at me and said, "You need to calm this guy down so we can help him. We won't have any sedatives until three this afternoon, and I don't want him to wait, if we can help it."

I took one look at the dog's feet and could tell why. All of them were bloody and raw, like he had been walking in some kind of chemical—and for a while too. I looked in the dog's eyes, smiled, and said aloud, "Hi, my name is Terri. This is Debra. She is a vet. We would like to help you with your feet. They look very sore."

He was white with cow-like brown patches on his back and stomach. His feet and legs were totally white from what I could see.

He looked at me and asked, *"What are you guys going to do to me?"*

"The doc is going to get something to make your feet feel better. I imagine she is going to wrap them up. If you can lie still while we do it, we can do it now. Otherwise, you will have to wait for drugs."

He immediately relaxed and lay still. He looked up at me and said, *"Just tell me what you're going to do and I'll be ok."*

Debra said, "I wish we knew what this was."

"Feels to me like a chemical burn. His feet are still burning, like he stepped in an acid or a chemical that would burn like an acid. I can feel his pain in my body, and that's what it feels like to me."

"Looks that way to me. Ok, we are going to treat it like it's an acid chemical," Debra said and had Jake get her some liquid.

Debra looked at me. "Don't stay in there too long (meaning in the dog's body). That's got to burn. I'm going to pour a little of this liquid on a small part of one foot. If it feels cool and soothing right away, I have the right stuff. If it burns, I'll have to get something else."

As she was about to pour, I said, "Wait a second."

She stopped and I told our little pit bull what we were going to do and how it should feel. I told him we'd stop if I felt it burn—or if he did, let me know. Then I looked up at Debra and said, "Ok."

"What did you do?"

"I had to tell him what we were going to do and how it should feel. And if he notices before I do, let me know."

She started to pour a small amount of liquid on the dog.

"Oh, that feels good!"

I told Debra, "He said that feels good. To me, it feels like it's cooling the heat."

Without looking up, she said, "Good, we have the right neutralizer. Jake, can you get me some more? Terri, keep talking to him so he will lie there and let us work."

"No problem. Just tell me what you're going to do before you do it, and then I can let him know what's happening."

Debra continued to work on his feet and I relayed the information to our patient, who stayed relaxed while the vet and her assistant put on a burn salve that felt very cooling to me. Then I helped hold the dog's legs up while they wrapped each foot with gauze. When Debra was pouring the neutralizing liquid on the last foot, we saw a flap of skin open on the side of it.

"Damn it! How does that feel to him?"

"Feels numb to me."

I asked our friend, who didn't feel anything either. He asked me what was wrong as he tried to look. I caught him and said, *"There is a tear in your skin on this foot. So we will have to do something different, I think. Let me ask the doc."*

I told Debra that the dog wasn't feeling any pain there. "I think it's numb right now."

"The chemicals have probably made it feel numb. Tell him I have to wash it out. Then I will use a local anesthesia and give him a shot in that area. I have to take off the flap of skin and then scrape the wound, so we get the chemical out and it can heal. Then we'll put on some more of the cool liquid and we can wrap it."

I told our patient. He said he thought it would be ok because he couldn't feel any pain, and would let us know if he did. I said the shot would also take away the pain, but he would have to lie very still so we could take care of his foot.

All of a sudden, I felt very thirsty. So I asked the pit bull if he was thirsty. *"Really thirsty,"* he said.

I looked at Debra and asked if he could have some water before she did the procedure. She said, "Sure. It's a local. Why don't we all get some water."

After everyone had a drink, I said it would be nice if we had some shade. We were out in the sun between Barns One and Two, and our surgery table was in the open air.

Debra said, "That's a good idea. Jake, can you get someone to figure out how to get us some shade—an umbrella or something?"

"How about an E-Z-up, one of those pointed tent-like things," I said. "They could just walk it over us."

Jake found another tech who returned with an umbrella to hold over us. Debra looked at the tech, then said to me, "Looks like your job of holding things has been passed on."

I laughed.

"Terri held an emergency vehicle flashlight over her head for at least an hour and a half last night while I did surgery."

The tech looked at her in surprise. "Do I have to hold this up that long?"

"No, I'm not that slow."

We all laughed and then went back to work. The tech did have to move the umbrella, though. Debra needed the light from the sun to see clearly so she could cut off the flap of skin. We began bandaging up the last foot, when we heard people coming up from the back of Barn One saying, "The food tent has spaghetti if anyone is hungry."

Debra looked at me and asked, "Are you hungry?"

"Yes, actually, I am. What time is it?"

"It's one o'clock. Why don't you take a break? We can finish up here. Bring me back some spaghetti."

I told our patient they were almost finished and to keep still. Then I pointed to a kennel Joe had set up and showed the little pit bull where he was going to go next. I said he'd be able to rest there.

"Could I have some more water and food too?" he asked.

I told Debra what he said, and I heard Joe say, "I'm already on it. It'll be in the kennel before he gets there."

I was looking up at Joe when the dog began to move. He was arching up, so I grabbed him and said, *"Hey there, you need to lie down."*

My face was close to his, and all of a sudden, I understood why he was arching: he wanted to give kisses! As I got him back in position, he kept licking my face and thanking all of us for helping him. I relayed his message and Debra said, "It seems to me that I'm doing all the work and you're getting all the kisses."

We both smiled, and at that moment, our pit bull headed her way with his kisses.

"I'll be back in a bit," I said and was off to the food tent. Jack and Shirley were cooking again—and boy, did it smell good! They saw me coming, and as I got to the tent, Shirley handed me a big plate of spaghetti. Jack pointed me to a red hammock chair and said, "You can sit in my chair."

As I sat down and looked up, he was right there with a fork, spoon, and napkin. "Take a load off and rest a bit."

"Thanks. Is it possible to take a plate back to the doc when I'm through?"

"Sure. I'll go fix her a plate right now. Spaghetti has a tendency to disappear quickly. I don't want you to have to wait for another batch."

The kindness of some people you meet during a disaster is always amazing. This couple had just heard about Katrina on the radio and had come and started cooking for anyone who needed food—at their own expense.

I offered to give them some money and Jack said, "No, it's our way of helping out. Tonight we are making stew. You best come back for that. My wife makes a killer stew. She's cutting up the vegetables now. It'll be ready about six, so get here any time after that."

"I look forward to it!"

It felt good to sit for a few minutes. As I got to the last of my meal, I slowed down and looked at my surroundings. To my left was a beautiful pond with grass all around it. To my right was the cooks' station with pots on two, two-burner stoves that Jack and Shirley had brought with them. Their camper was on the side of the tent, and I figured they had other things cooking inside there as well.

I took a deep breath and thought, "This really is a beautiful day. A little hot, but good."

I asked the cooks if they knew how hot it was. Jack said, "We keep trying not to look because we're cooking. But it's 102 degrees and the humidity is about 100 percent."

I finished my plate and sat for a moment longer. It had only been 20 minutes, but I felt I should get going. I thanked the cooks again and told them I couldn't wait for dinner. They handed me Debra's lunch, and I walked back to see her working on yet another dog in her open-air operating room.

She looked at me and said, "I'm really glad you're here. We have another one that I need your help with."

This latest pit bull had a terrible case of mange, a skin disease caused by parasitic mites. It was so bad that he didn't have any hair, was pink like a pig all over, and had sores oozing with puss. Debra checked him out and asked me to tell him we were going to give him a bath in a big bucket with something that would heal his wounds. Then she was going to give him a shot to make him feel better.

So it went for the next few hours. There was a dog with an open sore on her leg, the next one had a laceration on his side, and then another with a cut on her back. There were more paws to wrap up too.

At one point, a cat was brought in and immediately passed off to Debra. I could tell by the look on her face that this case was serious.

"What can you tell me about this one, Terri?"

I looked at the cat and felt immediate pain. "She's in a lot of pain, and it seems like her leg is broken."

"So now you're diagnosing too," she kidded me. "I can see

the leg is broken. How bad is the pain?"

"Really bad."

"Let's just leave her in the kennel until I can get a sedative and some pain meds. We don't need to be chasing a cat with a broken leg. We're going to have to amputate that leg or she won't survive."

While Debra went to get the drugs, I sat with the cat and started doing some Reiki on her. I spoke to my new little friend, telling her where she was and what was happening. I asked her how she broke her leg and she told me she had fallen out of a tree. She had spent several days in the tree when the water was high. As the water went down, she tried to get out of the tree to get some food (she hadn't eaten in a while) and that's when she fell.

As I continued the Reiki, the cat began to relax and put her head down. By the time Debra returned, she was almost asleep.

"What did you do?"

"I have been doing Reiki. It's a hands-on healing technique that allows the cells in the body to go where they need to. It can also help with pain. Usually I wouldn't do Reiki on a break until after it was set. But you said her leg has to be amputated, so I figured it was ok."

"Why would you normally wait?"

"Because the Reiki energy will heal the bone right where it is. So if the bone needs to be set, then doing Reiki would only make it worse. In her case, I didn't think it would hurt."

"You're right. She can use all the help she can get. Tell her I'm going to open the kennel and give her two shots—one for pain and one to help her sleep—until I can get her somewhere they can amputate that leg. We can't do it here. We don't have the right drugs."

I relayed the message, and our sleepy little cat was a real charmer as the doc opened the kennel and gave her the two shots.

"Just let her rest in there until I can get someone to help her."

Near the end of my work day with Debra, she showed me two lovely pit bulls and said, "What's wrong with them? I can't find anything."

I walked over to a cute boy and girl, and had a chat.

"They are just happy to be out of the water and on dry land—together. Nothing's wrong with them. They are brother and sister, though, so they should be kept together."

The doc put their paperwork together and sent them with a volunteer back to Barn Five.

It was now 7:00 p.m. Debra looked at me and said, "You're calling it a day. I need you back here tomorrow at eight o'clock. Ok?"

"Ok! I'm going to head for the food tent. They are supposed to have stew. You want some?"

She looked at her container of spaghetti and said, "No, I think I'll eat my lunch in a little bit."

I smiled and left for the food tent. A line of about ten people had formed, but when Jack saw me, he said, "Terri, I have your supper right over here."

Shirley was pouring a bowl just then. He handed it to me in front of everyone else, looked at the line, and said, "She was here a while ago and it wasn't ready yet."

I smiled at him.

"Your seat is over there," he said as he pointed to his red hammock chair and handed me a spoon and a fork. I took the big bowl of stew and headed for what must now be "my chair."

As I ate, the line grew longer and I looked at the other volunteers. They were chatting about how things were going. Some folks were dirty and some were not. Some seemed tough and others soft. There were all ages. Most of them were women, but there were a couple of men. I saw many nationalities. We certainly were different. Yet, I thought how we were all the same in our love for animals.

Jack brought over two Gatorades. "You look like a blue or

red kind of gal."

"Yes, both actually, when I drink it. But I'm good with my water."

"No, you're not. It's too hot. You need to replenish your fluids if you're going to keep up your pace. Take them both. You'll be surprised how much better you'll feel. There's a couple of coolers behind the tent filled with them, so make sure you drink at least one Gatorade to one water with this heat."

I twisted the cap off the red one and drank the whole thing in one tip of the bottle. "Wow, you're right. It actually tastes good—not sweet like it usually does."

"That's because you need fluids. So drink the blue one too. Then before you leave, take two with you. You look like you're going to do some more work."

"I'm supposed to take the night off, according to the doc…"

"Yeah. Yeah. I know my types, and you're not the type to rest. So take the Gatorade when you go, and make sure you drink water in between. Tomorrow they say they're going to have water here too. So get both."

"Thank you! And tell your wife this is the best stew I've ever had."

He grinned. "People think I married her because she can cook."

"That's a good reason."

"Naw, that's a bonus. Shirley's a real good person. But don't tell her I said that! I don't want her head to swell."

We laughed together as Shirley called to him, "Jack, we have more to do. Get over here. And I heard all that, so don't deny it."

"Busted! Coming, dear," Jack said as he went back to dishing up bowls of stew.

Just then, Inga came from around the side of the tent and asked me, "What are you doing after you finish?"

"Debra told me to take the night off and be back by eight tomorrow."

"So you're free for the night?"

"Yes. What did you have in mind?"

"The people who have been out all day doing search and rescue are about to come in with animals at the front. Do you want to help at intake again tonight? The vet you worked with last night is asking about you, said you were a big help."

"Sure, I can help."

"Great! He said that 'stuff you do' comes in handy."

We both laughed. I finished my stew and thanked the cooks. As I left, Jack said, "Breakfast is from six to eight. Will we see you?"

"Look forward to it."

"Terri, get some more Gatorade. You're going back to work, aren't you?"

"Yes I am. But you knew that before I did."

"You're just that kind of person, I could tell. And get some for your friend too."

Inga and I walked around the cooks' camper, took our Gatorade, and headed to intake. I hadn't really looked around Lamar-Dixon much since my arrival. I just saw the site from Inga's van the day before. As we walked the distance from Barn One to Barn Five, I asked, "Where's your van?"

"They took it to get some supplies, so we have to walk."

"That happens a lot, so we need to get used to this."

We walked in silence for a while, then she asked, "Did you sign out when you were done working with Debra?"

"Oh, no. I forgot."

"Good. You're still on the clock, so you don't have to sign back in."

I looked to my right and saw the horse ring between Barn Three and Barn Four. There was a young black horse in the ring, kicking up his feet and feeling free. There was a girl with him who was keeping him circling.

Inga said, "Looks like they are using the ring today to exercise the horses. Good. We have to pay extra for that.

HSUS is renting everything we're using. It's a huge cost."

"I can only imagine. But look at that beautiful horse having a good time. That's money well spent, I'd say."

Inga looked at me and then at the horse. "I think you're right," she said. "I have to stop at Barn Four to talk to the barn manager for a minute. Each barn has a manager, and I need to check in with everyone to make sure things are going well. Come on, I'll introduce you."

The manager of Barn Four was named Andy, and he seemed like a well-informed guy. He had short brown hair, big shoulders, and a very strong frame. I figured he was a body builder.

Andy greeted me, then looked at Inga and was all business. He told her how many more volunteers he would need for the night and how he was shorthanded again for tomorrow. Inga made notes and said, "I'll work on this and get back to you about who we can get."

We continued our walk to the vet station at the front of Barn Five to help with the incoming animals. Another vet, Mick, was there working with Chad. Mick was a middle-aged man of medium build with a little bit of a belly. What made him distinctive was his hair—he had a full head of brown curly hair, lots of arm hair, and his chest hair was sticking out of his scrubs. He looked like the kind of guy who would have to shave at least twice a day.

When Chad introduced us, Mick was checking in a dog. He glanced over his shoulder and said, "Hi. I'm busy here, Chad."

Chad smiled and said to me, "He's a little stiff around the edges, but he'll warm up to you."

"Did you tell him what I do?"

"Yes, and I told him you are really good with the aggressive dogs. But I don't think he heard me or it stuck about you being an animal communicator. He's probably what you would call a non-believer."

Mick finished with his client and was ready to hand off the

dog to someone to take him to the back for a bath. He turned, gave me the leash, and said, "Here you go. You can take him for his bath now."

I looked at Chad and said, "I can, if you like."

Chad took the leash from me and asked a woman standing near us to take the dog. "That's what I'm here to do—bathe and bed-down for the night," she said.

I looked at Chad. "I think your friend Mick might not want my help."

"Well, you can help me."

For the next half-hour, Chad and I checked in twice as many animals as Mick, who seemed to be getting more and more pissed off by the minute.

Suddenly he exploded all over Chad. (This sometimes happens in disasters—people can get pretty stressed out.) Mick thought that Chad wasn't giving complete physicals and told him he had better do them right.

Chad and I looked at each other, and he made what I thought was a pretty good decision at the time: he took a break.

"I'm going to go eat dinner. I've been here all day. I'll be back in a while."

Mick glared at him and said, "Fine, I can handle it."

Before Chad headed to the food tent, he asked me to help Mick if I could. "But don't take anything from him. If he gets grouchy, just walk away."

Mick was not in a good mood. I stood there for a while and it became apparent that he didn't need or want my help. When he finished the next dog, I decided to take him for his bath and get him settled. The woman who had taken the other dog earlier was back and asked me, "Are you sure? I thought you were supposed to stay with the vets."

"I think it will be ok," I told her. "Is that ok with you, Mick?"

"Yes, that's a very good idea. You go right ahead. I'll call you if I need you."

I took the small, brown pit bull and started our stroll to the back. Along the way, I saw the redhead who had helped me the previous night with Star and asked her how she was doing.

"I'm good. I thought you were helping the vets."

"This new vet likes to work alone. So I thought I would take this lovely boy for his bath. Is Star still here? I'd like to check in on her."

"Yes, we moved her, though. And guess what? This morning, the paperwork on her kennel that said 'aggressive' just disappeared," she said, smiling.

"Good! Is she ok?"

"Yes, she's such a delight. I've walked her twice today. After you finish this guy's bath, I'll have a kennel set up right here for him, then I'll show you where Star is."

My new friend and I headed to the back of the barn where the bathing ladies were. I could see they were all busy, but there was one empty space. "Can I give a bath here?" I asked.

"Sure, but be careful. You might end up all wet like we are," one of them told me.

"Thanks," I said. "Then I'll have a chat with my friend about shaking himself."

"Oh, that's right, you're the dog whisperer. Welcome back."

"Hello again. I saw you last night. You like being wet, I take it."

"Coolest place to be today!"

The water from the hose was, indeed, nice and cool. My new friend decided he wanted to drink before his bath. As he was drinking, I asked him if he would be kind enough to shake off after we left this area. Then I told him I would take him out to the back where he could pee.

"Ok," he said and looked at me curiously. *"You can hear me, can't you?"*

"Yes, I can. Do you want to tell me anything?"

"I'm glad to have a bath. I'm really dirty. I was floating in mud inside and outside for two days, standing on wood that would float by. Someone came and put me in their boat and

took me to a place that was dry land. I stayed there in a kennel for two days, and today I'm brought here."

"I didn't know there was a place in town that was like a shelter too. I thought this was the only one."

"It's just kennels lined up, and people brought us food and water. They didn't let us out, though, so I had poop and pee on my feet. It burns a little."

"Well, I'll take care of that. Nice clean feet for you. Right now!"

I turned the hose on his feet to get the debris off. I found the Dawn dish soap on the top of the wood fence and applied it generously to the pit bull, making sure his feet were well soaped. Before I hosed him off, I said, "You look very soapy."

The woman in the stall next to us laughed and said, "I think you used enough soap."

"I think you're right," I said, laughing. My little brown dog was all white bubbles. The hosing off continued until every spot was clean, and my friend had another drink.

"Boy, I'm thirsty."

Then, as if on cue, he started to shake. I touched him on the back and said, "Hey, we had an agreement."

He stopped and said, *"Sorry, I forgot. Can I go pee now?"*

The woman in the next stall looked amazed that he had stopped shaking. She smiled and pointed to the front of my t-shirt where I had gotten a few drops of water.

"Well, I'm not perfect," I said. And we laughed again.

I picked up my dog's leash and we headed to the back so he could relieve himself. As we rounded the corner of the bathing stalls, he said, *"Look out!"*

I knew what was coming. I stepped back around the fence, and he let go a good shake to get the water off. Then he let go again.

The woman in the other stall said, "Hey, can you teach me that?"

"Just ask them to wait."

She smiled again. "Ok, I'll try it. That sure must be something you've got!"

We headed to the back and the dog took a long pee. I asked him, *"What's your name?"*

"What do you mean?"

"My name is Terri. That is what people call me. What is your name?"

"I don't have a name. Sometimes they call me Stupid."

"Well, that's not right. You look pretty smart to me! I think you need a proper name. Would you like to pick one?"

"You mean people will call me by this name and I can have it?"

"Yes. What would you like to be called?"

"I don't know. What is a good name? Can you help me pick?"

"Let's see. You're smart, you're certainly handsome, and you look quite regal to me."

"Really?" He stood taller.

"You like to be clean. Just look how nice you are!"

"Yes, yes! That is me! So what is my name then?"

"How about Prince?"

"Really? You think that would be ok for me? It sounds like a really big name."

"It's the only name I can think of that fits you."

"I like it. Do you think people and animals will call me Prince?"

"Yes, I do. Here is what we'll do: I will put the name on your paperwork so that it will follow you from now on. And you can introduce yourself to the other animals here as Prince. Ok?"

"Ok! What do you think will happen to me? Do I have to go back? My owners just left us there. There was about fifteen of us, and they just left. They would try to make us fight. I'm not good at that. I liked all the dogs. I couldn't fight, so they hit me and put me under the house. When the water came, I chewed

through my rope and floated away on a big piece of wood."

"I'm really sorry that happened to you, Prince. You know, I think you're going to be able to pick new parents."

His eyes lit up!

"So you pick good," I said. *"Look in the mind's eye of the people who come to meet you. You know what I mean, right?"*

"Yes, I do. I watched my owner's mind, and I knew every time before he was going to hit me."

"Look into the new people's minds and pick who you like. Let them know that you are going home with them. Ok?"

"Ok! I like you, Terri."

"I like you too, Prince. Let's go find that redhead and get you something to eat."

We headed toward the front. When we got close to the middle of the barn, the redhead was waiting with a kennel set up with dishes full of food and water. Prince went right into his kennel and turned around to eat.

The redhead said, "By the way, my name is Suzanne. But everyone calls me Red."

"I'm Terri."

"You sure have a way with animals. You probably don't realize that when you come around, I can tell you're here before I see you."

"No, I didn't know that."

"It must be something in your energy. They can sense you and they all calm down. The barking gets quieter. I knew you were here about 30 minutes ago."

"That would be about right. I was up at the front."

"Oh, so you met the new vet?"

"Yes, I did."

"Everyone is staying away. It's like he's angry that he's here."

"Not a good thing at disasters."

"No," she agreed.

"He doesn't seem to want my help in the front today. He got mad at Chad, and Chad decided to go to dinner."

"Chad left? Hmmm...how about if, as we bring the pets back, you give them a little chat on the way to the bathing station. See if they are ok and tell them why they're here. It sure made a big difference for me last night."

"I'd be happy to. But first I want to say hello to Star."

"Let me go tell some of the other volunteers, so they can pass it along. I told them about you and they all want to meet you too."

"Ok. I'll wait here with Prince then."

"Prince, is it?"

"Yes, this is Prince."

"I'll add it to his paperwork. He told you his name?"

"No, he didn't have one. Seems he was at a fighting home, and they didn't have real names. So we picked a new one while we were out back."

Suddenly Prince sneezed and stood very proud, so Red could see.

"Well, he likes his name. I'll make sure that everyone knows it."

While Red was gone, Prince and I chatted about how he liked the food. He told me it was the best he had ever had and that the water tasted good. When I left him, he was a happy boy.

I headed with Red around the corner, and half way up to the front of Barn Five, I could see Star's beautiful coat. When Star saw me, she started dancing in her kennel and wagging her tail.

"Terri! Terri! Terri! You came back. Yay! Yay! Yay!"

"Hi, Star. Look at you, all pretty and still very clean."

Red told me Star had been a very good girl who liked her walks. They had moved her kennel to the side of the barn, so she could see the field and enjoy the breeze coming from that way.

I smiled at Star and said, *"You have a great new friend."*

"Can you open the kennel? I want to come out and see you."

"I think I can."

As I reached for the leash, I asked, "Red, ok with you if I

let Star out for a minute?"

"Sure. I think it's about time for her last walk of the night anyway. You can walk her and I will record it on her sheet."

The data sheets on each kennel contained whatever information we knew about the animal inside: where it was picked up (an address, intersection, building, or general area); whether it had a collar with a name on it; results of the veterinary exam; and when it was given food and water. We also documented when we walked each pet (we tried to walk all dogs at least twice a day; as time went on, this in itself was a major accomplishment) and what it did on the walk—pee, poop, or both.

"I'll write down that you're walking her, and then you can fill in the outcome," she said and giggled.

"Be happy to." I opened the kennel and was careful to make sure our guest couldn't bolt out. I reached in with the catch pole, and Star actually sat down for me so I could put the loop around her neck. She came out very gently and walked up to me. I was still kneeling, and she put her head down and burrowed into my chest. I put my arms around her and we stayed that way for a few minutes.

"I knew you would come back, because you said you would. I just want you to know I'm really glad you were here to help me and explain what was happening. I've been telling the other dogs about you. They all know now where we are and that we're safe. Thanks to you!"

I held on to Star while she was talking, then said, *"I'm just here to help and glad I can. I don't know what will happen, but right now, everyone is safe here."*

"I know."

I looked up and saw a group of about ten volunteers had gathered around us. It was one of the many times that there wasn't a dry eye in the house, mine included. I told everyone what Star had said, and more tears flowed.

"Come on, Star, let's go for a walk." I stood up, wiped my

tears, and headed her to the back of Barn Five.

When we got there, the stars were coming out again. We stood quietly for a while. I looked up and pointed, *"See, Star, look at all the stars in the sky that you're named after. What a pretty night."*

Star was looking in the direction of the campsite where the people who were evacuated from New Orleans were now living. We could hear music beginning to play and it had a nice gentle sound to it.

"What's that?"

"The humans who were evacuated have a campsite over there. It's their own area. That is their safe place. Seems they have a band tonight."

"It sounds nice."

I kneeled down beside Star again to look at the scene from her eye level. Often, I get a whole new perspective when I do this. Sure enough, from Star's view, I saw the flicker of lights from the area where the band was playing. *"Looks like a nice and peaceful night, doesn't it, Star?"*

"Yes."

Star leaned against me. As I put my arm around her shoulders and gave her a hug, she leaned into me even more. I had to catch myself because I almost lost my balance.

"Oops!" I said.

"Too hard?"

"No, I just wasn't ready for it."

I sat up higher on my knees and said, *"Ok, go."* She leaned hard against me and I leaned back. It was an experience I hope to never forget. Just me and Star in a very peaceful moment at Lamar-Dixon, out behind Barn Five.

After a while, I told Star we should get back. She had done her business when we first got there, so I got to my feet. As we arrived at the barn, Red was there and I could see tears in her eyes. She had seen us out back, and it had touched her heart. She said, "I was coming to get you, because we need your help. But I didn't want to interrupt such a lovely moment."

As we put Star in her kennel and marked her chart, Red told me about a dog that was charging his kennel and wouldn't let the vet check him out. I said I would go see if I could help.

When I arrived at the front of the barn, a crowd had gathered. About twenty people were standing in a circle around a black pit bull spinning in his kennel. The two guys who had brought him in said he started right after they got him to camp.

The men looked at me and one said, "You're the behaviorist they were talking about?"

I could see some of the women who were around when Star and I had our moment before our walk. I said, "Something like that." (I've learned, at times like this, it is better to just agree, or say as little as possible, until I can figure out what's happening with the animals.)

"Do you have a name on him?"

"No," said the man, shaking his head. He and his partner were sunburned and looked exhausted, like they had been through the ringer. "This is the last dog we have to check in, and it's not willing to comply."

"Can we get a leash on him?" I asked.

He handed me a catch pole and said, "I think you better use this, just to be safe."

I asked the crowd to make some space and ignore us. "I'm going to hook him up and take him for a walk in that field," I said, pointing behind me.

Inga, who had come over to check things out, heard what I said. She told everyone to stand back and give me room, "Go back to what you were doing and let Terri handle this."

She looked at me and said quietly, "You got this?"

"I think so. We'll see."

"Be careful."

Mick, the new vet, had been watching too. He didn't look like he was interested in placing a thermometer in the dog's butt, let alone getting anywhere near the animal.

I glanced back at the black pit bull in the kennel, trying not to look directly into his eyes. I wanted to let him know I wasn't a threat. I stopped for a moment, looked at the ground, and took a deep breath. I knew he saw me.

I said to him, *"Hi, my name is Terri. How about if you and I go for a walk? I need to attach this stiff leash to you so we can walk together. Would that be ok? It will get you out of the kennel, then you can pee."*

I took another deep breath. Inga was still trying to disperse people, so I waited until the crowd thinned out a bit more. Some of the volunteers backed up a little.

I noticed, on my second deep breath, the black pit also took a breath and released a big sigh. That was a good sign. I glanced at him again, looked into his eyes for just a moment, and said, *"You want to go for a walk?"*

"Yes, get me out of here!"

"Ok. I have to crack the door open and put this leash on. It has to go around your neck. Then I will tighten it so that it won't fall off, and we can go. Ok?"

I saw his eyes moving back and forth between me and the crowd of people. He decided I might be the better plan and said, *"Ok."*

I placed the heel of my foot by the kennel door and the toe of my shoe up on it, so when I loosened the latch, he couldn't bolt out. I slightly opened the kennel at the top of the door and slid in the fully opened, looped end of the catch pole.

I said to him, *"Your head has to go in the loop so I can tighten it and we can go."*

He looked at the loop for a moment. He looked at me, then he looked at the people—and he looked at me again.

One of the two guys said, "You gonna loop him?"

"Do you want to do this?"

"No."

"Then do you mind if I do it my way?"

"Ok," he said and backed up, then sat down in a chair that was nearby. All the while, I held the loop at the front of the kennel.

I caught Red out of the corner of my eye. "Hey Red, would you like to get a new kennel ready for our friend?"

"Sure!"

I looked at the vet and said, "Mick, do you think it might be a good idea for this guy to just rest tonight? Then he can get checked tomorrow."

I saw a smile come over Mick's face. He was not thrilled about the thought of doing an exam on this dog—and he knew that tomorrow, it would be someone else's problem.

"Yes. I think that's a good idea. We just need to document on his paperwork that he needs a vet exam, and keep him near the front."

Mick took a step closer to the kennel, and the dog charged the door. Fortunately, I had a firm hold on the door with my foot. I thought, "Really, Mick? Really?" I knew we would have a huge problem if the pit bull got out, and I would probably be sent home.

Mick immediately backed up, realizing how stupid it was to come closer. "He looks ok to go through the night. No open wounds I can see."

"Wow," I thought to myself, "We have the vet's approval." I saw the crowd of volunteers glaring at him—like they were thinking, "Stupid move."

I said aloud to the dog, "Did you hear my friend the vet say you are ok for tonight? So let's take you to pee and relax a bit. Then my friend Red will get a nice kennel set up for you."

I looked to the side so the dog could see the open field. I thought it might help him with the claustrophobia I knew he was feeling. Red nodded that she would get a kennel ready, and I looked back at my pit. I took another deep breath—and this time, the dog joined me.

"Boy, that feels better, doesn't it?"

He looked directly at me this time and said, *"You can hear me?"*

"Yes."

"Can they?"

"No."

"Good. Those men were very pushy. They dropped my kennel twice on the way to the truck. Then I'm in the back of the truck for a long ride and lots of sun. As you can see, I'm a black dog—it was hot. I'm thirsty. They didn't give me any water. Or food either. Now I'm here with you."

I watched my pit as he was telling his story and glanced once at the men who brought him in. I said, *"I'm sorry. I don't think they had any food to give you. From the looks of you, you're a big boy, so they probably had trouble carrying you to their truck. I doubt they had anything in their pickup truck to cover you. The good news is that you're out of the town with the flood, and I can hear you. If you want to, we can go for a walk. Then I can take you to a clean kennel, and you can rest tonight with the other dogs that have been brought here to be safe."*

I paused and then added, *"But you have to put your head in this loop so we can go."*

"How about some water on the walk?"

"I'll see what I can do."

I looked over to where Red had been standing, but she was gone. I was sure she was getting the kennel ready. I saw a woman who had been at our huddle before and asked her, "Can you get me three bowls with water in them, and put them out there in the field? Our guy is thirsty."

She lit up and said, "Yes, I can," as she grabbed another gal to help her.

I looked at my friend and said, *"Do you want to go for a walk and get some water? I think the crowd is wondering if we are going to stay like this all night. I would love to see the looks on their faces when we head out of here for a walk. How about you?"*

He looked at the people again, then stuck his head in the loop of the catch pole. The crowd hushed, and I let him stand there for a moment to get used to the loop around his neck. I could feel the crowd's surprise at my slowness to tighten the loop.

"I'm going to tighten this, but it will be loose enough for you to breathe. Ok?"

"Ok."

I slowly pulled the loop until it was tight enough that he couldn't back out of it, but loose enough so he didn't feel like he was being choked.

"That ok?"

"Yes."

"Ok, let's go."

The kennel door was facing Barn Four. As he came out, I needed to swing him around on the catch pole to face the opposite direction, so we could head straight to the field. When the door flung open, the crowd backed up again, not knowing what my friend would do.

"You're with me," I told him, and off we went to the field. We got about five yards into the darkness and stopped. I took another deep breath, and he did too.

"Those people are nuts," he said.

I smiled, thinking he might be right about some of them. *"Their hearts are in the right place. And the hard part is over for you."*

He took another deep breath and started sniffing the dirt. *"Ok if I pee? I've been in that hot truck for hours."*

"Sure. Help yourself."

I was upwind from him and could tell by the odor of his urine that he hadn't had any water in a while. Just as he finished, I saw a flashlight beam and the two ladies headed our way with three bowls and a gallon of water to fill them up. I said to them, "How about we just use one bowl. I think he's feeling better now."

"Are you ok with these gals standing in the area while you drink? They will stay about 10 feet away, and I will keep my eye on them."

"That would be ok."

I asked them to stand back, and he headed for the bowl.

"More, please," he said as he emptied it.

We refilled the bowl three times. *"You should stop now. We want that water to stay inside you."*

"Yes, ok. But can I have more later?"

"Yes, you can have more later, and there will be some in your new kennel too."

Suddenly the three of us saw it—a flash of white teeth, smiling in the darkness.

"Is there food too?"

"Yes, that will be in your kennel too."

"Are those men going to come and take me again?"

"No, I think you're finished with them."

"Good. I like the way it feels here."

"Of course. You should. There are lots of women here to help you. They'll take you for a walk in the morning and in the afternoon. They'll bring you food and water too."

He looked up at me and said, *"So where is the food? And I could use a nap."*

"Ok if the ladies walk with us? Because I have a feeling they'll be helping you tonight and tomorrow."

"Ok."

I explained to the women what was going on and we all walked together back toward Red, who we saw under the lights on our side of the barn.

"Look," I said aloud to the pit bull, "There's Red at your new kennel, and it looks like you have some new friends waiting to talk to you too."

The smile on the pit kept getting bigger as we got closer to his new clean kennel. He saw which one was his and went in with no fuss, no muss. I placed my foot in front of the door, while I released the loop from his neck and slid it out. Then I latched the door and said, *"You ok?"*

He looked around, still smiling, and asked, *"Is this food for me?"*

"Yes, that's for you. Help yourself."

As he ate, I asked, *"Do you have a name? I would like to add it to your paperwork."*

"Pete," he said between chews, *"It's Pete."*

I let the women know that he said his name is Pete. I looked at him and said, *"Pete, will you be ok with these people and be nice on walks?*

"Yes. Can I have more food?" His bowl was empty.

I told Red that he said he is still hungry. "Can you feed him again in a couple of hours, or before you leave? I don't think he's eaten for a while."

"Sure," she said. I let Pete know that more food would be coming in a little while, and that he might want to rest for a bit.

"I think I'll go back up front and check things out," I said to the women. As I rounded the corner in the center of Barn Five, I saw a beautiful golden retriever walking with a volunteer toward the back. I said to her, "He's a beaut. Not our typical dog of the day."

"No, he's not a pit—definitely a rare breed for us."

At that moment, I heard him say, *"My head hurts."*

I asked the woman if this dog had seen the vet.

"He just saw him, and he said he's ok."

"Just a second. Let me look at him," I said as I asked the golden retriever where his head hurt.

"Right on top, near my left ear."

As I started looking at the dog's head, it did seem fine. Then I pulled his hair up and saw there was a slice in his head that had matted over where it had bled. I showed it to the volunteer.

"Oh my," she said. "You might want to take him back up to the vet."

"I think he might have missed this. It can sometimes be hard to see blood on redheads."

"Do you want to take him? You found it."

"No. I think it might be better if you showed him. I'll be behind you a few steps."

She headed back up to the front with the retriever. I spoke

to a few dogs in their kennels as I worked my way there. All of them seemed fine, so I continued on.

As I rounded the corner at the front of the barn, the vet was looking at the retriever's head. The woman said to him, pointing at me, "There she is. She's the one who told me his head was hurt, way before she looked at him."

Mick looked over at me and asked, "How did you know he had a cut?"

"He was complaining his head hurt. So I looked at it, and there it was."

"He was complaining his head hurt—and you heard him?"

I looked Mick right in the eyes. "Yes."

Mick shook his head. "He needs to go to Barn One for stitches. Who wants to take him?"

"I will," I said.

"No. I think you should stay with me until we finish."

I smiled.

He looked at the volunteer and asked her to take the dog. I told her to ask for Doc Debra. "Tell her Terri sent this one down. She'll take care of him."

As they started toward Barn One, I could hear the retriever say, *"Thank you!"*

Mick looked at me hard and said, "I don't know what it is that you do, but maybe you should stand behind me and let me know if I miss anything."

There were about ten more dogs to process. After Mick examined each one, he looked at me—and I shook my head "yes" or "no" and told him what I was picking up. After getting my input, he finished the exam and sent the dog to the bathers.

There was one other dog that had to go to Barn One. It was a pug with mange. But Mick could see it, so all I said was, "He is really itchy."

Mick thanked me for my help. "If you're back here tomorrow night, you can help me again if you like."

"Thanks, Mick. Let's see what tomorrow brings. I think I'll

call it a night."

I enjoyed a leisurely walk toward Barn One. As I passed the barn, I heard a familiar voice. It was Doc Debra. "Hey, Terri! Can you tell this guy what we are going to do to him? Since you're the one who sent him down here. Who knew I would be getting referrals in a disaster!"

She laughed as she waved me over. I saw the retriever was now on Debra's makeshift operating table. I told him what was going to happen as Debra explained it to me.

Then the doc asked me, "What are you doing now?"

"I was headed to the showers to get ready for tomorrow."

"Good answer! Bright and early, right here. Got it?"

"Got it," I said as Debra injected a shot. It looked like she had better drugs now, because the retriever went right to sleep.

"The cat with the broken leg was taken to the vet hospital. Looks like she is going to make it too."

"How is Lucky?"

"See for yourself."

I could see the black Lab was sleeping. "No bandage?" I asked.

"He kept standing up and it slid all over. So we are just watching him and letting him rest. Tomorrow we might even let him get out of his kennel a bit."

"You mean his mansion of a kennel?"

Debra smiled. "Now go get your shower and I'll see you tomorrow."

"See you in the morning," I said as the doc started to shave the retriever's head and stitch up his wound.

I walked to my tent, got out my headlamp, and dug out my clothes for tomorrow. After a hot shower, I lay down in my tent and wrote my notes. I really couldn't believe all that had happened in just one day. I talked to so many animals that they were all becoming a blur.

I noticed it was 10:07 p.m. when I put my head on the pillow. That was the last thing I remembered until my alarm went off at 7:00 a.m.

CHAPTER THREE

Thursday September 15, 2005

Buzzzz. I shot awake at the sound of the alarm and turned it off quickly, just in case Inga next door was still sleeping. I looked out through the front of my tent and saw the morning light shining.

I grabbed my clothes for the day. I could sit up in my two-man pup tent, so dressing the top of me was pretty easy. However, it took me a few minutes to figure out how to put on pants while lying down. Next came socks and boots.

As I stepped outside, I heard Inga was up. I put on my gadget belt with my flashlight, multi-tool, and axe. (My pants still had the stuff in them from yesterday since I hadn't used any of it yet.) When I bent over to blouse my pants in my boots, Inga came out.

"Where are you headed?" she asked.

"To the cooks' tent. They said they would have breakfast between six and eight."

"Sounds good. I'll take us up in the van."

She drove all the way to the back of Barn One and parked next to the cooks' camper in the grass.

Jack gave us each a plate full of food and we sat down in the hammock chairs. Inga said, "I want to talk to you about something. I think you should start working with the HSUS group that goes down to New Orleans and does search and rescue. You're trained to work with aggressive dogs, and they need your help."

"Ok, I have to let Doc Debra know, though."

"Sure. I think she will agree with me."

We finished eating and walked over to the HSUS incident command motorhome behind Barn One, where about twenty people had gathered for a quick meeting. I found out more volunteers would be coming, but for the next couple of days, this small group was the only one that would be allowed into the city for animal rescue. All of us had to get an official pass at the Emergency Operations Center (EOC) located downtown.

Inga whispered to me, "Go over by the front door of the motorhome. You'll see some boxes that have HSUS t-shirts in them. Take four in your size. Put one on and put the rest in your tent. By the time you get back, I'll have someone to be your partner."

I hurried to the boxes, got the shirts, and went to my tent to change. When I returned, Inga was standing with a man in his 40s. He was about 5 feet, 7 inches tall. He had a very round face with stubble from not shaving and a moustache that looked like he kept trimmed. He had on round eyeglasses and was wearing blue cargo pants, a white t-shirt, baseball cap, and black boots like mine.

Inga waved me over and introduced me to Perry Nelson. In his Southern accent, he said, "Good to meet you. That's my truck right there. I have a cooler in it and I'm going to fill it with ice, water, and Gatorade. So why don't you go to the food tent and get something for our lunch from the canned foods—something that might taste good even if it's cold."

At the food tent, Jack and Shirley gave me a puzzled look, thinking I was back for more breakfast. I said, "Ok if I take some canned goods? I think I'm going down to New Orleans today to do search and rescue."

Jack walked me over to the shelves of canned food. He pulled out some stew and said, "This one is good, even if you can't heat it. You want to look for something that has a pull-top. The rest are useless to you unless you have a can opener. And take some napkins and some plastic spoons and forks. I'll go get you a bag."

He returned shortly. I thanked him and put four cans of stew in the bag with the utensils.

Perry appeared around the corner of the tent and said, "Where'd you get that t-shirt?"

"Inga told me to go get one by incident command. Let's see if we can get one for you."

Inga was at the boxes, sorting shirts. She gave Perry two and said, "You two be careful in town. I'll see you tonight. The state vet has given us a curfew, so everyone needs to be out and through security by six o'clock. We want to be able to keep going in and getting animals out, so remember that."

We headed back to Perry's truck. He stopped at the driver's-side door and changed shirts. I thought it was nice that he turned away from me to change. I figured he was a little shy—and it also let me know the type of man he was.

Perry's truck was a bright-red, official-looking vehicle with red police lights on top. There was an insignia of a police badge on the door with the words "Search and Rescue." He had an official radio and could listen to what was going on. In the bed of the truck was a huge pile of boxes filled with new wire kennels.

"Let's see where the others are and catch up with them," he said as he pulled out the radio and called our team leader. No response. He called again. And again, no response. "I guess we're out of range. We shouldn't be. But I know where they're going, so we can meet them in town. We have to take a back way in because the town is closed off from people entering. It's about an hour's drive from here."

As we left Lamar-Dixon, Perry slowed to a stop at the guard shack to let them know we were headed to New Orleans to do search and rescue and that we'd be back a little after 7:00 p.m.

They exchanged pleasantries and Perry introduced me as his new partner.

"Always talk to the people standing on the road or at the guard shacks," he told me as we drove off. "They will remember you and let you ahead of others when they can."

I said, "Being pleasant with people is the way I was raised. You never know what kind of day someone is having, and if you can make them smile and feel good, then I think it comes back around tenfold."

"Karma," he said. "You and I should get along just fine."

I thought, "Perry's a nice guy."

Before getting on the interstate, we stopped in Gonzales at a gas station and convenience store so Perry could get doughnuts for his breakfast. While I waited, I breathed in the sweet aroma of the alfalfa growing in the fields nearby. It was pretty here. The land was flat and looked like farm country.

As we talked on our drive, I found out Perry was from a small town in Louisiana, about three hours away. He was a former ambulance driver and did search and rescue with his local sheriff's department. He was currently working on oil rigs off the coasts of Texas and Louisiana. He worked fourteen days on and fourteen days off. He was the only medic on the rig. Whenever someone was injured, it was his job to get the person stable so the medevac helicopter could take them to shore for treatment.

Perry said the pay was good, but that nothing much happens, because the rigs are very safety conscious. Then he laughed. "My job's pretty slow. Lots of Band-Aids, though."

Right now, he was on his fourteen days off. He said he couldn't keep watching everything on TV, so he told his wife he had to come help. He packed up his equipment and drove the three hours to Lamar-Dixon.

I asked him if he had trouble getting in because the roads were closed. He pulled his wallet out, opened it, and showed me he had a police badge from his work with search and rescue. "Between the vehicle and the badge, I just sailed through."

I smiled. I was in very good company.

I told Perry that I lived in California and HSUS had flown me out to help where I could for two weeks. I explained how I had worked with the vets and at intake the last couple of days. When he asked me what I did for a living, I told him the truth.

"I'm an animal communicator. I can hear what they say, so I can relay messages back and forth. I can also feel their pain in my body, so that's why it's helpful for me to work with the vets."

He asked what I did with the vets. I told him I was working with a surgeon and could tell her when the animals were waking up and explain to them what was going to happen. This allowed her to do some surgeries that she wouldn't have been able to do with the limited drugs they had on site.

He looked at me for a moment and said, "I can see why they flew you out here. I'm riding along with Doctor Doolittle! Wait until my wife hears about this—she will want to meet you!"

When Perry was finally able to make radio contact, our team leader, Will, told him our other vehicles had just hit traffic where the police had the interstate blocked off. They were turning people away. He asked us to get close to them so we could go through security together.

Less than 10 minutes later, Perry and I came up to what looked like Los Angeles freeway traffic, and it went on for miles.

"The police are turning everyone back, even if they live here, because it's not safe yet," Perry said. "Last I heard, no one but emergency vehicles and officials were getting in."

I looked at the line of traffic and thought, "We'll be here forever." It was about 10:00 a.m. and I figured we weren't going to get a lot of search and rescue done today.

Perry called Will to notify him we had caught up to the traffic at the 7-mile marker. Our leader said they were at the 3-mile marker and had been sitting in traffic for about 20 minutes. He told Perry, "I'll leave your name at the checkpoint. We'll wait for you on the other side."

Perry looked at me and said, "You game for some fun?"

"Sure!"

"Ever ride on the divider?"

"No."

The interstate had two lanes in each direction, with a big dip in between. There was grass growing about knee-high in the dip. The edges of both roads were graveled and tilted toward the center for drainage.

"Look official," he said and smiled at me. He turned on the lights on top of the truck, and onto the side of the road we went, tearing through the gravel!

I smiled, amazed at all the cars we were passing.

"Don't look so happy. We don't want to piss anyone off."

We rode the edge of the road, all 7 miles to the front of the traffic. The policeman at the blockade waved us toward him. Perry pulled out his badge and told him who we were and what we were supposed to do.

The official looked at his badge and our t-shirts. "HSUS. You guys are good. Thanks for helping. There's lots of animals downtown. Good luck."

Perry asked him how his day was and who they were letting in. He said it was still only officials and he was turning back everyone else. "Some folks are trying to sneak in different ways, but we've been able to keep most people out. You be careful—there are still downed trees that are hard to get around, and we aren't sure if the electricity is off. So watch out for electrical wires, they might be hot. The electric company has been working 24/7 to try to get things turned off, then we can let residents down there. But it's not safe yet."

"Thanks. Has the rest of our crew been through? They have a large horse trailer and three SUVs."

"No, not yet."

"I think they are in the traffic right behind us. Please let them through when they get here. We have to meet at our check-in point and get started."

The officer smiled and we started down the empty interstate. Perry took the next exit. "This is a short cut to where we are going. Heard about it from my last partner, so I thought we should try it out."

We drove about 2 miles, made a left turn, and headed toward what Perry said was town. I hoped so. I had no idea where we were. The houses in this area looked pretty normal, with lots of greenery and trees.

"How far to the disaster?"

"About 5 miles. This area just got a lot of rain. We have a site in town where there's a temporary animal shelter. We'll go there first, then head to our check-in point and meet the others."

We drove through some nice neighborhoods. The houses were set on one- and two-acre lots. It looked like a great place to live. Perry told me this area had been evacuated too, but most of the people owned these houses as their second homes and they got out early.

As we continued down a two-lane road, we heard the radio come alive. It was Will. "Team One, this is team leader. We have just cleared the blockade and can wait for you on the side of the road."

Perry and I smiled at each other. "Team leader, this is Team One. We passed through the checkpoint about 10 minutes ago. Didn't see you there, so we figured you were headed to the town shelter to drop off supplies."

"How did you get ahead of us!"

"I don't know sir," Perry responded, stifling a laugh. "We are headed to the shelter. We can meet you there or at the check-in point. Please confirm which location."

"You get to the shelter and wait for us to arrive. Stay at the shelter. Is that clear?"

"Yes, sir! Heading to the shelter and will wait for you to arrive. Team One, clear."

We both burst into laughter. Chuckling, Perry said, "I didn't see the horse trailer. Did you?"

"I didn't know I was supposed to look for a horse trailer."

It was another 10 minutes to the shelter. We went through a second checkpoint and were just fifth in line, behind two police cars, an ambulance, and a large flatbed truck.

Soon, we passed the Audubon Zoo. Perry said they had decided to stay put instead of evacuate, which seemed to work out. They lost some animals, but most were ok.

Perry had to maneuver around fallen trees and electrical wires that were blocking several streets. After turning around a few times, we went down a street where we saw large electric-company trucks. Crews were working to fix the broken lines and replace the downed poles. They had cut up trees and laid the debris along the sides of the road for someone else to pick up and remove. In some places, there was just enough room for our truck to get through.

We passed a house that had a 16-foot boat sticking halfway out of the front of it and continued to work our way along the littered streets. Soon we arrived at a parking lot that had been turned into a makeshift shelter. There were E-Z-Ups over kennels to keep the afternoon sun off of the animals. I saw dogs in several kennels and people helping them.

Perry parked in the shade and said, "You can get out now. We need to wait for Will to get here."

He reached into a container in the back of the truck bed and pulled out what looked like a bag of medical supplies. I followed him to the vet's station. The vet was delighted, and he told me Perry had always been able to bring him what he needed.

They continued to chat while I looked at the dogs they had in the kennels. Most of them were pit bulls and they all seemed to be very happy. A woman who was cleaning kennels came up, and I introduced myself. I asked her if these dogs were going to the Lamar-Dixon site.

"No. They'll stay in town. The vet over there is from the Louisiana state veterinary hospital and these animals are under their direct care. Some of the animals have been transported to other shelters outside of Louisiana, and they are waiting for the trucks to come back to take more of them out."

She noticed my t-shirt and added, "We're glad HSUS is here to help—there's so much to do."

About 15 minutes later, a large horse trailer, two SUVs, and an animal control truck pulled into the parking lot. As the volunteers got out of their vehicles, I spotted a man who I thought might be Will. I figured I was right when I saw him quickly go over to Perry.

"How long have you been here?" asked our team leader.

"Oh, only a couple of minutes—you guys are fast."

Will smiled. "Good. Well, let's have a meeting and get started. We are short on time today. We'll meet over by the horse trailer."

As everyone headed that direction, Will noticed me and asked, "Who are you?"

"My name is Terri Steuben. I'm Perry's new partner."

Will was a thin, small-framed man, and at about 5 feet, 5 inches, he was just a little taller than me. He had glasses and a roll-up fishing hat with a wide brim. He wore tan Dockers, a beige short-sleeve shirt with a white t-shirt underneath, and ankle hiking boots—not your typical disaster-response outfit. He looked brainy, like a computer geek. (I later found out he was. He had been sent from the EOC to see how our groups worked in the field.)

His assistant, Sandy, wore tennis shoes, jeans, and a dark blue t-shirt. Her hair was tied back in a ponytail that was sticking out the back of her baseball cap.

The man in the horse trailer, Buck, was pure cowboy—and he dressed the part from his Stetson to his boots. The rest of our team included three animal control officers, Cindy, Sharon, and Anthony, who were from Ohio. They wore what I assumed was their uniform: blue military pants with side pockets, black military boots, and a white t-shirt with the logo of their humane society on the front.

Lastly there was a man from Louisiana, Glen, who had self-deployed. He started volunteering when he heard the news about Katrina. He was thin but well-built for his 5-foot, 7-inch frame. He had brown hair and wore a white t-shirt, jeans, and black military boots.

Will looked like he felt anything but at ease in the field. He pulled out a map and gave us some instructions and directions to the check-in point, then we headed there in a caravan.

We soon came to a very old bridge with large metal sides. All of a sudden, I heard a bell ringing.

"We aren't going to make it," Perry said.

I looked ahead and saw the bridge was moving. It was a draw bridge, and there was ship coming our direction to go through the passage. Perry hopped out of the truck, got into the back, and pulled out the cans of stew I had gotten from the food tent.

"Lunchtime! It's a little early, but we'll be waiting here for 15 minutes. I don't think we'll get another break later, so I would eat if I were you."

I got in the back of the truck, sat on the side, opened my can of stew, and watched the magic of the draw bridge rising so the small ship could pass.

"You know your way around," I said to Perry.

"I've been down here since Monday. This isn't the way I would have gone, but Will's in charge. He came out with us yesterday for the first time and just slowed us down. You watch. He'll send people out to get one animal, come back, drop it off, and then go get another one. My truck can fit four dogs at a time. The animal control truck looks like it can hold six or eight, and the SUV, at least three. This is gonna be an interesting day. Yesterday we only got twenty animals. Took forever, and we left here almost at dark. Today they want us to be out and past that first blockade at six o'clock. It's eleven now—how much do you think we are going to get done?"

"Has anyone tried to talk to him?"

"I don't think it's worth it. He doesn't like me and I don't like him. So I don't think I'm the one to say anything. I just let him bumble around. At least today, we get lunch," he said, smiling.

I laughed and ate my stew, enjoying the old bridge and its moving art show. I thought, "It's almost noon and we haven't rescued any animals yet. By this time yesterday, I was doing surgeries with Doc Debra. Let's see what the day brings. If it doesn't get better, I can always go back and help her."

We crossed the bridge, and about 10 minutes later, we were close to our check-in point. Perry pointed, "Down that street is the Lower Ninth Ward shelter. Some of the local animal control people have set up a temporary shelter there and have been helping catch strays. Keep that in the back of your mind. If you need anything, check there first."

He turned right into a deserted gas station and convenience store that had obviously been flooded—the ground was now covered with dried, cracked dirt. "Welcome to our check-in point. Use your gloves and don't touch anything with your bare hands. Do you have HAZMAT training?"

"Yes."

"Good, then you know what I'm talking about. Lots of chemicals have floated through here. When the levees broke, this whole area was flooded—above one story in some areas—in about 60 seconds. Think of all those garage and kitchen sink chemicals!"

We all got out and unloaded supplies from our vehicles: canned food and kibble for both dogs and cats, cat litter, and lots of brand-new kennels and carriers that needed assembling. We began putting them together as Will looked at maps with the addresses where we needed to check for animals.

He called us over. "I want you animal control people to go out and get these animals. Bring them directly back to me here and put them in the horse trailer. Then I will have new ones for you to get."

Cindy looked at the list he had given her. "There is only one address on here. Where's a map of the area so we can find it?"

"We only have one map. I will draw you a map for each animal to pick up. When you bring it back, I will have a new map for you."

Wow! I couldn't believe it. I could see the frustration on Cindy's face, and I knew everyone was feeling the same way. I wondered what he had in mind for Perry and me, and whether he thought we were qualified to go get animals.

"How many addresses do you have total?" I asked.

"Right now, we have fifteen. I'm going to the EOC to get more addresses. While I'm gone, I want you and Perry to assemble the kennels. You can head out and get your passes for tomorrow after I get back."

"How about if you look at the addresses and see if several are in the same area—let us all get more than one dog at a time. Each vehicle can carry several dogs."

"Hmm, I will see what I can do. But you two get busy on assembling the kennels. We'll need about thirty today."

"Ok," I said, although I was thinking, "This process needs to be fixed somehow, but I'm not the boss."

Perry didn't say anything. He turned and headed to the kennels. In about 30 minutes, we had them all put together and stacked up.

When we finished, Cindy was just getting ready to leave. Perry walked over to their truck. I followed and heard him say to her, "If you just happen to see an animal and it walks right up to you, it would be a shame to leave it out there—if you know what I mean."

"I think I do," she said and smiled.

Our instructions were to go get pets at the addresses that people had called in. If we found stray animals outside along the way, we could only pick up those that looked sick or very thin. All of the others could eat at drop sites where we put out food and water. We would be told at a later time when we could bring them in.

When Will got back, he told us to go to the EOC and get back as soon as we could, so we could keep the pick-up process going. We got in Perry's truck and headed out of the area. I asked him why Will was doing things that way—it just made no sense.

"He's scared. He doesn't like to be outside and in all of the chemicals. He's freaking out. He's a computer guy who is supposed to be in the EOC on the computer. I don't think he's been outside at all—he's gonna burn today. Will is also afraid that if people get hurt when they go out to get a dog, he will have to go get them. Then he would have to go further into the chemicals. You'll see when we get back. By yesterday afternoon, he was literally shaking from the stress. This isn't a good job for him."

The directions to the EOC took us to the Hyatt Regency hotel in downtown New Orleans. I saw all the high-rises standing tall—some had glass broken out of their windows.

There was a line of about fifty people in front of the Hyatt, which was being guarded by military troops with rifles.

"That's the National Guard. They have been here a few days, helping to keep order and policing the area at night to keep the looting down. There are still people here who wouldn't evacuate," Perry explained.

The line moved pretty fast. Our IDs were checked at the door, and we were directed to a banquet room that was serving as the EOC. At the door, Perry asked to see the person in charge of the animal section so we could get the passes we would need for tomorrow.

We waited outside about five minutes and were met by Kathryn (Kat) Destreza, animal services director and chief humane officer for the Louisiana Society for the Prevention of Cruelty to Animals. She was about 5 feet, 6 inches tall, and had jet-black short hair that stuck straight up. She looked to be in her 30s and was wearing an official uniform: blue pants, black military boots, and a white short-sleeved dress shirt with the LASPCA insignia.

We introduced ourselves and told her we needed official passes. Kat escorted us into a huge room full of computers, cameras, and big-screen video monitors. There were about 150 people, all busy looking at their computers or TVs.

Kat took our IDs. She returned in 10 minutes and handed us our IDs and the new passes. "Starting tomorrow, you'll need to show these to get past the blockade. They are really going to crack down. There are too many civilians getting in, and the police are having to escort them out. So how's it going outside?"

We explained the problems we were having with our team leader's one-at-a-time approach. She asked for Will's phone number and said she would talk to him. We also told her we needed bigger vehicles to hold more animals—and more maps.

"We actually have different names for the streets, now that the signs are gone or twisted in the wrong direction," Perry said. "But maps would be helpful to count the streets. Some people have had to purchase their own."

Kat gave us ten copies of the map as well as an address list with some new animals we needed to rescue. She said, "Also please make sure you check the feeding spots. Drop bags of food and change the water there, so we can start getting some of the dogs and cats used to an area. Then it will be easier to pick them up."

"Will do," we said and headed out the door.

By the time we returned to the check-in point at 1:30 p.m., poor Will was literally fried from the sun. Everyone else was there too, still working on getting all of the animals from his list. They had picked up ten and had five to go. The list we had gotten from Kat had fifteen more.

We had started to tell them about Kat and the EOC when Will's phone rang and he excused himself.

"There are some changes to today's plans," I said, handing out the maps and address lists. "Let's divide them up and go get them. We also need to drop more food at sites where there has been food on the ground before. Open up the whole bag up so the animals can get to it. Or dump it on the ground and keep the bag. Also get the water jugs from our supplies and leave plenty of water for them to drink. It's been two days since water was dropped, and we have to cover the whole area."

We divvied up the addresses and checked the maps. Then we all exchanged cell phone numbers and decided we would call each other, or Will, every hour, unless we had an emergency.

Will was still on the phone when Perry and I got in our truck and headed to the area he had chosen for us. I started looking at the map.

"You can put that down. I know where we're going and can show you the ropes. It's easier to remember if you see it. Count the streets or make new markers—like that downed tree or the pink house."

The main road through the area had dirt on it and had been traveled quite a bit in the two weeks since Katrina hit. The side streets looked more like dried riverbeds with cracked pieces of dirt. It was hot again. The temperature was 100 degrees and the humidity was about 102 percent. (I don't know how you get 102 percent humidity, but that's what they were saying.)

Three blocks down the main road, Perry said, "I want to show you something. We aren't allowed to take this dog out yet, but I want to get him before I leave. Or if I can't get down here, I want you to get him out."

We turned right, went a half-block, and he stopped the truck in the center of the road. We got out of the truck and I joined him as he walked over to a yard with a chain-link fence. All of a sudden, a little black puppy ran toward us! I couldn't believe it. Still here, still alive, and doing quite well from the looks of it.

"Why can't we take him?"

"This one isn't on the list. So I've made sure to come by and feed them, check that they're ok, and give them water everyday I'm here. I've been hoping the family would return to get them. I'm just waiting until they let people back in tomorrow or the next day to see if the family comes back. In the meantime, I've been taking care of them."

"Them?"

"Yes, there's a grouchy Shih Tzu male, I think, that is very protective and taking care of this little guy. They have been staying in the house. The door is open, so they get in the shade during the day."

I saw where Perry had left food and dumped water when he was there before. Now he climbed over the padlocked driveway gates and asked me to hand him a bag of puppy food. He placed the bag on the ground and used his knife to make a slice down the center of the bag and t-shaped slices on the ends. He opened up the bag like a bowl, and the puppy went to the bag to eat.

I gave Perry a water jug and asked if we had something bigger than the makeshift bowl he had been using—something the puppy couldn't tip over.

"Yeah, why don't you go get me one of those litter pans in the back of the truck, and I'll put the water in there."

I returned with a litter pan, and as Perry poured the water in it, I tried to explain to the puppy he could drink the water and sit by the dish if he wanted to. I talked out loud to him so Perry heard what I was saying.

Suddenly the puppy stepped into the litter pan. *"I can just sit here and drink!"* said the little guy. We both laughed at the sight of the puppy drinking the water while sitting in it.

I started to hear growling not far behind Perry. On the other side of the fence, the neighbor's dog had noticed us and was not happy with our visit. He growled and snapped in our direction, then charged the fence. His barking brought out the Shih Tzu from inside the house.

Perry just made it back over the fence by the time the Shih Tzu got to the gate, growling mad. We stepped back and I said aloud, "We brought you food and water—and your little friend is ok."

The Shih Tzu decided it was time to drink, and then I heard him say he was going to eat too. He had accomplished his goal of getting Perry off his property and his guarding duties were over.

Next we walked over to the neighbor's house to check on the barking dog. He was a vicious pit bull and not friendly at all. Perry looked on the ground and said, "I can't believe it. I spoke to the owner two days ago. I asked him if he had food for the dog. He said he did, but I don't see it. The owner said this dog is too vicious to take off the property, so he's just leaving him here."

Perry walked around to the side of the house, looking for signs of food and water, while I chatted with the dog. He told me his owner didn't leave him any. *"He wants me to die here because he thinks I'm bad. But he is the one who told me to be bad—and now he isn't telling me what else to do. So I'm guarding the property like he wants me to. But what else should I do?"*

"If you are nice to people, they could take you away from here. And then you might be ok."

"When I'm nice to people, my owner beats me. So I don't know what to do."

Perry returned and said, "That guy lied to me. I think he is trying to starve this dog so he doesn't have to deal with him. He has had some trouble with animal control complaining, so I bet he is just going to starve him out."

I looked at Perry and told him what the dog had said.

"Well, he may have to stay here for a while, but I'm not going to let him starve while I'm around."

He got a bag of food out of the truck, cut the top, and poured it over the fence. I got the water and said to the dog, *"You should eat now, and while you have your back turned, we will put the water in a bowl. If you don't see us do it, you won't have to defend the property."*

He immediately turned his back to us and started eating. I could tell it had been a few days since he had last eaten. I slid a small litter pan under the fence, and Perry figured out a way to pour the water through the fence and into the dish. We stood up, and the dog came over and took a huge drink. We waited and refilled the pan before returning to our truck.

It wasn't easy for either of us to leave those dogs behind, but we had to comply with the guidelines from incident command. In disaster response, if you can't follow the rules, they don't need you and will send you home. You are there as an extension of the police, firefighters, animal control, military, and all of the officials who have extensive lifesaving training. You must be flexible and even-tempered to be able to work in these conditions. Both Perry and I understood the rules and why the dogs had to stay where they were, at least for now.

We headed down the road, and Perry showed me all the places where he was putting food. Almost all of them were empty. We took out bags and dumped food on the sidewalk or made bowls out of the bags, depending on whether or not the dogs in the area were nice.

One spot had to be a drive-by food drop. As I got in the back of the truck, Perry slowly went around a corner and said, "Drop the food off the left side and then get down in the bed." I wondered why we were doing it this way, but did what he said. I opened the bag and poured it off the left back corner. Just as I was ducking back into the bed, there was a thunk on the side. I peeked over the top and saw a dog had bounced off the side of the truck—all four of his feet were flying and he was snapping and growling. "Quite a feat," I thought as the dog headed back to the food.

"What do we do about water?" I yelled.

"We come back in 10 minutes. He'll be full, so we won't have that much to worry about."

We went around the block, and I did two other drops. Sure enough, when we came back around the corner, our bouncing boy was lying under a tree. Perry told me to get in front and handed me a gallon of water. He pointed on the side of the street to a tinfoil pan—the kind used to cook a roast. "I'm going to stop when your door is right above it. Open the door and pour. Then we leave. If I see him coming, I'll let you know and just shut your door."

As I opened the door, I asked our friend to lie there until I was through, then he could come get water after we left. He didn't move. I poured the water, closed the door, and said, "Ok, we're good."

"You said something to him, didn't you?"

"Yes. I asked him to lie there while I did that, and he was kind enough to do it."

"The idea from animal control is to feed all the strays down here, so they don't pack up and we can get them out sooner. If the dogs are full, they don't need to fight. They are actually calmer now than when I started. You should have seen the first day I tried to feed that guy. It wasn't pretty."

"I can only imagine."

"You should've been here then. I could have used you. Now I have someone else for you to meet."

We drove a few more streets and came across a small golden retriever. We stopped and got out of the truck. Perry set a kennel on the ground, handed me a catch pole, and said, "I need you to ask that one to come out of the yard. Then put him in the catch pole and bring him to the kennel. He has a bad foot. If he's off the property, then he's considered a stray. I'll get the paperwork and write down that we got him right in front of this house. Then we can take him to get his foot taken care of."

Perry walked to the cab to start the paperwork that would follow this dog everywhere. If his mom and dad came looking for him, they could locate him through the information we recorded. By the time Perry came back with the paperwork, I had the dog in the kennel.

Perry took off his hat and shook his head. "How did you do that so fast? I tried to get this guy for two hours the other day. Did you use the catch pole?"

"No, I just asked him to get in and go with us. I said we have food and water and we can take him out of this mess. He walked right in. I think he's tired of being here."

Perry smiled, and we lifted our first catch of the day into the back of the truck.

We accomplished a lot in the next hour, then headed back to the check-in point to drop off four dogs we had rescued from the streets. We wanted to get them in the shade of the gas station. As we turned into the lot, I could see twenty kennels sitting in the shade next to the gas pumps, and we added our dogs to the group.

Sandy the assistant was there and told us the others were doing well. "They have brought in most of the animals we have addresses for. There are just a few more to do. We might be out of here earlier than yesterday, because our trailer is almost full."

We asked where Will was and she said he had heat stroke shortly after we left. "He looked like he was about to pass out. Someone came, put him in an air-conditioned car, and left. He just got himself all stressed out, and then, boom, that was it."

We told Sandy we'd be back in an hour, and Perry and I headed out again. He gave me a quick tour of parts of the Lower Ninth Ward that I hadn't seen before, pointing out landmarks and hazards.

We went about two miles and he said, "Beyond this point is St. Bernard Parish. I'm going to drive you through there so you know what it looks like in case you need to come down here. Be careful if you have to drive into any water or muddy areas, because we don't know how deep they are. Someone got stuck over there two days ago, and we had to get a big truck to pull them out."

We pulled up to a T-intersection and Perry stopped the truck in the center of the road. He pointed to the house just ahead to the left and on the corner. "There's three pits here. Let's go see if they're home. They aren't the nicest, so I feed them in the corner of the property. They won't leave their yard, so we're safe in the street."

I followed Perry to the corner. The house was on cinder blocks, but its roof had collapsed. He said, "The dogs just stay here and they look healthy. So until we can take them, I feed them here. You will need to remember these guys when I'm gone. Let's go around back and see if they're here. Maybe someone picked them up already. We don't want to leave food if there's no one here."

I followed Perry down the street, along a wood fence with planks that were pointed at the top. When we got to the gate on the far side of the house, Perry opened it and said he didn't see anything. We both walked in the yard. He headed across to the far side of the house while I walked up to the back.

I peeked in the window on the back door and could see the kitchen in front of me. It looked like the living room was to the left, but beyond that, it was daylight—the far side of the house was missing.

The door was open about an inch, and at first, I didn't see anything. All of a sudden, there was a grey flash in the house. It was headed outside. I yelled to Perry, "There's one coming your way fast!"

He ran to the gate. A grey pit bull popped his head out from underneath the house, looked at Perry, and then saw me at the kitchen door. I knew I wouldn't make it to the gate in time, so I went inside and closed the door behind me.

I heard Perry yell from the other side of the fence, "Are you ok?"

"Yes!"

"I'll go out front to distract them."

At that moment, I spotted a hole in the living room floor. The grey pit popped his head up through it and saw me in the kitchen. I grabbed a doorknob to my right and it opened. I headed into a bathroom and closed the door, just as the pit, snarling and growling, hit it with his full weight. I thought, "Great! Now I'm stuck!"

I looked around to see if there was an exit point. The bathroom did have a window, but there were bars on it. I stopped for a moment, took a deep breath, and said to all of the dogs, *"You should go see the man out front. He has food for you."*

I imagined myself being invisible. I waited about a minute, then peeked out the bathroom door, ready to slam it shut if necessary. I had seen Perry pull out an extending metal stick when he was headed for the gate and realized I didn't have anything to defend myself with. There was my axe, but I didn't want to hurt the dogs unless I had to. They would have to get pretty close before I could use it, and if there were three of them, I could be surrounded very easily. I thought, "Boy, Terri, do you have yourself in a bad spot."

I looked out through the kitchen and opened the door a bit more. I didn't see the grey pit anywhere, not in the kitchen and not poking his head up through the floor. I had no idea if he might be waiting right around the corner. But I decided to make my move.

I tried to be very quiet. I left the bathroom and headed to the back door. I went out the way I had come and through the back gate. "Whew, I made it," I thought.

As I walked to the front of the house, I saw Perry flinging a can of dog food at all three of the pit bulls—one black, one brown, and, of course, one grey.

"You ok?" he asked.

"I'm good."

"That was close. Thanks for letting me know. I haven't run that fast in years, and I just made it out the gate. Where'd you go?"

"I went inside."

"That was smart."

"Yes, until the grey pit popped his head up through a hole in the floor and headed at me. I ended up in the bathroom."

"I figured if I got some food out, they would come over here and you could get out."

"Good idea. They look hungry."

"Why don't you go get a bag of food and I will keep them here. Dump the bag over there, where you see the kibble. Then we can put the water here while they're eating."

As we finished up and headed back to the truck, Perry said, "Keep in mind that someday we have to come back and get these guys out of here. For now, they have food and water, and you can keep feeding them."

We drove to what looked like an old church, where he pointed to the second floor. I saw the faces of three dogs looking out at us. "They aren't too happy when I try to go inside. I think they belong to the family that lived up there above the church, so maybe they're the minister's dogs. I have a ladder on the side of the building. I'm going to show you inside what to do, and then I'm going to go up the ladder and in through the window. You'll need to make some noise and occupy the dogs while I leave food and water. Good thing you have boots on—you're gonna need them."

I wasn't sure what he meant, until he opened the door of the church. There was mud everywhere. When the levees broke, the water flooded the whole church and moved the pews around. But, quite miraculously, the candles that had been lit on the mantle for prayers were totally untouched, as though holding space and light for the powers that be. I could feel that God liked this little church—the energy was quite happy.

Perry took me up a narrow staircase and showed me a door with a padlock and chain on it, which I imagined were meant to keep the dogs safe and people out. He said I should pound on the door to distract the dogs when he was ready.

Perry left me, climbed up the ladder to the window, and made a noise to signal me to start knocking on the door. The dogs immediately headed my way. As they barked, I told them we were giving them food and water and we would return with more. I also said that when we could, we would get them out of here.

The dogs got really quiet, so I wasn't sure if they were by me at the door or if they were heading for Perry.

All of a sudden, I heard a noise right behind me and I jumped. It was Perry.

"You ok?"

"Yes, but I didn't expect you to be right there!"

He laughed. "Let's go. Today was the easiest this has been all week."

As we walked back through the church, I picked up a candle on the floor and placed it on the mantle with the rest of them. Perry looked at me, smiled, and said, "I do that every day I come in here too."

When we got back in the truck, he asked, "What were you saying to the dogs?"

"I told them what you were doing—giving them food and water—and that when we could, we would come and get them out of here. Until then, we would bring them food."

"This is the first day I've been able to get the food and water down without interruption. I actually thought they were gone, it was so quiet. I poked my head in the window and I could see the three of them sitting by the door. One had his head tilted to the side. It looked like they were all listening to you. That's quite a gift you have there."

We drove back to the check-in point, and as we arrived, we saw that almost all of the dogs were loaded on the horse trailer. We decided we had perfect timing. We helped load the last six dogs on the trailer. Buck said he was going to head out, because it would take him longer and he had to drive slower than the rest of us.

"Do you want us to follow you?" Perry asked.

"Naw, I'll call if I have a problem."

"Well, we'll stay close, just in case."

Sandy walked over to Perry and handed him Will's radio. "You ok to lead everyone back to Lamar-Dixon? I have to head over to the EOC and check in. Then I'll see how Will is. Poor guy, they ended up taking him to the hospital."

We gathered everyone together for a debriefing, then headed back home. Perry and I were in the lead, and the other two vehicles followed us. The ride back to Lamar-Dixon was beautiful, as the sun came down and made for a pretty sky.

About a third of the way back to Lamar-Dixon, we passed the truck. Perry got on the radio and told the team that we were going to get gas. He asked the last SUV to follow Buck back and to radio us if they needed anything.

We got off of the interstate and pulled into a gas station. As Perry filled the tank, he said, "I have to find another way to get gas—this is getting expensive. I heard about a place in New Orleans I might be able to get gas. We should check it out tomorrow—that is, if you're ok to ride along again."

"I sure am! That sounds good to me."

At 7:30 p.m., we drove up to Lamar-Dixon and I got to see another side of the site. There was a line of vehicles with animals in them at the front entrance. Perry passed the entrance and went in to the right to avoid the line, since all of our team's animals hadn't yet arrived.

"No sense slowing things down. Looks like they have a

few more people tonight to help out. Where do you want me to drop you off?"

"By Barn One. That's the vets' barn and I want to check on some animals I helped with yesterday."

"Ok, I'll go meet Buck at the front. See you tomorrow morning at the meeting. It'll be at six, so we can get people downtown earlier in the day."

I said goodbye and headed to the vets' area to check in. I could see Doc Debra was working on a white pit bull. She glanced up and caught my eye. "Get over here. I need your help."

Standing next to her at the table were two people who seemed very concerned about the dog. Debra told me they were the owners and that they had a terrible time getting back into New Orleans to get their dog.

The woman kept saying, "They told us it would just be overnight and we would be back, but we couldn't take our pets. They loaded us on a bus and we got out just before the flooding. I was so worried about Gizmo that I couldn't sleep! So we finally went a different way and got him out, the poor boy."

The dog had been at their house for fourteen days before they figured a way to get him. They were told to come here because there was vet care available.

The woman was very emotional. "Oh, dear God. Please help our dog!"

Debra said to a vet tech, "Take these folks to the food tent and get them something to drink and eat. It's going to be a while."

After they left, Debra said, "I'm glad you're here. You need to tell Gizmo what we have to do."

All of the dog's feet were raw and one foot was probably broken. Debra had already sewed up his left shoulder—it looked like she had put in about twenty stitches to close a 5-inch slice. Now there was a drainage tube in it.

I started to talk to Gizmo about Debra giving more medication to sedate him, so they could finish his feet. I said they would probably take him to the hospital, when he was stable, to x-ray his foot.

He looked me in the eyes and lifted his head. *"You can hear me! You can hear me! Oh, thank God! They left me! They just left me!"*

I looked at Debra and said, "I need a minute here."

"I'll go get some things I need. Be back in a few."

I touched our friend on the side and held his head. I kept looking at him as he talked and gave him time to get out everything he needed to say. *"They left me! I can't believe it, they left me! I waited! I waited! They weren't coming! I crashed around the house in the water and I couldn't get out. I stood on something for two days in the water. I couldn't get out. I waited! I waited!"*

I said, *"I am very proud of you! You are an amazing dog. I am very proud to be holding your head right now. You are so beautiful."*

"I waited. When the water started to go down, I had to jump back in it, because I was up high on the white thing (refrigerator). I was afraid I wouldn't be able to get down. So I jumped in again and swam to a countertop in the kitchen. I don't know how I ended up in the kitchen. I couldn't tell where I was. It was dark, and then there was water, and I was standing up to breathe, and then it was dark again. It seemed like it went on and on. They left me! Can I go home with you? I hurt. I hurt really bad. Am I going to be ok? Oh, ouch! I can't stand it. It hurts. It hurts."

The dog was so exhausted that he could barely hold his head up, and he rested it more and more in my hand. *"Doc Debra is going to do all that she can to help you, and I'm going to stand right here and explain it all."*

Finally, he took a deep breath and exhaled. I said aloud, "See, here comes the doc. She is going to tell me what she is going to do, and I then will tell you."

"What is this thing for in my shoulder?" Gizmo wanted to know. I knew it was a drainage tube, but I asked Doc Debra

to explain it to me. I thought if he heard it from her, it would make him feel more comfortable, given all the rest she would have to do.

"He wants to know what you have already done with his shoulder and what the tube is for."

She explained that she had sedated Gizmo when he first came in and was screaming with pain. She had stitched up his shoulder so it would heal. Then she put the tube in, because the wound would heal from the inside and the tube would let the extra fluid out. In a couple of days, they could remove the tube.

"I think it will heal ok. But now I need to do something to your feet—all but this one," she said, pointing to his left back foot. "This one will need special attention, but I think we can get the burning to stop."

She looked at me and I looked back at our boy. Gizmo kissed me on the nose and reached his head up toward Debra. She lowered her head and he kissed her nose too. We both saw the trust in his eyes.

The doc poured saline on his feet to cool the burning. Every time we moved him, he screamed with pain. When the burn salve was applied to his feet, I could feel a little relief with each foot.

"That's good cream," I said to Debra.

"I stole it from the human hospital this morning. They can get more, and it has been a life-saver here."

She was good at getting supplies she needed for the animals. I imagined some people just gave her things because she would keep at them until they did. She was my kind of gal.

A vet tech came over with a cell phone in his hand and told her it was the call she was expecting. I heard her talking about our pit bull. It sounded like they were trying to get space for Gizmo to get x-rayed and stay at the animal hospital. He needed to be stabilized and would require constant care.

When she ended the call, she explained, "It'll be an hour before they can get here. I need the vets to transport him so he can go right in. If his owners take him, they will have to wait out front. I don't want this guy to wait—he has waited long enough."

As I explained to Gizmo what was going on, he agreed that he had waited long enough. *"I am so tired. It hurts. It really hurts."*

"I know. You are very brave."

I looked at Debra and said, "They just left him."

"I know. It's terrible. I can't imagine doing that. I would stay with my guys, no matter what. Poor Gizmo, this has got to be very painful. But he looks more relaxed now." Then she smiled and said, "We needed you today. How was your day?"

"Our group got out thirty more. They should be here soon, if they aren't here now being checked in. I think they're all healthy, though, so none of them should be headed your way."

Gizmo kept looking back and forth between Debra and me. Our chatting about other things was helping to distract him a bit from the pain. He said, *"I know you're helping me. I can feel it. Thank you! I feel better."*

I smiled, looked him in the eyes, gave him a big kiss on the head, and said aloud, "I am very happy to help such a brave dog. You have made my whole day, just letting me touch such a beautiful boy. Thank you!"

Debra chimed in, "I'm lucky to be the one here to help you, because you are such a good patient."

He screamed again. *"My foot! It hurts."*

"I know. That's the foot that needs more help. We are waiting for people to come and get you. They will take you to the hospital, so they can x-ray it and see what can be done to make it better."

I asked the doc what she thought they would do, and then let Gizmo know what to expect. I said, "At first, the pain will be really bad, but then it will get better. After a week or so, you can probably put a little weight on it. And as time goes on, you will be ok again. Right, Doc?"

"Yes, I think you are going to be just fine. It will take a little time, but you will heal."

She finished wrapping the third foot, then decided to wrap the broken one to keep the burn salve on it until they could get Gizmo to the hospital.

Just then, the pet ambulance pulled up to the front of Barn One. It was getting ready to transport another dog to the hospital.

"Hold that ambulance!" Debra yelled, then glanced at me.

I knew what to do. I told Gizmo that the doc was trying to get him a ride now. We waited a few minutes. I saw Debra talking to the vets up front. As she came back toward us, I saw a vet tech take off running to the back to get the owners.

"He's going now! They have room and he can ride with another dog. I had to explain that my case is actually in worse shape and needs the hospital ASAP. When I told them all what was going on, they decided the broken foot could have a passage."

"Gizmo, you're going! Gizmo, you're going to the hospital right now. Ok? They went to get your mom and dad, and I bet they will follow the ambulance."

"Ok. I can go now?"

"Yes. They have to get a spot ready for you. You're going now."

"Yes, yes, yes, yes, I want to go!"

Two men from the ambulance carried over a stretcher to get the dog. I quickly explained what was going to happen, and he asked, *"Are you coming?"*

"No, Gizmo. These men know what to do. You are in good hands."

I was still holding him as the men approached the table. The pit started to growl. I told him things would be ok, then looked at the men and said, "I wouldn't make any sudden movements. Tell him what you're doing when you're doing it—and preferably before you do it. Then I think you'll be ok."

"Gizmo, you be good for these guys."

One of the ambulance drivers said, "You're the pet whisperer."

He leaned down near Gizmo's head and spoke softly, telling him that they would carry him to the ambulance and take him for a ride. Then the man stood up and looked at me. I looked at Gizmo. *"You ok?"*

Our boy reached his head up again and kissed me on the nose. He looked at Debra and he had to kiss her nose too, before they could leave.

Gizmo's mom and dad came over from the back just as we lifted Gizmo on to the stretcher—and, of course, he screamed in pain again. The doc told the ambulance guys what pain meds she had given him and suggested they wait until they decided on surgery before giving any more.

I told Gizmo that it might be a bumpy ride, but when he got to the hospital, they would take care of him. The men carried him to the ambulance, with his mom and dad hurrying along after. I saw one of the guys give the couple what looked like a business card, so they would know where to go. They hurried to their car near the front of Barn One and followed the pet ambulance toward the front gate.

I looked at my watch. It was now 9:30 p.m. and I had missed dinner. It was quiet at the vets' station, so I went to the food tent. The cooks had gone to bed already. I checked the canned food supplies and got out a can of stew with a pull-top for dinner, a small can of fruit for dessert, and a couple of plastic sporks. I started to leave, then grabbed another can of stew in case I'd need it tomorrow.

As I headed to my tent, I saw the showers looked empty. Dinner would have to wait until I was clean. Apparently I got a shower at just the right time, because several other women were standing in line as I left the building.

Back inside my little pup tent, I ate dinner by the light of my headlamp. It was nice and quiet. I set the alarm on my clock for 5:00 a.m. and wrote in my journal.

I thought for a long while about Gizmo and hoped he was ok. I got a message in my head that he was better since they gave him something for his pain, and he was resting now.

I smiled and closed my eyes.

CHAPTER FOUR

Friday, September 16, 2005

It was still dark when the alarm went off. The sound shot me awake, and I felt like I was late for something! I looked at the clock: 5:00 a.m. I took a deep breath and lay back down for a minute to get my bearings.

"Yep, still in my pup tent, still at Katrina," I thought. As I stretched, I discovered my legs and shoulders were a bit sore. I felt for my headlamp, turned it on, and looked down at my feet to get the clothes I had laid out. I began my morning ritual of dressing my top half while sitting up and my bottom half while lying in a prone position—I was getting good at this. I saw the light from my headlamp was tracking across the top of the tent. I laughed to myself, thinking if anyone outside spotted that, they would wonder what the heck was going on in here.

I sat up and took a look at my foot, which had lost a thin layer of skin the day before. It seemed fine, so I pulled on my boots. As I finished, I looked by the doorway of the tent, where lots of little visitors were enjoying the few remnants of food left in the cans from my dinner. I quickly got out of the tent and saw the ants had made one straight line into the tent and into the can of stew. I grabbed the can and put it outside. I told the ants to get out of the tent, otherwise I would have to use my bug spray to help them along.

As I headed to the restrooms, I placed the can in the trash.

When I returned, I was delighted to see the ants had left. To keep the rest of my food safe, I decided to spray around the inside perimeter of the tent—it would have time to dry before I returned that night. I got the rest of my gear and headed to the food tent to see if the cooks were up yet.

It was 5:45 a.m. and Barn One was quiet. The animals were still sleeping and so were some of the vets. I checked on Lucky, who was resting peacefully.

As I rounded the corner, Jack and Shirley were just getting out their pots and pans. He said, "You're up early. We missed you yesterday."

I told him I was downtown doing search and rescue. "There are lots of dogs running loose, and we are trying to get them out. It looks like the flood went through and moved everything this way and that. There is dirt everywhere—and dried mud. There are a lot of trees fallen on the roads, and the electricians are working around the clock to get power lines out of the way. They aren't sure which ones are hot or dead, so it's still pretty dangerous. And it's very toxic too—lots of chemicals from garages, kitchen sinks, you name it, not to mention all the businesses, like paint stores, with toxic chemicals. I heard there was a spill from an oil rig offshore that they are trying to keep quiet. But the oil could be coming from something else."

Shirley said breakfast would be a while, so I grabbed a can of stew and walked over to the morning meeting. A group of fifteen people had gathered by the HSUS motorhome, and I saw Perry coming my way with a plastic cup of coffee in hand. He told me he had a chance to re-charge a couple of extra radios overnight. He had stayed with a friend in his trailer and had gotten a good night's rest.

"I think I had a good sleep too. I closed my eyes, and a few moments later, the alarm went off."

Hank, the meeting leader from HSUS, lifted his bullhorn. "Thank you for getting up at the crack of dawn. We want to get you into New Orleans as early as we can. Because of the curfew, we need to have everyone out of town at six o'clock. We are working on moving it to seven, but the police aren't budging on that right now.

"With all of your combined efforts, we are bringing in about 300 animals a day. Thanks to you, we have some very happy, and very relieved, animals that we can now hopefully reunite with their human families and get back home.

"I realize that, for some of you, there's lots of driving. Because of the small size of our vehicles, you have to go back and forth two and three times a day, an hour each way, to bring back just two or three animals at a time. We are trying to get some larger semi-trailers, and hopefully some air-conditioned vehicles, to transport the animals. They should be here later today. So tomorrow you will be able to make drop-offs in town and go right back to your areas to bring in more animals in one trip.

"We are also working on transporting animals from here at Lamar-Dixon to other shelters around the entire country. If you know of any facilities that might be able to take animals, let me know and we can set up their transport.

"I have been given some addresses for different sections of town, where we have been asked by the owners to go into their homes and retrieve their pets. It's still not safe to let in the general public. The large sandbags along the levees are beginning to seep water, so be careful. If it looks like it's beginning to flood, get out of town.

"As for entering homes and rescuing pets: tape any windows you might need to break, because we don't want animals cutting their feet and needing to be rushed back here. Be mindful that people live in these homes—they don't want to see their front door smashed in when they return. When you can do it easily, drop out a window air conditioner and use the window as an entrance. Look around the house to see if there is an easy entrance. Keep in mind that when you break down the door, the animals can get out and lost—then we are not doing our job. Break a doorknob that can be easily replaced. Then close the door behind you so the pet can't get out while you're looking for it.

"Most importantly, expect the unexpected. Remember you're dealing with frightened and sick animals that have been abandoned and traumatized by this disaster. Any of them might react aggressively. The pets don't know you. You're an intruder. Look out for watch dogs and keep yourselves safe."

Perry tapped me and whispered, "That's where you come in."

Hank finished up, saying, "Those of you with partners, working in teams: you will be with the same teams again today. So go over to the left and I will pass out intake forms to the team leaders. Those who need partners or who haven't been into town yet: stand off to my right and we will get you set up soon. We want to make sure you are with an experienced team leader."

Perry and I walked over to the rest of our crew. Buck, Cindy, Anthony, Sharon, and Glen were already standing together. I didn't see Sandy and thought she might be at the EOC. I figured Will was still in the hospital from his heat stroke.

Perry looked at me and said, "Why don't you go get our paperwork while I get my radios handed out. I think I have enough for everyone."

I walked up to Hank as he was giving the day's forms to the team leaders. The city of New Orleans had been divided into sections to make it easier for teams to work each area and get out the most animals possible. At this time, there were seventeen areas (it would later grow to thirty-five), but we didn't have enough people to cover every area.

He gave me the Lower Ninth Ward. "Great," I thought. "One day I'm a newbie and the next day I'm considered team leader of the worst hit area in Katrina!"

I headed back to where my group had been and saw

everyone had dispersed. Perry was at the truck. "I told them to go get their supplies, then meet back here."

We filled up our cooler with ice, water bottles, and blue and red Gatorade. We drove in between Barns Two and Three and loaded up as many flattened kennels as we could. Perry then started looking for litter pans. Volunteers had brought in truckloads of donated items and the supply area was becoming one giant mess.

I noticed two men at the front side of Barn Three and asked Perry who they were. He didn't know, so I went over and introduced myself. They told me their names were John and Ernie.

"We were evacuated from New Orleans. We're staying in a camper over there," said Ernie, as he pointed to the evacuee section of the site. "We're bored. There's nothing to do there, so we thought we would come and help. But they don't want evacuees doing search and rescue. They said we have already been stressed enough—and we can't help with the animals, because we don't have training. So we've been looking at all this stuff."

"You wouldn't happen to know where there are litter pans about this size," I asked, as I held out my hands in the size of an 8.5x11-inch sheet of paper.

Ernie's face lit up. "I saw litter pans over there." He raced along the barn, climbed over a couple of piles of supplies, and came up with the litter pans we needed.

I whistled at Perry, motioned him over, and asked what else we needed. He said dog food in bags and cans, plus some canned cat food. "Dogs love the cat food—makes it easier to catch them."

Ernie thought hard. "I think there's bags of food halfway down on the left, and the canned cat food is on the right in Barn Two."

He went right to what we needed, but the cat food he found wasn't in pull-top cans.

"Have you seen a can opener yet?" I asked.

"No. I'll look for one for you and set it aside." He went a little further into the piles and scored some food in pull-tops. As Ernie located our supplies, John, the quiet one, put the food and pans in our truck. We were all loaded up in no time.

"Thank you both," I said. "I think you have found your jobs—looks like you two are our new supply managers."

Ernie's smile widened. "I think you're right!"

"You don't need any animal training to organize this area. When trucks come in, direct them to where you have the stuff organized. It would help all of us to get out quicker. If you don't mind doing it."

"It's better than sitting around."

As we got in the truck, I saw Ernie and John pointing to the right and left, figuring out how they would put the supplies in order.

We stopped at the food tent to pick up something for lunch, then gathered the rest of our crew. Cindy and Anthony were in their animal control truck. Sharon was with Glen in a cargo minivan he had rented to replace the SUV.

"It cost the same and it's better for hauling kennels," he said. "We can bring back more animals, because we can keep them longer in the air conditioning."

It was 7:30 a.m. when we left Lamar-Dixon. Buck would bring the horse trailer to our check-in point at the deserted gas station in a couple of hours.

As we came upon the traffic backup before the blockade, Perry got on his radio and asked if both teams had good tires. "Put on your flashers and follow me—and look official!"

We all drove along the center of the interstate, passing the stopped cars, for about a mile. When we got to the blockade, the same officer from the day before was there. He recognized us, quickly checked our passes, and waved our team on.

We went through the second checkpoint and stopped at the downtown shelter to see if they needed anything. We left them a few kennels and some water, then headed to the deserted gas station, our check-in point. As we drove up, we saw a dog tied with a small rope to the front door of the convenience store.

"Some of the locals who have stayed know we are here. They're dropping off strays so we can help them," said Perry.

We pulled in, unloaded the vehicles, and put our newest rescue in a kennel with food and water. Next we set up our office on the tailgate of Perry's truck. He and Cindy figured out who would take each address on our list.

When they were done, I said, "If you see any strays, feel free to get them. Let's just see how we do. If you get hurt or have trouble catching a dog, call on the radio and Perry and I will come assist you. Check in on your radios on the hour and let me know you're ok. We'll meet back here before we head to Lamar-Dixon. And remember, if you need anything..."

"...call Terri the team leader on the radio," they all chimed in, smiling.

Before going to our first address, we went by the black puppy's house to make sure he and his protective Shih Tzu were ok. We then headed off to see what we might find.

Perry stopped at an intersection and I spotted the house we were looking for. It was one level, and like most all of the houses in the area, was built on cinder blocks. A tree had smashed in the roof, and one whole side of the house was missing. Everything was covered with dried dirt, even the bushes were filled with it. The backyard fence was down—not a good sign.

We got out and Perry looked at our notes. "There are supposed to be three dogs here, tied up in the yard. But I don't see or hear anything, do you?"

"No," I said, taking everything in. I looked down at the street to my left. What I saw next startled me so much that I actually jumped backward and cried out, "Oh no!"

Right in front of me were the remains of a dog. He was hard to see because of all the dirt. With the heat and the exposure, he had melted into the road. It looked like there was a rope attached to him.

I kneeled down to see if he might have a collar, but there was just a rope. We couldn't tell if he had chewed through it or if the force of the water had snapped the rope and he ended up here.

"Do you think this is one of the three?" I asked.

"Hard to tell. He could have floated here from anywhere. This area filled up with water in about 15 minutes when the levees burst. People were in their attics and on their roofs, just trying to get to somewhere dry and safe."

"Should we do anything for this guy?"

"No, not yet. The local animal control will be setting up an area for deceased pets. Don't touch him...the toxins."

We left him there and walked over to the backyard. It was tough trying to see through all the dirt.

Soon I heard voices in my head.

"I'm over here!"

"Me too!"

"Me too!"

I looked where I was hearing the voices. The dogs blended in to their surroundings, but I could see that all three of them had passed when the area flooded. They were attached by their ties and couldn't get above the water. They had all drowned right in their own yard.

I took a moment to tell them they could go on to heaven, that it would be ok. They said they already had, but came back to tell their parents. I told them that we would let their mom and dad know they had passed. The dogs were glad to hear that, then said they were just going to stay awhile and play in their yard.

I looked at Perry and told him what they said.

"I'll do their paperwork," he replied.

We were driving to our next address when I looked to my right and told Perry to stop. I thought I had seen something. I got out of the truck and looked more closely at the house. It took a minute for me to see the dog.

It was a brown Lab, blended in with all the dirt. *"I can't get out! I can't get out! Help me! Help me! I can't get out!"*

I said to Perry, "We have one."

He turned off the engine, got out, and came over to me. We could see that the Lab was chained to the house. He was all wrapped up and couldn't move more than a foot in any direction. Perry got out a kennel and I grabbed a catch pole. We headed over to our Lab.

"I can't get out."

"I can see that. We're here to help you and get you to a safe place."

"I'm thirsty."

"We have water and food."

"Food? Really? Food? I haven't had food forever!"

I told Perry, "He's hooked up. It looks like the chain is embedded into his neck on the front and side, and it has healed around the chain. Do you have bolt cutters?"

As he headed back to the truck, I kept talking to the Lab. *"Hang on, we are going to get you out of here. My friend is going to help us. We have a nice kennel over there for you. You can rest and eat. We will take you to a place about an hour away, where all the animals are going so they will be safe. I think they will have to look at your neck to get this chain out. In the meantime, let me put this leash on you so we can all go together. I want you to stay with us, and we can get your neck fixed, ok?"*

"Ok. My neck does hurt. But it was bad days ago. It is better now...healing."

"Yes, I see that. You look like a good healer."

"I am."

Perry returned with a pair of bolt cutters and I backed up to give him some space. I explained what I had told our Lab he was going to do. "I said you are going to cut his chain, but leave some so the vets can get to it to remove it. Then I will walk him to the kennel, put him in the back of the truck, and give him some food and water."

"Ready?" Perry asked.

I looked at the brown Lab. "Ready?"

"*Yes!*" he responded.

I nodded at Perry. He pushed on the bolt cutters. He was going to have to cut twice because the chain was thick.

I said, "One more time and you're free, ok?"

The Lab looked at me and said, "*Ok.*"

Perry looked at me and said, "He really is talking to you, isn't he?"

"Yes, and he's ready."

Perry pushed the bolt cutters together again, and our friend just stood there.

I said to the Lab, "*Let's see if you can move, ok?*"

"*Really, I can move?*"

"*Yes, let's see.*"

He began to take a small step. When he realized he could actually get away from the building, he froze. He looked at me and said, "*What about my mom? She said she would come back.*"

"*Your mom had to leave here, right?*"

"*Yes.*"

"*Now it's your turn. You see, your mom and all of the people have to stay out of this area because of the flood. My friend Perry and I are going to take you to a place where your mom can find you. I'm sure she would like to find you there. We can get in touch with her because this is your house. She will want to be with you again.*"

The Lab thought for a moment. I imagined that, after all this time of waiting for his mom and then seeing us arrive instead, it was a lot for him to digest.

"*You have food?*"

"*Yes, as soon as we put you in the kennel. And there's water too.*"

He looked me in the eyes. *"Ok."*

He led the way, and we went out a white gate that was in front of what once was a very nice, small home. He headed for the kennel and got inside. I held the door with my foot, released him from the catch pole, and latched the door. We lifted him onto the back of the truck. Perry had already put a dish of food in the kennel, and I poured the water through the side into the bowl.

Our Lab was very hungry. He ate the food in two bites.

"Let's let your tummy rest a bit, then we can have some more, ok?" I said.

"Ok, but I'm still hungry."

I tuned in and could tell he didn't feel full. *"All right, maybe just a bit more. Your tummy has probably shrunk a bit, and I don't want you to get sick."*

Perry added more food and it was gone in a flash. Then our Lab got a big drink—I filled the water dish three times before he stopped. He turned in a circle and lay down. *"Oh, it feels good to lie down. I think I'll just take a little nap."* In an instant, he was asleep.

Perry looked at me and asked, "He ok?"

"Yes. I don't think he has had much sleep for quite a while. He's exhausted. But he knows now he is safe, so he relaxed— and there you go."

"Night, night," I said aloud to our Lab. "We are going to see if we can get more friends for you. So just rest."

Perry took out his can of orange spray paint and wrote on the side of the fence: "PICKED UP 1 BROWN LAB FROM YARD 9/16/05 TAKEN TO LAMAR-DIXON."

We got in the truck and continued down the street. Two houses down, we saw a spotted pit bull. And it looked like he was tied up to his house too. We moved our sleeping brown Lab to the front of the bed, close to the cab, and he didn't move.

We slowly headed toward the pit. As soon as Perry unlatched the gate, he started growling and fussing. We were lucky he was stuck because he looked like he could be mean. He was, most likely, a very good guard dog. As we moved a little closer, I started chatting to him, telling him that we wanted to get him to food. But he just wanted to get loose and protect his yard.

"Well, there is a big section of fence missing along the side of your house. So I think you might be safer with us."

Again I talked about the food and water. He was thirsty, he said, but he had work to do. So far, he had been able to keep everyone away with his growling.

"I can see that. You have a very fierce growl and snarl."

"Don't touch me or I'll bite you!"

"We just want to take a look and see what we can do to help you out of this situation."

I looked at Perry and said, "That looks like coaxial cable for TVs tied around his neck."

"You're kidding! What kind of nut would use that? Are you sure he just didn't get tangled up in this?"

"I can see a tied knot."

"Can you get the catch pole on him? He's not very happy."

"Give me a minute."

I kept explaining to the spotted pit what I wanted to do, and he was having none of it. He had a job—and that is what he was going to do.

"You have been here almost three weeks with no food or water. I think you should have a break. I'm sure your parents fed you. Maybe not all the time, but it was never this long, was it?"

Spotty stopped growling and looked at me. *"No, but they missed lots of meals. They like to drink. Then they would fall asleep and I wouldn't get dinner. Sometimes they didn't wake up in the morning and I wouldn't get breakfast."*

"How about I take you to a place where you will be fed two times a day, morning and night, and get to go for a walk on a leash."

"Off the property!"

"Yes, we would have to go off the property."

"I have to guard! That is my job!"

Perry looked at me. "Are you making any headway?"

"It's taking time, but I think I'm making progress. Can you distract him for a second?"

Perry took the bolt cutters and banged them on the house. Spotty snarled and growled in his direction. When he took his eyes off of me, I looped the catch pole around his neck and pulled it just tight enough to hold him.

The pit tried to flip around. *"I'm guarding and you have to leave!"*

"Ok, but we're taking you with us."

Perry had trouble getting close enough to the cable to cut it off of his neck. But we figured we should get it off, because if Spotty continued to be aggressive when we took him to the shelter, the vets wouldn't be able to get close to him.

Whoever tied up the pit had put a square knot in the cable—and because Spotty had been pulling on it, there was no way for us to untie it. I looked at Perry and said, "Let's both take a deep breath, relax a minute, and let Spotty calm down."

As we did, Spotty sighed in relief too. We all calmed down.

"Perry, see that cardboard box behind you. Cut a piece big enough to put between you and the mouth of our friend. If he bites that, it's ok."

Perry pulled out his pocket knife and cut a good size piece out of the side of the box. I said, "Let me put it between you and him, while I hold the catch pole. When you cut the cable, I'll swing him away from both of us."

"Ok. I hope this works."

I wedged the cardboard in and Spotty went after it, fussing and twisting. All of a sudden, Perry reached in and cut the cable. I swung our spotted pit away, and he could see he was free from the cable. I headed him to the side where the fence was missing and walked him toward the street. I said to Perry, "I'm going to take him for a little walk while you get the food in his kennel."

"Be careful with that one. Let's see what he does."

I walked with Spotty down the street for a while, and then turned him to head back. He stopped dead in his tracks when he looked at his house. *"There is nothing to guard here anymore. It's all gone."*

"I'm sorry."

"I couldn't see it from where I was tied. They just told me to guard the house, they would be back. They will be mad."

"Spotty, the water flooded this area."

"I know, I was here. Slammed me up against the house. I almost drowned, but the water went down."

"I'm glad you're ok. The water made the damage, Spotty. Your parents will be glad you're ok."

"You think so?"

"I know so. I would be, if you were my dog."

"Now you want to put me in that cage?"

"Well, it's the best way to take you to the shelter. It's an hour away, and we have to take you and put you in a bigger truck so you can get there. Do you think that would be ok?"

Spotty stood there for a minute. *"Food's in there?"*

"Yes, it's already in there...Let's just do this!" I said, as I swung him in a circle right in front of the kennel. Then he walked right in! I put my foot on the door and released the catch pole.

Spotty looked up at me and said, *"You tricked me."*

"Yes, but now you can eat."

He gave me a big smile, then put his face in the bowl. While he was eating, we lifted him up into the truck and Perry completed his paperwork. I poured water in his dish, and as he took a good long drink, I told him we were going to go get some more friends to ride to the shelter with him.

He took a deep breath, like he was smelling fresh air for the first time in a few weeks. He had been pinned tightly to the rotting, moldy-smelling wood on the house. He smiled again and sat down. *"Oh, this feels good. I haven't been able to do this for a while. I'm going to sit here and breathe."*

We got in the truck and headed in the direction where the levees had broken. The floodwater had come through so fast in this area that a lot of structures had washed away. We found the location of another address and Perry said, "There's supposed to be a house here."

It was totally gone! It looked like a vacant lot, and we couldn't even see any cinder blocks where the house had sat. "This is the place," he said. "The houses to the left and the right are 13 and 17, so 15 should be right there in the gap."

I looked at the paperwork and said, "I hope the dog got out."

"Me too. This is a little eerie. Let's move on."

I gave him another address two blocks away. The street was mostly mud, and it was getting deeper by the second. When the mud came up to the middle of the tires, we knew we couldn't go much further. The address we wanted was 35. We saw 33 on the left and 37 on the right, but when we looked where 35 should be, it was gone—just like that other house. Most likely, they were on the same path of destruction, and the strong floodwaters took both houses away.

Our paperwork showed we were supposed to get a dog at this address, but I wasn't picking up any sense that one had passed or was in the area. So we decided to get out of the mud and went to another address in the direction of our check-in point.

We pulled up and saw a beige pit bull, tied up and stuck on the side of a house. We walked toward our new friend, who was tied with quarter-inch wire that had been put around his neck and then twisted like a bread-bag tie. I spoke to the pit and told him what we were going to do. This guy didn't seem to mind—he just wanted out of there.

I placed the catch pole over his head and tightened it a little. Perry tried to untwist the wire, but he couldn't get it to budge. When he went to the truck to get the bolt cutters, I explained to the dog what we were going to do. He was fine with all of it, but said, *"Just get me out! Just get me out! The water is coming again! I can feel it—the water is coming. I will drown this time for sure!"*

"We're going to get you out. Just hang on."

Perry was able to place the bolt cutters in a spot that would free him, and after a bit of maneuvering, the wire finally gave way.

This was one happy dog! As I led him on the catch pole toward the truck, he danced and hopped, then danced and hopped some more. *"I'm free! I'm free! I'm free!"*

"Are you hungry?"

He stopped. *"You have food too?"*

"Yes, and water."

"I'm going with you!"

"Let's put you in a safety kennel—your food is in there. Then we'll lift you up and I'll get you some water."

He went into the kennel easily, and as we picked him up to put him in the truck, he said, *"Um, um, really good. Um, um, really good. Water too, um, um."*

Our truck was looking full now, and I said to Perry, "I think we should head back. It's getting hot and we can get these guys into some shade."

Spotty said, *"Shade! You have shade too!"* Then he looked at our beige pit and said, *"These guys have everything."* Spotty, it seemed, was doing just fine.

As we drove to the check-in point to drop off our boys, I asked Perry, "Why do you think no one has gotten these guys before now?"

He thought for a moment. "Some of the volunteers are afraid of what might be a vicious dog, so they just drive by. But keep in mind, I've been here a whole week and I didn't see these guys until today either. It could also be no one had bolt cutters to get them out."

We met our team and loaded the dogs in Buck's horse trailer. As we ate lunch, Cindy mentioned one of the pick-ups on her list was for a couple of cats in a house out of our assigned area. Perry looked at the address, knew where it was, and said we'd take it.

He and I drove to a two-story townhouse in a nice neighborhood—not at all what we were used to in the Lower Ninth Ward. It looked like there was no water damage at all in this area. I pulled out two carriers as Perry got duct tape and cardboard out of the truck. He taped a window panel on the front door and cracked it with the butt end of my axe. The piece fell on the floor, and he reached inside, unlocked both the deadbolt and the doorknob, and opened the door. I closed the door behind us, and he taped some cardboard over the small hole, so our kitties wouldn't get out and lost.

We went directly up a flight of stairs to another level, where the majority of the living space was. We saw one cat sitting on the sofa and moved slowly toward him. But when he spotted the carrier, he jumped off and hid behind the sofa, against the corner of the wall. I told Perry to stand at the end of the sofa and keep him busy. I put a towel over the cat, pulled him up, and dropped him into the carrier.

"One down, one to go," I said.

We had trouble finding the second cat. I tried to hone in on where he was and got something from the kitchen. Sure enough, he was behind the washing machine. I placed the carrier at the back of the washer and started talking to him about our food. He was scared and afraid to move.

"If you get in the carrier, we can take you to your mom and dad," I said, as I tapped him on the butt with the catch pole to prod him along.

"Ok!" he said and zipped into the carrier. We had to move quickly so he wouldn't dart back out, and we got the door closed just in time.

Perry went over to a desk and started looking at some papers. He said, "I want to find the owners' cell number so I can call them to get their cats back. They aren't used to people. If we take them to the shelter, they could get lost for days."

He settled on a prescription bottle in the medicine cabinet, called the pharmacy, and asked them to contact the owners and give them his number.

Was this how we should have done it? Probably not. But it worked.

We met our group back at the check-in point. Together, we had saved fifteen dogs, four cats, six birds, four cockatiels, and two parakeets. When we were all ready to go to Lamar-Dixon, Perry said, "I want you guys to head back to camp. Terri and I have to check on something."

After the others left, we got in the truck and Perry said, "Remember that guy I told you about? Where I might be able to get gas at a discount. I want to check it out."

We drove downtown and passed the EOC at the Hyatt and a bunch of TV news trucks with large antennas on top. Perry turned into an area that had a fence in front of it. There was a man standing inside who opened the gate, let us in, and showed us where to fill up.

Perry walked over to the man to pay for our gas. He came back to the truck and told me, "It's free for those of us helping with the disaster relief. We can bring the other two vehicles tomorrow. The guy said whoever is helping us is ok."

Next Perry suggested we grab dinner. He parked on the street near Harrah's Casino, a local landmark that had flooded.

"Where do we eat?" I asked. "Everything is closed."

He pointed to tented area with tables and chairs. Behind it was a huge naval ship. "The U.S. Navy is cooking for all of us helping with the disaster."

We had both been eating cold canned food the last two days and a hot meal sounded great. Sure enough, they let us in, and Perry and I had a wonderful buffet dinner. As we left, I asked one of the sailors if we could come again. He said, "Of course, bring your friends helping with the relief. I would just as soon feed you as I would the news people—at least you guys are working."

On our trip back to Lamar-Dixon, Perry told me that tomorrow would be his last day. He needed to head back home, because he had to go to work on Monday and wanted to see his wife. He hoped I would find someone else to go to New Orleans with—and he'd see what he could do to set me up with another partner.

As we arrived back at camp, Perry got a phone call from the couple who owned the cats and he made arrangements to meet them later. We went to the intake area, where Buck's truck was just getting to the front of the line. We stayed to make sure all of our animals were checked in and bedded down for the night.

Perry headed out to meet the cats' owners, and I walked to Barn One to see our brown Lab. I also wanted to find out if the vets had heard anything from the hospital about Gizmo.

Doc Debra waved me over. They were still working on the Lab, trying to figure out how to get the chain out of his neck. They had given him a sedative, so he was knocked out. They were debating whether to cut his neck to release the chain or try to pull it out and let it heal. The concern was about infection inside the wound that would be left. I told the doc that he said he heals fast and he's very strong.

"How's Gizmo?" I asked.

"Gizmo is going to be ok. His foot isn't broken. They left on the wraps I did to heal his feet. X-rayed him right through the bandages. They said they didn't want to touch him because he was still in a lot of pain. They're going to keep him for a couple of days, give him fluids, and then send him back with his mom and dad."

As I turned to head to my tent, I looked at my watch. 10:00 p.m. Wow, time flies when you're busy.

I needed a shower. I had to wait for two people who were ahead of me and was amazed I had hot water. "What a great facility," I thought.

When I got to my tent, I laid out my clothes and realized I would have to find a laundry soon. I pulled out my last pair of clean pants. I still had some t-shirts left and a few more pairs of socks and undergarments.

I had my headlamp on and could see that all of my ant visitors were outside where they should be. I wrote quickly in my journal, set my alarm, and laid my head down.

CHAPTER FIVE

Saturday, September 17, 2005

I was saving a dog at a house in New Orleans, when I was startled awake and realized I was dreaming. It was 5:00 a.m. I turned off the alarm and lay back down for a minute. I decided to imagine that I helped my dream dog to safety, and then I could begin my day.

I stretched and found that different areas of my body were sore this morning. I dressed sitting down and got out of the tent to blouse my pant legs. It was still dark as I headed to the restrooms. Everything looked just like it did the night before when I walked in the dark to go to bed.

I went to Barn One to check on the dogs. I knew Lucky was doing fine. I found our brown Lab, who no longer had the cable embedded in his neck. He now had a pretty pink bandage and pink bandana tied around his neck. He sat up as I arrived at his kennel. The vet tech told me he was doing well and explained they were using the headband to keep him out of his wound.

I asked the dog how he was doing.

"They have fed me twice, and I got to walk over there to go potty. I have nice water. Look," he said, as he looked down at his full water bowl.

"You're doing very well. Everyone will be glad to hear it."

"I am, I am. Thank you!"

I asked the tech about the spotted pit bull that had been

tied with the coaxial cable. "They had to take that one to the hospital. The cut was deep, and they needed anesthesia. He's a little concerned about people touching him. But last I heard, he's all stitched up—and a tech was sitting with him when he woke up. He's going to be just fine."

"Good. Thanks for letting me know Spotty's ok. I'll tell the responders who helped bring him."

I headed over to the cooks' tent and saw their camper was gone. They had vanished! I looked at the canned goods—the supplies were getting slim. I remembered the can of stew I had in my tent and thought I should grab a few more, just in case. I still had some jerky I brought from home and a few other munchies from the convenience store in Gonzales, but figured now was a good time to stock up.

I walked over to Perry's truck and set the cans in the back. I pulled out the cooler and took it over to two freezers that were where the cooks' camper had been. Stacked next to the freezers were cases of Gatorade and water. I grabbed a case of water and mixed a case of red and blue Gatorade. I loaded the cooler with the drinks and ice. Perry strolled up as I took it to the truck.

"Hey, where's the cooks' camper?" he asked.

"I don't know. Looks like no breakfast today."

"Maybe they had to go home."

We saw people were beginning to gather at the meeting spot behind Barn One and we headed over. Hank came out of the trailer with a handsome man who didn't look dressed for disaster response.

Hank began the meeting. "We have a very special guest here today. He is president and chief executive officer of HSUS. He has come to see how we are doing in our rescue response and serve as the spokesman for our efforts. Ladies and gentlemen, Wayne Pacelle."

Everyone applauded as Wayne took the bullhorn. "I want to thank you for being here and taking time from your lives to help us with this disaster. I think you should all give yourselves a round of applause because, yes, you are heroes. You're here. You're doing the work. You deserve the credit. I and all the people at HSUS are very thankful for your help.

"I want you to know we are currently in negotiations with this facility, because we are close to exceeding our limit of 2,000 animals—thanks to all of your great work in rescuing them from New Orleans. We will keep transporting animals to other shelters around the country, so we can continue our efforts to get as many as possible to safety.

"I'm going to turn you back over to Hank now. I have a meeting to attend. Tonight, I will do the debriefing at eight o'clock. We will meet by Barn Five, where you bring the animals for check-in. Be safe today—and get us some more animals. See you tonight."

Everyone applauded. Hank said, "Thank you, Wayne. Some of you might have noticed that the great cooks we had are gone. Unfortunately, the Health Department was here yesterday while you were in town, and several changes have been made. They said the cooks' camper wasn't up to code and told the couple to quit cooking for everyone. We are now going to have food delivered. The bad news is that breakfast won't be here until eight, so none of you can have it. Dinner will arrive at six-thirty, so most of you might miss that too. I'm sorry. We are working on getting the food here when you are."

Perry winked at me and I smiled back. We had our new dinner location, thanks to the Navy.

Hank continued, "The canned food, in what will now be called the 'Relaxation Tent,' will also be removed later today. Another Health Department issue. So please help yourselves to any canned goods you'd like.

"Also, we have had to move the volunteers who were sleeping in Barn Three with the horses to a different location. Apparently, people and animals sleeping together is a problem—and the food there has to be removed too. I know this doesn't affect you, but I just want to keep you informed of the changes.

"In addition, we have had some animals disappear from camp. A few volunteers came to help one day, then returned the next day and claimed animals as their own. Most of the animals they are trying to remove are the purebreds and what they think are fighting pit bulls. That stops now. Security at the front gate will begin checking vehicles for any animals leaving Lamar-Dixon—and if they don't have the proper paperwork, then they will be detained and possibly arrested. There will be police security at the front gate now, instead of volunteers. But you all don't have to worry about that, because you are BRINGING IN animals."

Everyone laughed at that.

"There was a dog that escaped camp yesterday. So we are working on tighter protocol for all people handling animals to make sure they have training. Again, that doesn't apply to any of you. Ok now, what does apply to you? Wayne Pacelle will hold tonight's meeting, then Eric Sakach will be taking over as incident commander.

"As we all know with disasters, things change from one minute to the next. So thank you for being flexible and understanding the changes as they come down the line. I also hear that the head of the Louisiana SPCA will be coming here to help with our rescue efforts. They are actually the ones who are in charge of our relief effort, so be respectful when they arrive. They are very happy with the work you are all doing.

"Finally, thank you for all your help—and be safe today."

I headed to the front with the other team leaders and got the list for the Lower Ninth Ward, then went back to the truck. Perry and I drove to Barn Three to pick up more kennels and supplies for our day in New Orleans. There, we saw the rest of our crew getting supplies. But I didn't see Ernie and John, and I wondered if the Health Department had kicked them out. It was evident that they had been working, though. The supplies—kennels, food, and water—were beginning to look in order.

Just then I noticed Ernie coming from the middle of the barn. I smiled and waved to him. "Hi, Ernie. I'm glad you guys are ok. I heard the Health Department was here yesterday, and our cooks are gone."

"They tried to kick us out too. Then someone asked them if they were going to stay and sort this all out—and, surprise, surprise, they let us stay."

We laughed together and he said, "I have something for you." He walked over to what looked like their office area, reached between two boxes, and pulled out a can opener.

"Yay! Now we can take food without pull-tops. Thank you!" (It is amazing how excited you can get over such a small thing. But in a disaster, a can opener can be a life saver.)

I gave Ernie a big hug, which surprised him. "John will be very sad he missed that."

"When you see him, tell him I have a hug for him too."

"You were right, Miss Terri, people have been very glad we're here. We now have jobs and it makes us happy to help. There's a lot of donations coming in, so it looks like we're going to be here for a while."

Our team was ready and we headed to New Orleans to see what the day would bring. We made a quick stop at the convenience store on our way out of town for doughnuts and snacks. Perry again reminded me it was his last day and asked me if I knew what that meant.

"You want me to take care of the puppy."

"Yep."

"Be happy to." I knew we were headed to check on the puppy one more time.

We arrived at the check-in gas station and I pulled out the list of animals we had to get. I gave it to Perry and Cindy and they went to work dividing up the addresses. Everyone else got busy taking kennels off of vehicles, putting dishes in stacks for supplies, and helping each other. No one had much to say, but the feeling in the air was light. Buck was on his way and would arrive about 10:00 a.m.

We had a little meeting, and I told the team that both the Lab with the embedded chain and the pit bull with the cable were doing fine. I also said this was Perry's last day. He blushed when everyone applauded all his good work.

Perry said, "After everyone is finished loading up this afternoon, Terri and I want to take you somewhere before we return to Lamar-Dixon."

"It's a surprise," I added.

Perry told us he would have to take his radios with him when he left.

"I guess we'll have to go back to using cell phones," I said. "So we don't forget, let's pass around some paper now and make sure we have each other's numbers."

We all agreed to check in on the hour. I told them Perry and I had been watching and feeding three chows, but they kept walking away each time we tried to get them. "No more of that—the idea today is to get as many animals as we can!"

As we all drove off, I heard the radio come alive. It was Anthony. "We like you, team leader, just in case you didn't know."

Then Cindy came on. "I like you too."

Glen and Sharon followed, and Perry picked up our radio. "I like you too, team leader. And just so y'all know, team leader is a little red."

I took the radio from him and added, "Seems the color red is going around today. Now all you kids get to work and be careful." In response, I heard laughter coming from the team.

Perry and I went to the food areas to see if we could pick up the three chows—two black and one brown one—that appeared to be siblings. When we pulled up to the first area, they were waiting for food.

Instead of putting food out, I took my catch pole and placed it on the ground, with the loop end opened in a circle. Next, I emptied a can of cat food into the center of the circle. One of the black chows headed toward the loop. As he began eating, I lifted the loop over his head and told him I was going to take him somewhere that's safe and has plenty of food. I was able to get the catch pole around him and let him finish eating. Then he went into the kennel and I placed it in the back of Perry's truck.

Meanwhile, Perry had caught the brown chow, so we were down to one dog. The other black chow, who seemed to be the ringleader, didn't want any part of what we were doing. He darted around the corner of the building, then poked his head back out to watch us. I tried to tell him we wanted all three dogs to go at the same time, but he was having none of it.

Perry said, "Let's follow him in the truck and see if we can wear him out. Then we can keep him with the family."

The black chow slowly jogged down four blocks in front of us, not going off of the road. All of a sudden, he went toward a house, darted under it, and was gone. Perry said, "We'll check back at the food site later to see if we can get him, otherwise we'll leave some food for him."

I told the black chow, *"We are trying to take all three of you to the same place, so you can be together and have food all the time. Meet us this afternoon at the food drop and we can take you with your brothers."*

I didn't hear any response from the dog. I hoped he was thinking about it and would see us at the drop.

We took the two chows to the check-in point and headed out again. We had been told initially to rescue only those animals that looked the most distressed and leave food for the others. The size of our trailer also limited the number of animals we could take out in a day. So there were several animals that Perry and I had been feeding—now we decided it was time for them to get a break, and we would get them out of here.

The roads had been drying out the last couple of days, and

we were able to get further and on to a few more streets that had been flooded before. There was still about an inch of mud on the ground and on the sides of the road, but it had dried and cracked.

We turned a corner to get to our first address. Perry pointed and said, "Well, we can't go that way."

Directly in front of us was a house. It had come to stop in the middle of the road after floating away in the flood. Perry put the truck in reverse and we went around the block to get to our address.

We parked in front of a house that looked all closed up. We walked over to it and listened to see if we could hear anything. Perry lifted the window air conditioner and it dropped out, on to the ground. He said, "Let me lift you up there. You go look for the Rottweiler, and I will make sure he doesn't come out the window."

"Ok," I said.

Perry lifted me up and I went in the window, hands first. I was glad I had on both my plastic gloves and my leather gloves, because there was dried dirt everywhere.

As I stood up, Perry moved the air conditioning unit under the window and used it as a step stool so he could see in the house.

"I'll go look for our friend," I said.

"Be careful. We don't know if the dog's nice. Always assume the worst, and then you're not taken off guard."

I started through the muddy, dirty house. I was in what looked like an office. I headed to the hallway and tried to close the door, so the dog couldn't get to where Perry was. The door wouldn't close all the way—the water from the flood had soaked it and made it swell. I looked through the bedrooms and then headed to the living room. Everything had been moved around, like you'd expect from a flood. I saw the watermark was about a foot from the ceiling, and now, because of the heat and humidity, the walls had begun to turn moldy green and grey in some places.

As I moved from room to room, I kept saying aloud, "Hi. Anyone home? I hope you'll come with me. It's time to get out of the house and get some fresh air."

I rounded the corner to the living room and saw her in the kitchen. The Rottweiler was lying on a sofa cushion that had floated up on top of a 1950s diner-style kitchen table. I could tell she was using one of the chairs to get up and down—its red vinyl cushion was somewhat visible, while the rest of the chairs were still completely covered in dried mud.

"Hi there," I said. "Look how pretty you are!"

She stared at me, then started to get up and move away. I took a step back and said, "It's ok. You look comfy there. Please stay."

"What are you doing in my house?"

"I'm looking for you."

Her ears went up. "For me?"

"Yes, I would like for you to come with me to get some food and water. I can take you to a place that's dry and has good air. It's kind of stinky in here, don't you think?"

She paused and looked around. "It didn't look like this before."

I waited a moment. "I can see that's a nice table you're on and a nice cushion to rest on. Do you feel ok?"

"I'm tired and sore. My tummy hurts and I'm thirsty. Do you have water?"

"Yes, I do. But it's outside. Would you like to come and meet my friend? His name is Perry. He likes dogs too."

"How did you get in? The doors are all blocked."

I looked around to the living room and saw the sofa had floated in front of the door. Behind my Rotty, the refrigerator was standing in front of the kitchen door.

"I came in the office window, where the air conditioner was."

"It hasn't worked in days."

"I know. What do you think? Would it be ok if I put my leash on you and we went out together?"

She seemed very tired. I assumed this one hadn't eaten or drank since the flood. I said, *"I'll just move very slowly so you can get used to it. And then when we are hooked together, we can go. Ok?"*

I heard Perry outside the window. "Did you find him?"

I looked at my Rotty. "Yes, I found her. I'm just chatting so we can leave together."

"See, that is Perry. He wants to meet you too."

As I got closer with the catch pole, our girl didn't move. I placed the loop over her head and then tightened it gently so we could go. *"Are you ready?"* I asked.

"Yes. How are we going to go out?"

"How about the window in the office?"

"Ok. Let's go then."

I gave a little tug on the catch pole. She got up and stretched. She climbed off the table using the red chair and said, *"The water was up to the table for a long time. I had to stay up there to be out of it."*

"I'm sorry."

The dog stopped in the living room and looked around. *"I guess I'm not coming back here, am I?"*

"I don't think so. At least not until everything is fixed."

"Good," she said, surprising me.

She led the way to the office. I got close to her when I tried to open the door and she leaned on my leg—she seemed very weak. She looked me in the eyes and said, *"Thank you! Thank you for coming for me. I have waited a long time."*

I felt her words down to my soul. I stopped for a moment and looked deep into her eyes. *"It's definitely my pleasure. I'm just sorry we couldn't get here sooner."*

Tears welled up in both of our eyes, and I said, *"But we aren't out to the fresh air yet, so let's go. What do you say?"*

"Yes, let's go."

I pulled open the warped door and we saw Perry looking at us through the window. "This one ok?" he asked.

"This one is fine and really ready to go. Right, young lady?"

"Young lady? Our paperwork says it's a boy."

"Wrong. This is a girl!" The Rotty looked at me and the little nub of her tail began to wag.

Perry smiled. "Well, little lady, let's get you out of there. Terri, can you lift her out to me?"

"Yes. I think she needs to see the vet. She is terribly dehydrated."

"We'll take her back to check-in so she can rest in the shade. If we need to, we can call the vet at the downtown shelter, then either take her there or have him come over if they are slow. We'll call on the way back—maybe he can meet us."

"Did you hear that, little girl? We are even going to get someone to help you feel better. Ok?"

She looked up at me and smiled. *"Thank you,"* she said.

"I have to pick you up by the front and by the back. I will hand you to Perry, and then he will take you to the truck."

She just kept smiling and looking at me. Tears came in her eyes.

"Honey, you are going to be ok."

I looked at Perry, who also had tears in his eyes. "Let's get her out of here," he said.

I picked her up, putting one arm around her front and one around her butt. I did it gently so she could get the feel of her feet being off of the floor, and I held her securely so she would know I had a good grip. I said, "Honey, I will put your butt out first. You might feel like you're dropping a bit, but Perry will catch you."

Our Rotty looked surprised when she went down, and I saw the relief on her face when Perry caught her. She licked his face, as the catch pole followed out the window and the handle fell on the ground.

Perry said, "I have you, girl. I think I'll just carry you to our truck."

He walked slowly away with her. I looked down at the

ground and it took me a minute to figure out how to get out of the window without landing on the air conditioner, which was now tilted the wrong way. I had to jump to the other side of it, away from the house. I was tickled with myself when I landed on my feet—much better than when I went in the house hands first!

Back at the truck, Perry was on the phone with the vet. He already had our girl in the kennel, resting in the middle of the road. She had drunk some water and eaten some food.

"We can go," he said. "The vet will meet us at check-in and take a look at her."

"Do we need to put the A/C back?"

"No, I think they'll have to demo this place. Don't worry about it."

We put the Rotty in the back of the truck. She looked me in the eyes and said, *"The fresh air smells really good."*

"That's my girl! Just keep breathing, Honey. We're headed for your new place to stay. Enjoy the ride."

She was smiling now. Perry stood by his door and smiled too. "What did you call her? Honey?"

"Yep, that's it. Honey."

He got in the truck and filled out her paperwork. He put the name "Honey" on it, with a note: "Named by the rescue responders." We knew she belonged to someone, but anyone who would see her paperwork from this point on would get that info and realize she was a sweet dog.

Perry started the truck and drove slowly so she could smell the air and take in her new freedom. We never discussed both of us being in tears—we understood each other and nothing needed to be said.

The vet was waiting for us at the deserted gas station. He looked at Honey, checked her temperature, and decided that, as long as she was drinking and eating, she would be ok. He said it was probably the fumes from the mold that made her weak, along with her prolonged time without food or good drinking water.

Buck was there too. He said he would keep her in the shade and give her a little more food in a couple of hours. So we took off again to see if we could get more animals before noon.

It was about 11:30 a.m. when Perry and I headed to our next address. It was in another area that was drying out. He pulled to a stop by the front of the house, and as I got out of the truck, I heard what sounded like a cat crying. I looked to my left and saw an orange cat with a white chest sitting at the side of the house. It had seen us pull up.

I said, calling out the window, "Hello there. Would you like to come with us?"

With that, he started talking and talking and talking. He was tired of being out here and having the dogs chase him like he was food. He had to hide all the time and could only eat the food that got set out late at night.

"Yuck! It was dog food! Do you have any cat food? I'm starving for good cat food, any cat food! Dog food is dry. It's ok, but it's dry and not as tasty as cat food. I don't know how they eat it! You going to that place the dogs are talking about? I hear it's away from all of this dirt. Are you? Can I go?"

I looked at Perry and said, "Get a carrier ready. I think this guy is thumbing a ride. And open a can of good wet food for him."

As I got out and closed the truck door, the cat looked at me and asked, *"What do I have to do to go with you?"*

"If you would like to go with us, just come over here. I will put you in a special carrier and off we go."

"Ok," he said and started to walk my direction. Just then, Perry dropped the carrier and our orange kitty stopped in his tracks.

"It's ok now. My friend is done dropping things. Perry, you're through dropping things, aren't you?"

"I hope so, but no promises."

I smiled, looked the cat, and said, *"Coming?"* Then I kneeled down and waited. He slowly walked over, still chatting about how the dogs had chased him for days and how he got away by coming into the flooded area.

"I don't like water, but it kept me safe from them. Look at me! I'm filthy. I need a bath. I need my bed. I need my nice home that floated away. I need my mom. Have you seen her?"

"No, but we can go look for her. I can take you to the place the dogs are talking about. Then your mom can come find you there. Ok?"

"Ok. Do they have cats there, or is it just dogs? I don't want any more dogs chasing me."

"I think we can take care of that. You will have your own spot and your own food. I think they will even get you some litter..."

"Litter! I used to have the best litter! It was soft on my feet and smelled nice. Oh, they have litter?"

"They do. They have cats too—and birds and horses and cows and a couple of goats and bunnies."

"Really? All of those animals? Not just dogs?"

"Yes, I have seen them for myself," I said, as he walked in front of me and looked up. He was still talking, but to Perry it sounded like he was crying. Perry asked, "Is he ok or does he need the vet too? I can call and see if he's still there."

I asked the cat if he was ok physically. He said, *"Yes,"* but it came out like, "Are you kidding? Of course, I'm ok."

He quickly added, *"But look at my hair! It is a mess! My mom is going to have a fit."*

I smiled. *"Let me give you a lift to your new home, and we can get you out of here. But first, we have to go into this house and get some dogs too. Are you ok to ride with them?"*

"If they are in their own house, I'm good."

I kneeled down and reached out for the cat. He stepped closer and rubbed against me. I picked him up and went around the back of the truck, where Perry had the carrier open and food inside. He went right in and curled up.

"Free! I made it, didn't I? I made it."

"Yes you did. You're free now, and you made it."

We went up to the next house and looked at the door. It had been opened by someone else. We gently said, "Hello, anyone home? HSUS. We are here to pick up the dogs. Hello!"

No one responded. Perry was able to close the door and we looked around to get our bearings. The interior was painted blue with white trim, and I could tell it was quite nice before the flood. It was well lit with windows and light colors, unlike many of the homes that were very dark and hard to see inside.

Perry went down the hallway, looking for two dogs—our paperwork had no breed or description listed. He got to a bedroom and saw that a dresser had floated in front of the door. He gave it a bit of a push to see if he could spot anything inside the room. Sure enough, there were two little dogs sitting on the bed. It looked like they had been in there the whole time.

I helped Perry push and the dresser gave way. We made a one-foot gap and Perry squeezed through it. He went to the bed and picked up a small black dog that looked like a terrier. The other dog was a miniature pincher. He handed me the terrier and I headed to the truck to introduce my new friend to our orange cat.

The cat didn't pay this terrier any mind—I guessed he'd been chased by much bigger dogs. I put the little guy in a kennel and waited for Perry. After a few minutes, I went back in to see what was going on. "Perry, you ok?" I said, as I came through the door.

"Yes, I am now. He decided to get underneath the bed and I had to get him out."

I looked at Perry and tried not to laugh. The front of his sheriff's t-shirt and pants were now quite muddy. The dog had his paw on Perry's face, which was also covered in mud. "Not a word," he said. "I got him."

"Well, that's the main thing. But I think you're taking a shower before you head home," I said and laughed.

I opened the kennel door just enough so he could put our

two friends together. While I did the paperwork, Perry tried to clean himself up as best he could with the hand sanitizer we kept in the truck.

We decided it was lunch time. As the truck began to roll, the cat started crying and Perry asked what he was talking about. I listened for a minute. "Keep an eye out for dogs. He is telling everyone that he is free. Their dinner is leaving. They are on their own."

We met everyone at the check-in point. They had figured it was time for lunch too. Someone had stopped for sandwiches and brought enough for all of us. After Perry and I took care of our animals, we sat on his tailgate to enjoy our meal.

As we finished, we saw some vehicles coming over the bridge. This was odd, because we were the only ones in this part of town. Perry said, "DEA, Drug Enforcement Administration. Probably looking for drugs."

They pulled into our lot, got out of their vehicles, and introduced themselves. They were in the area to help check for drugs and any deceased bodies. The EOC was beginning a count and trying to locate as many people as they could.

The agents mentioned where they were headed, and I said, "We have to get a couple of animals out of houses over there. Want us to show you where you're going?"

"Sure," one of the men said. "We'll have to check the houses first, and then you can have the pets."

"Ok, but you have to shut the door behind you when you go in, so you don't let the animals out. If you do, you're chasing them."

One of the agents looked at me hard, and Perry said, "The lady is right. You're chasing them if you let them out."

The guys from the DEA ended up being very nice and very helpful. They actually broke into two houses for us, so all we had to do was get the dogs—two pit bulls and a border collie, all ready to go and happy to see someone to let them out.

The DEA continued down the street. After checking each house, they marked the front with spray paint, noting whether they found people or toxic materials. Below that, they marked it if they found pets (dog, cat, etc.) and if they were deceased or alive.

They agreed to call us when they found any live animals, so we could come and get them. But we didn't hear from the DEA the rest of the day.

It was nearing 3:00 p.m. when we returned the three dogs to the trailer at the gas station. Perry said, "We need to check on the little guy."

We arrived in front of the house to feed the puppy and his pal and saw the water dish wasn't quite empty. We didn't hear anything. Nothing at all. Perry asked, "What do you think?"

"They are used to seeing us in the morning. I would check the house."

All of a sudden, we saw the little squirt racing straight for us to say hello. I said, "I think it's time they came with us. We can look for something in the house that has their information on it and get in touch with the owners. I don't know if I will have a vehicle tomorrow, so I'm not sure I can get back down here. Let's just take them."

Perry smiled. "I think you're reading my mind. You get this little guy a kennel and I'll go get the Shih Tzu."

I put the puppy in a kennel with enough food for both of them. It took Perry some time, but he finally emerged from the house, holding the Shih Tzu in both hands against his side. I asked, "You ok?"

"Yes. He's all bark." He handed him to me and I saw our Shih Tzu was a girl. As soon as she was in my arms, she started growling at Perry. "Women—they just don't like me," he said, shaking his head.

I laughed and took the Shih Tzu to her puppy. The two snuggled and were obviously glad to be in the same kennel. The puppy definitely wasn't a Shih Tzu, but he was "hers" and she was taking care of him nonetheless.

After Perry found something with the owners' name on it,

we went back to the check-in and gave the two dogs to Buck. He said he would call them on the way back to Lamar-Dixon so they could be reunited with their pets.

We headed out one more time. I wanted to pick up a brown Lab-mix puppy we had fed on the other days. I figured she would be an easy last-catch. She was also about the age to go into her first heat—and I knew that would be better for her to do away from all the loose males in the area.

We approached the corner where I had given her food, but I didn't see her anywhere.

I thought about the previous day. When I put down food, water, and a snack, she had actually started to walk away with the snack. I told her to come back and eat some food. *"I'll watch out while you eat. Then you can have some water and take the snack for later."*

She did exactly what I said: she gave me the snack, ate some food, and drank some water. Then the puppy looked at me, took the snack back, and headed down the street.

Now, Perry stopped the truck and I got out. I looked all over the place and started to get anxious. I understood exactly how Perry had felt about his puppy. I was feeling the same way. I didn't want to leave her here. I stopped for a moment and took a deep breath.

I said in my head, *"Where are you, Brownie? It's time to go. Today, you can go with us, but you have to come right now. Right now, to the spot where I fed you yesterday. Ok? Hurry, we have to leave soon."*

While we waited, I got a kennel out of the truck for her. Perry looked at me and said, "If she doesn't show up soon, we'll have to leave her for someone else."

I kept saying, *"Brownie, come on. Come on, Brownie. It's time to go! I can take you today."*

Where was she? She was always right here. Finally Perry said, "I think we'll have to leave her."

"No. She's coming. I can feel it. Let's just wait a bit more."

"We've got about two minutes and we have to meet the group."

So I said out loud, "Brownie, where are you? We have to go. You need to be here now! Now, Brownie. Now!"

The streets were quiet. There was no noise. But I could feel her, and I knew she was close. "Come on, Brownie, let's go! Come on, girl! It's time."

Perry sighed and said, "I think we have to go."

I swallowed hard. We lifted up the kennel and put it back into the truck. As we headed to the front, I suddenly heard her barking at me! *"I'm coming! I'm coming! I'm here. I had to bring my friend. She couldn't be outside. They would eat her. She's too small."*

I looked down the street and shut the door to the cab. Perry stopped too. We both saw them coming: Brownie and her little friend, a Yorkie who couldn't have been more than four pounds.

I looked at Perry as he broke into a smile. I said, "She had to bring her friend—and the other dog can't go as fast."

Now it made sense why, when my puppy finished eating, she left with the snack—she was taking food to her friend. Today, when I told her we would take her, she made sure her friend would be safe too.

Brownie ran into my arms and looked at her friend. I picked up the Yorkie and hugged them both. *"Oh Brownie, you are the best protector ever. She is adorable!"*

Brownie told me she was her sister and her name was Penny. They were staying together at their house, but she would go out to get food. Water was a problem, she said, but she had pulled one of the gallon jugs we left behind all the way to their house for her sister.

I handed Penny over to Perry and said, "I will make a kennel for two, so we can keep them together."

Brownie looked up at me and said, *"Thank you for coming for us."*

"Why didn't you tell me about your friend? We could have

taken you sooner."

"You told me that you were getting the sick ones first and then would come back for us. We weren't sick."

I hugged Brownie again, as I lifted her up into the kennel with Penny. I asked her what her real name was and she said, *"I like Brownie. Will you call me that?"*

"Done! You're now officially Brownie."

Perry filled out the paperwork and noted: "Brownie and Penny: Keep together, found in the same home."

On the road back to the check-in, we spotted a black terrier. He was dragging about 15 feet of rope that was tied around his neck. Perry said, "We, at least, have to cut that off so he doesn't get caught and strangle himself."

"Or, we can just take him with us."

Perry smiled. "Let's see if he's friendly."

When we got close, I grabbed my catch pole and hopped out of the truck. I stepped on the rope and then worked my way toward the dog, who was very surprised, and not very happy, that I was threatening his freedom.

Perry got out of the truck and took the rope, so I could focus on catching him. Perry actually had to lift the rope to hold up the dog, so I could snag him with the catch pole. The little guy was becoming very upset, but I got the catch pole on him.

As Perry took out a kennel, I could hear Brownie trying to talk to our new black friend and help calm him down, but he wasn't having it. Perry said, "Do you have him? I have to cut off this rope before we put him in the kennel."

"Yes, go ahead."

Perry had to work to keep his hands from getting bit. Once the rope was cut, I walked with the dog like he was on a leash and he calmed down. I told him where we were going and that he was safe. *"The rope is off of your neck. I'm sure it doesn't feel that way now, but you can stay free."*

I walked him close to the kennel. We did a circle and in he went.

We got to the check-in point and added our new friends

to the horse trailer. I told them all that Buck was going to take them to a nice place, where there were already lots of animals and they would be taken care of. As Buck headed out, the rest of the crew looked at us, wanting to know about their surprise.

"What have we been waiting all day for?" asked Cindy.

"You'll have to follow us," I said.

We headed to the downtown lot where we had gotten gas the day before. The same man was there, and all three vehicles were filled up. Cindy asked how we pay and the man said, "You don't."

I told her that it is free to us, because we are doing search and rescue, so she could stop here every day and fill up before leaving town.

Then I said to Cindy, "You hungry? Perry and I were thinking of getting dinner on the way back."

"Sure, but there isn't any place here."

"Tell Sharon and Jeff to follow us. We're going to dinner."

We caravanned the two blocks and I motioned for them to park. We parked, and Cindy said, "I need a picture of us in front of Harrah's—no one will believe the casino is closed."

After we posed for pictures together, I asked if everyone was hungry.

"Are you kidding? I'm starving," Anthony said, then stopped and looked at me. "Are you fooling us, boss?"

"No. Just come on," I said, as Perry and I headed toward the ship. They followed us like little kids who were getting away with something.

The sailor from yesterday was there and he smiled at Perry and me. We told him we had our other responders with us and asked if that was ok.

"Of course. You all look like you could use a good meal," he said and pointed to the buffet. The team welcomed the chance to set aside our canned goods! We all had a lovely hot dinner—and most everyone had seconds.

Bellies full, we went back to Lamar-Dixon. We met Buck, just as he was pulling up to the front of the intake line. We unloaded our rescues and relayed everything we knew about the animals. As Perry was collecting his radios from our crew, they asked me about tomorrow. I said, "I guess we'll just gather at the morning meeting and see what happens."

A few minutes later, Wayne Pacelle arrived near the front of Barn Five, pulled out the bullhorn, and called everyone over for the evening debriefing. Folks gathered around.

Wayne thanked everyone for their hard work and said that the site was filled almost to capacity. "We might have to suspend our search-and-rescue efforts until we can get some of our animals relocated. A big, air-conditioned truck should be here tonight from Texas. It will allow us to rescue an even larger number of pets, but we are still working on relocating animals from our site.

"Also we will be receiving more volunteers to help us in the next couple of days. The restrictions on going into town are becoming more stringent. So make sure you have your proper documents with you whenever you go to New Orleans, and show them to anyone who asks. We've had a few problems with people who are not a part of our rescue just helping themselves. The authorities are trying to shut that down, so keep your eyes open. If you see anyone who's not a part of our group, don't approach them. Just get their license plate number, let authorities know the whereabouts, and they'll handle it.

"We'll have a morning meeting behind Barn One at six o'clock to tell you about the day's events. Thank you, and see you all tomorrow. Have a good night's rest."

I gave Perry a hug and told him to keep in touch. I thanked him for all of his help and wished him a safe trip home—after a shower, of course. We both laughed.

I spotted Inga across the barn at the main check-in and went to see her. We caught up on what each of us had been doing over the past few days. Then I said, "My partner is leaving with his truck, so I'll be without a vehicle. If I can get another partner, I can continue to rescue. If not, I guess I'll work with the vets."

"Let me see what I can do."

"Great. I'm going to the vets' barn to check on the dogs I've helped with and some of the ones my team brought in."

Back in Barn One, Doc Debra was in full swing. I spoke to a couple of dogs and cats that she asked me about. She said the brown Lab had been transported to the hospital and was doing well. I smiled, but was sad I didn't get to say goodbye. The other two dogs we had worked on were doing well and were waiting to go to the hospital.

A woman walked up to me and said, "Are you Terri?"

"Yes."

"I'm Christie. I hear you need a vehicle. Come with me."

I said goodbye to Debra and followed Christie to the front of Barn One. As we walked, she told me she worked with a regional humane society. When we got to the spay/neuter van that Inga had been driving a few days before, Christie said, "Hop in."

We got in the van and she said, "Inga tells me you have a tent in the corner by hers. Show me which one it is."

We drove to the far corner of the site, where I pointed out my little pup tent. There was a fifth-wheel parked along the fence directly in front of us and a huge semi-truck in front of that—its trailer was specially configured for animal transport and the side was marked "SPCA of Texas." I assumed it was the big truck for search and rescue that we had been told about. In front of that truck was another fifth-wheel.

Christie said, "Texas is here."

We went over to meet the Texas folks. They had folding chairs set out and offered us each one. We sat down and chatted for a while.

Christie talked about how she had helped with the water

evacuation, but had to quit because she cut her thumb and couldn't be around the toxins with an open wound. She said there were a couple of men who had been in and out of the water without wet suits or waders—they got really sick and were taken to the hospital.

The Texans talked about their trip here and the flat tire that delayed them a day. They were waiting for a replacement driver—the driver who came with the truck was sent home because he appeared to be drunk.

I told Christie I once drove school buses and have a Class B driver's license. "Whatever you need, I'm here for two weeks."

"Inga told me you have already worked at intake and with the vets for three days, and you've been in New Orleans doing search and rescue. She also said you're a pet whisperer," said Christie.

"That's what I do for a living."

"Has it helped in New Orleans, your being able to chat with the animals?"

"Yes, it has—at least according to my partner, who is leaving tonight."

I saw Perry's truck coming our way and flagged him down. As he got out, I could see he was clean. I introduced him to Christie and the Texas group, and Christie pulled him aside. I went back to chatting with the Texans.

When Christie and Perry returned, I again said goodbye to Perry and he headed out.

Christie handed me a set of keys. "Here are the keys to the van I drove down here. I'm going home tomorrow, but they want to keep it for a while. I can't think of any better use than search and rescue. If you take the van, it will be easy for you to get a partner, and then you can continue your work. Just take good care of her—I want her back in one piece."

"Of course," I said, thanking her. "I will do my best."

I went to my tent, got my casual clothes, and headed to the showers. I was tickled to have a vehicle—now all I needed was a partner.

I was especially tired after the day we had, but I still wrote in my journal. Then I put in my ear plugs (those new neighbors were getting noisy), set my alarm, and "boom," I was out.

CHAPTER SIX

Sunday, September 18, 2005

Buzz. Buzz. Buzz. There it was again: the alarm. I turned
it off, and as I lay there for a moment, I remembered my new
neighbors. I didn't hear anything. "Of course," I thought, "I
have ear plugs in." I pulled them out—and it was still quiet.

I got ready and stepped out of my tent. It was barely light, but
on the way to the restrooms, I could see the outline of the fifth-
wheels and a few more tents. New volunteers were arriving.

I remembered I had the keys to the van and drove over to
load up supplies. Then I figured I would eat a can of stew
while waiting for the morning meeting to begin.

I didn't see Ernie or John, but by now, I knew where
everything was kept. I loaded the van with kennels, litter
pans, and two-gallon water jugs. I also found a 15-foot
extension catch pole and a regular one. I took a box of plastic
gloves, a cooler for drinks, antiseptic hand cleaner, and
neon-orange spray paint for marking houses. I even spotted
another can opener.

Next I drove over to where Perry would park, behind what
was now the Relaxation Tent. I filled up the cooler with ice,
blue and red Gatorade, and two cases of drinking water.

When I was done, I saw everyone was gathering for
the meeting. Wayne came out of the incident command
motorhome, and as he started his briefing, I felt a tap on my
shoulder. I turned and saw Kat, the woman from the Louisiana

SPCA I had met at the EOC downtown. She whispered, "Meet me by the water tower in 15 minutes. I have my own group going downtown and I'd like for you to join us."

"I need a partner."

"I'll find you one. I need to get a few more people, then I'll see you there."

I headed to the van. I figured going with her would be good. There were a lot of new people in the HSUS meeting this morning, and I would rather be with others who had experience and knew what to do.

I backed out and went toward Barn Three to avoid the crowd of newbie responders. I drove to the water tower and parked by my tent. Two of the Texans were sitting in their folding chairs and asked me to join them. I said, "Is this where Kat is coming for her meeting?"

"We don't know. The head of the LASPCA is supposed to come and brief us about what we're going to do today."

Kat pulled up a few minutes later and asked, "Terri, did you work with a group yesterday? Inga told me you were a team leader."

"Yes, I did."

"Go get your team."

I hopped in the van and headed back to the HSUS meeting. I parked behind Barn One and could see my group in the crowd. When Cindy spotted me, I waved her over and said, "Get everyone and meet me. You'll see me in a spay/neuter van at the front of Barn One. I'll show you where we're going—I have a new group for us."

"Gotcha. Meet you in a minute."

She waved to the others, who had been watching us, and they headed to their vehicles. I met them in front of Barn One and they followed me to the Texas trailers. I told them we had been invited to join the head of the Louisiana SPCA and do search and rescue with her.

Kat asked everyone to circle around. "As some of you

know, I stole you from the group by Barn One, because you've already been into town or you are a qualified animal responder. Now, I know the Texas folks and a few others of you are new. Why don't you all introduce yourselves so everyone knows who's here."

There were two women and a man from Texas, who were all in uniform: black jeans and red t-shirts with their SPCA logo printed in white. Another gal was with HSUS and had brought her own vehicle from Texas. And there was a short woman in her mid-30s from New Mexico, who said, "My name is Jackie, but everyone calls me Jax."

Kat said, "Terri, don't you want to tell everyone what you do?"

"I'm an animal communicator."

Kat smiled. "She's been doing some wonderful things while she's been here. She worked with the vets for three days and has been doing search and rescue for several days too. So if you get stuck, ask her."

Some of the Texans' eyes lit up. I wasn't sure if it was from surprise or if they were thinking, "Oh no, we have a nut with us."

As everyone partnered up, Jax and I were left. We looked at each other and smiled. I said, "I have a van."

"I'll get my gear."

Kat stopped us and said, "Hold on a minute, I have to let you know some things. First off, we need to find supplies like kennels and food."

I said, "Along the sides of Barns Two and Three. Tell Ernie and John that Terri sent you, and they'll fix you up. Also I suggest we stop at the convenience store in Gonzales—it's on the right, before you get to the highway—to get snacks and sandwiches or something for lunch. There's no food in town."

Kat smiled. "I like that idea. When we get to the blockade, turn on your flashers and we'll all go through at the same time. We'll meet at a location down by the bridge near the Lower

Ninth Ward. Terri, is that the area you've been working in?"

"Yes, all of us have," I said, pointing to my group.

"Today, we are going to meet the National Guard and they'll be escorting us. There are people in town who are shooting things up, so the Guard will be with us if we need any help. Let's hope not. But, if anyone is afraid to go downtown, please say so now. I would rather you stay here, so we don't have to bring back just one person."

No one said a word.

"We're all a go. Get your supplies and meet me back here in 30 minutes."

When Jax came back, she was carrying a big, black backpack and a large, ball-peen hammer with a 26-inch handle. She waved it and said to me, "Ole Faithful. Don't go to any disasters without her. She's real handy for breaking locks."

"Great! You're our official wrecker," I said.

She chuckled. "I'll wear that title with a smile."

Kat had everyone exchange cell numbers, and our procession of seven vehicles, with the big Texas SPCA truck at the end, left Lamar-Dixon.

As we drove to New Orleans, Jax and I got acquainted. She worked in animal control in New Mexico, and she headed out to help when the call came. We chatted for a while and then she said, "I can tell you have some powerful gifts. I can feel them—it's the Navajo in me. But do me a favor: don't turn any of mine back on. They scare the bejesus out of me. You are sensitive to energy, and that's enough protection for both of us."

I smiled and said, "Ok, but the only person who can turn on your gifts is you."

When we arrived at the blockade, I saw the right lane was blocked off with orange cones and a large sign that said, "Official Vehicles Only." Kat headed right for it. She stopped at the front gate and let the officers know we were coming through. As I drove by, I saw the man who had been there every day since I arrived. I introduced Jax, so he would know who she was. "Happy hunting," he said and waved us through.

The second checkpoint was about the same, except the man at the blockade had radioed ahead that I now had my own van. (It didn't dawn on me that they were in touch with each other.) As I drove through, the official bowed and said, "Your highness, so glad to see you today. Congratulations on getting your own vehicle."

I had begun to find out that disaster responders are a pretty tight-knit group—and they watch out for each other. I was proud to be a part of this team.

We drove on the main dirt roads through town and stopped just before going over the bridge to our old check-in point. On the right was a brick building that the National Guard had commandeered for its headquarters. We parked along the side of the road and waited about 15 minutes while Kat was inside. When she came out, she waved for us all to follow her. We made a U-turn and went to an empty parking lot about two blocks back. We were to wait for the National Guardsmen to meet us, and then we would head out. We unloaded our extra supplies along a fence at the side of the lot. The big truck pulled to the back, so it would be easier for us to get in and out for drop-off.

Soon seven military vehicles arrived—four-door Humvees painted in sand camouflage. Each carried three or four men, dressed in camouflage, with rifles, helmets, and all the gear. The commander talked to Kat about who would go out together and what areas they would cover before we needed to return at 4:30 p.m. He told her the Guard was there to protect us, not rescue animals. The commander handed off the men to Kat and said, "Gentlemen, she is in charge. You will follow her orders."

"Yes sir!" they responded. Then the commander left and returned to his headquarters.

Kat had the men introduce themselves and then partnered

them off with all of us. Jax and I were paired with Sergeant First Class Thomas (or Sarge to his troops), Sergeant Porter, and Private Clark. They eyed us up and down, and from the looks on their faces, they were not happy to have babysitting duty.

Next Kat asked those of us doing rescue to introduce ourselves. When it was my turn, I could tell Thomas was not thrilled. Everyone else had gotten animal control officers.

The razzing began immediately. "Hey, Sarge, you have a good day with your animal communicator, while we go and get dogs."

He smiled and tried to brush it off, but I could tell it was a problem for him.

Kat handed out the new addresses for locating pets and gave me a list. "I think you're familiar with the Lower Ninth Ward, so take your team and get going."

I looked at the list and thought, "Thank you, Perry! I know where most of these are."

Thomas asked if he could help us locate the addresses. "I think we're good," I replied.

I handed a page each to Cindy and Sharon for their vehicles. I said to Thomas, "You ready to head out?"

He looked surprised. "Yes, ma'am."

Jax and I got in the van and pulled out behind Cindy and Anthony, who were being followed by their Guardsmen. Sharon and Glen got in line right behind us. Meanwhile, the rest of the groups were still looking at maps, trying to figure out where they were so they could get started.

As we went over the bridge, I saw Thomas smiling and waving off the other guys, as if to say, "We are first. Ha, ha!" We pulled into our old check-in gas station. Cindy and Anthony needed to pick up some water jugs. Sharon and Glen grabbed a couple of kennels.

I told the sergeant we would be here just a few minutes and then gathered together the team. "Look at your list and see if the addresses are in an area you're familiar with. If not, let's switch. And you know the drill: call me on the hour to let me know you're ok. Instead of returning your drop-offs here, take them across the bridge to the big truck and then come back and get more animals. If you see something walking around, feel free to pick it up. It would be a shame to let anything stay down here longer than necessary—and I didn't hear any instructions about feeding and leaving today. Did any of you?"

Everyone was smiling and no one said a word.

"Ok! You know where they are, let's go get them. We have a big truck to fill."

We drove off with our military men in tow. When Jax and I stopped at the first house where we were supposed to get a dog, I said, "Get out your plastic gloves and your leather ones—there are lots of toxic chemicals here, so only touch the things you need to. We'll get out a kennel, open the door, and put two dishes in it. We'll only put food in now, and will fill the water later. Also set a dish with water in it outside of the kennel, so the dogs can drink as soon as we get them out."

I took my catch pole, started toward the house, and said, "Let's go see what we need to do to get this guy out."

I looked around the front and sides of the property. There wasn't any way to get into the backyard, so I figured the front door might be the best. "Jax, get Ole Faithful and see what you can do on the doorknob. Try to leave it so the owners can replace as little as possible when they return. The noise will probably scare the dog, so make your hits count."

Porter wanted to help break the door down, but Thomas stopped him. "We are here to protect."

Porter seemed disappointed. However, Jax was delighted they couldn't help, because she was "The Wrecker."

I said, "Before you hit the door, let's talk. If the door opens, close it until I can get ready to enter. Then, when I do, close the door behind me."

"Behind you and Sergeant Porter," corrected Thomas. "He

will go with you to keep you safe. If the dog is vicious, we have to keep you safe."

"Ok. The first thing is: you will not be shooting anything today, especially animals. If one growls at you, you will back up and let me handle it. These animals have been through enough. That's the way it is, or you can stay outside until I return."

It seemed for a moment that we might have a bit of a standoff. Then Thomas said, "Porter, you go with her."

Jax hit the doorknob. The wood on the door was rotten from the moisture, so the lock flew into the house. I grabbed the door and pulled it shut.

"Good job!" I said to Jax. "When I come out, keep the guys clear, so we have a direct path to the water dish, ok?"

"Yes, boss."

I stepped through the door first and shut it behind me. I said to Porter, "Hang outside a minute, so I can make sure the dog is not right here. We don't want it to get out."

He waited. I let my eyes adjust to the darkness and the interior of the living room began to appear: sofa, chair, and TV. The drapes were shut to keep the cool in, I imagined. I didn't see a dog, alive or dead. I said, "Porter, step in the door, stop, and let your eyes adjust. Jax will shut the door."

He slipped in lickety-split, and Jax pulled the door shut and held it closed. After a few moments, I told Porter to follow me down the hall. There was light from outside shining through one window, and as we went down the hall, we saw that furniture had floated everywhere. We passed the bathroom, where the tub was filled with dirty water and there were dog footprints on the floor in the mud.

I saw that the end of Porter's gun was close to my left leg. I looked at it and said, "What are you doing?"

"I'm going to keep you safe."

"I'd feel a lot safer if you aimed that thing toward the wall."

He smiled and actually pointed it further away from me. I

pointed to the dog tracks in the carpet and put my finger to my lips, motioning him to be quiet. As we approached what looked to be the master bedroom, I saw the bed against the far wall. Suddenly I spotted in the darkness a large dog lying on the bed.

I stopped, relaxed, and said aloud, "Hi there. How are you?" The dog didn't move, until he saw Porter come up behind me, then he began growling—and not in a nice tone. I'm not sure what triggered him, but I said to Porter, "It might be the uniform. Back up and stay there. I'm going to shut the door, so we can at least keep him in this room and make it easier for us to catch him. You stay in the hall, and when I tell you, open the door. But not until I ask you, ok?"

"Yes, ma'am."

I stepped into the room, talking to the dog as I went. *"My friend is going to stay out here. I think I'll just come in and chat, ok?"*

He made no movement, but the growling had stopped. So I kept chatting. I closed the door and the room got even darker. I held up my catch pole between the two of us and waited a moment for my eyes to adjust again. When they did, I saw we had a lovely Rottweiler, probably a male. *"Look at you. You're beautiful!"*

He just kept lying there, looking at me. *"Who are you?"*

"My name is Terri. I've been sent here to get you out and take you to a safe place. Is that ok with you?"

"I'm guarding. I have to guard the house for my mom. She said she'll be back. You shouldn't even be in here, but I'm tired."

"I see. You look very handsome, though, I must say. Are you ok?"

"I'm not hurt, if that's what you're asking."

"Yes, that's what I wanted to know."

I realized this Rotty was exhausted, but willing to defend if he had to. I let my catch pole go down to the floor, then took a deep breath and let the air out. *"Hot in here."*

"Yes, it has been hot for days."

I got quiet for a moment, thinking about what to say next, when the Rotty said, *"Look at this place—it's a mess! My mommy is going to be so mad at me. She told me to guard it and she would be back. She left, and the water came, and I had to swim for three days. I thought I was going to drown! Then the water started to go down, and everything was all muddy and moved around. Look at it. It's a mess."*

I looked around. *"You did everything you could. The water came from the levees bursting and it flooded this area. I'm so sorry. I'm sorry you were all alone."*

"No food or good water either."

That was my cue. *"I have water and food right outside and a way to take you to a shelter where your mommy can find you. She can't come here to get you. They are keeping all the people out. But they are sending people like me to come and get you, so I can take you to somewhere that's safe. Would that be ok with you?"*

He looked around at the mess. *"Do you think my mommy would be ok if I left?"*

"I think she would love for you to leave, and then she can find you at the shelter."

"Ok. I guess I can go with you."

"You see this stick-like leash I have on the floor? I need to attach it to you, so we can walk out together and I can keep you safe. Would that be ok?"

"I guess so."

Just then, Porter interrupted our conversation. "Ma'am, are you all right? Ma'am?"

"Yes, sergeant. Just give me a little bit more time and I think we're good."

I said to my Rotty, *"That is Sergeant Porter. He's getting excited to see you too. How about I put this loop on over your head. I will tighten it a little so we can walk out together. Ok?"*

"Ok."

I moved slowly so I wouldn't startle my Rotty and talked to him the whole time. After the loop was over his head, I began to tighten it. When I got it to just the right spot, I said, *"So what do you think? Are you ready to go?"*

He stood up on the bed. *"Yes, I am very ready."*

"I'm going to let you go first. So you go right by Sergeant Porter and out the front door. I will follow you all the way. Ok?"

"Ok."

"Sergeant Porter, open the door and get out of the way."

He gently pushed open the door. My Rotty jumped off the bed and took a dash toward the door. He passed Porter and we headed down the hall. I tried to keep up with him, but kept slipping on the mud in the hallway. I started laughing and said aloud, "Look at you go!"

Porter hollered over my head, "Stand aside!"

I saw Clark had come in the house and was standing at the side of the living room. He flattened against the wall and said, "She's coming! Open the door!"

Jax opened the door and our Rotty headed outside. Thomas was standing by the kennel and the dog made a beeline for him. The sergeant didn't know what to do, so he froze. The Rotty jumped up, excited to see him, and put his muddy paws all over Thomas' pants. I pulled the dog off, pointed to the water, and said, "Look here."

The Rotty went for the water. I yelled to Jax to get the water bottle so we could fill the bowl again. She was still near the front door, so Thomas picked up the water jug from the van and re-filled the bowl.

I said, "That's good for now. We don't want him to throw it up."

The dog looked up at me. *"Thank you. You brought all these people to take me to my mommy?"*

"I sure did. They're all happy to see you too. Now, let's get you some food."

I turned the Rotty on the catch pole in a circle and he went right in the kennel. *"Here is your food, and we will get you some more water soon."*

The Rotty smiled at me. *"Thank you."*

"You're welcome."

I said to Thomas, "Sorry about your pants."

"Not a problem. Last I heard, he was growling and not happy. Now look at him."

"If you explain to the animals what's happening and where they're going, then they're ok. Just like we would be. If you try to manhandle them and yank them out...well, I wouldn't want to go either. Would you?"

"No, I guess I wouldn't"

By now, everyone was back near the kennel. I looked at Thomas and said, "Thank you for getting the water. That was a big help. I know you're not supposed to help us, but I appreciate it."

"Well, he looked really thirsty."

"He was. Jax, why don't we lift him into the van and go get another one."

"You will not!" Thomas declared.

I looked at him and said, "What?"

He looked me in the eyes, smiled, and said, "Porter and Clark will put him in the van for you. Right, gentlemen?"

"Right, Sarge!" they yelled.

The ice had been broken.

We went to the next house and the next and the next. The animals just kept coming. We made several drops back at the truck—and every time we brought animals to the lot, we were the only team there.

We checked on another house and didn't find any dogs. The whole side of the house was missing, so I figured they had gotten out. When Clark and I went around to the backyard, we saw a beautiful, red-and-white rooster, sitting in all of his glory, all by himself. Nowhere did we see a chicken coop or anything resembling a coop, yet there he was.

Clark asked me, "Do we take that?"

"Yes, I think we should. I've seen some roosters and chickens up at the shelter, so he'll have company. I'm actually surprised he's still alive and not someone's dinner. This must be one tough rooster."

I asked Clark to get a towel from the van, so we could scoop him up. The rooster was in no hurry to go anywhere. He just stood there like this was his yard. I walked up close to him and scooped him up in one swoop. Clark wanted to carry him back and put him in the kennel, so I handed him off. "You ok with him?"

"Yes, I grew up on a farm."

"Then our rooster is in good hands," I said as we headed to the truck.

The phone rang every hour from both Cindy and Sharon. Everyone on my team was pulling in dogs by the carload, which made me very happy.

Cindy called about 1:00 p.m. "We got him. We got the last chow, the third one from the other day that ran away from you and Perry."

"Awesome! How did you do that?"

"We followed him on the road for about 20 minutes. I think he was ready to go, because he just stopped and let me put the catch pole on him."

"Good job! I want to be there when he sees his family."

At that moment, I saw what looked like a dog lying in some water on the road. I actually felt him before I saw him. I stopped the van and asked Jax to get out a kennel.

"Do you see one?" she asked.

"I think so."

I got out of the van and slowly walked in the direction of what I thought was a dog. I kept saying in my head, *"Is that you? Are you there? I can feel you. Do you want to come with me? I have food and water. I can take you somewhere that's safe."*

All of a sudden, I saw movement in the water. A beige

dog started to get up and looked right at me. I could tell he weighed about 20 pounds and was very thin.

I kneeled down. *"I can take you, if you'd like to go."*

I realized I didn't have my catch pole—I had just moved toward the energy I felt from him. I held up my hand behind me like a stop sign, so no one would come our direction. I wanted time to chat with this little dog. I said, *"I have food. I have good water."*

He was about 20 feet from me and started to move slowly my direction. I stayed put—waiting to see if he would come over to me or dart away—and kept talking to him. *"Look at you. You're so handsome."*

He looked at me like I was nuts. *"I'm all dirty,"* he said.

"You look handsome to me. I can only imagine how you must look after a bath. Were you sitting in the water to cool off?"

"All you can do is sit in it. It's bad to drink. I have seen some dogs die drinking it. You have good water?"

"Yes, I do. I'm having my friends get some out for you right now—and they are also getting you a place to rest."

He slowly walked in my direction. When he was about 5 feet from me, I said, *"Come on, let me take you out of here."*

With that, he walked right up between my squatting legs, curled into my chest, and gave me a big hug. I could feel the love coming from him and his delight to be free from his burden. It was now over, and he could rest.

I held him for what seemed like a long moment. *"How about if I carry you the rest of the way."*

"Really? I'm very tired."

I gently put my arms around his chest and his behind, lifted him, and slowly carried him back to the van. He looked up at me, and I tipped him up like a baby cuddled in my arms. He put his head on my neck, leaned against me, and closed his eyes.

So he wouldn't be startled when he saw everyone, I said, *"I have some wonderful friends who are very excited to meet you."*

"Ok, but I'm kind of tired right now."

"That's ok. I want you to have some water and maybe some food. Then you can rest on the way to the shelter."

When I got back to the van, there wasn't a dry eye to be found. I placed our little friend in the kennel and put the water bowl inside. He drank quite a bit, and I asked him if he wanted more. He said he did, so I filled the water bowl again.

"Food!" he said, as he noticed it was there. He grabbed a mouthful and looked up at me. *"I knew you would come. I knew you would come for me."*

I smiled and got tears in my eyes too. *"I'm just sorry you had to wait so long for me to come."*

"You're here now." He smiled, then looked around. *"These your friends?"*

As I introduced the dog to everyone, we were all wiping tears from our eyes. I said to Thomas, who was doing the paperwork, "We need to make sure this one sees the vet. Put that in large print. He is not feeling the best. I'll see how he feels after the food. That might be all he needs."

Thomas looked at me. "You can tell that?"

"Yes, I can feel it in my body. I'll check him in a bit."

"Wow, that's amazing."

"Let's go. We have more to bring home."

As the day went on, Jax got a few dogs and so did Porter. All in all, I thought we had a great day—it was the best one yet for me.

At 3:30 p.m., the big truck was full. We had a meeting at the site with our military friends. Kat thanked them all for their help. We said our goodbyes and told them we hoped we would see them tomorrow. I asked Kat if my team could follow me back to Lamar-Dixon, and she let us leave together.

We filled up our gas tanks and arrived just in time for dinner at the Navy ship. Then we headed back to camp and waved at the Texas gang as we passed their caravan on the interstate.

We all parked at the front, so we could help unload the

animals when our truck arrived. There was almost a hush as people saw the Texas SPCA truck come in—it was massive compared to the other vehicles. Realizing it was full of rescued animals made everyone's heart sing with joy!

It took us an hour and a half to unload all the animals from the truck and process them with the veterinarian. (They called another vet to the front to check the animals from the cars.) The vet climbed in the back of the truck and used it like a private office to examine our rescues. It was a new vet, but he had heard about me. He asked me to stand by and let him know if any of the animals had problems. After about fifty animals, he began to rely on me and the processing got a little faster.

When we got down to the last three pets, I said to the vet, "If you're good, I think I'll head out."

"Sure, go ahead. Long day for you."

It wasn't over yet. The beige dog had been sent to Barn One and I wanted to check on him. I also wanted to see the three chows reunited. I asked Cindy where they were.

"You missed it. They were all glad to see each other. Come on, I'll show you. They're so happy."

We walked halfway down the barn and I saw them side by side in their kennels. The brown chow was in the center and the two black ones were on either side. The brown chow kept turning back and forth between the other two. I said, "Let's turn them so the backs of the kennels are together. That way, they can all nose each other and the two black chows will feel closer."

We re-arranged the kennels. The three dogs put their noses together, then looked up at us, smiled, and thanked us. Next they curled up as close as they could get to each other and went to sleep.

I said to Cindy, "Let's check the paperwork and see that they all stay together." We wrote in large print: "These three chows stay together—siblings." We also wrote it on the paperwork of each kennel, just to be sure.

I told her I had a dog to check on in the vets' barn and

would meet her later at the debriefing. When I got to Barn One, I saw Doc Debra working on a red mix-breed puppy. When she spotted me, she said, "Hey, come over here. I need you to calm this guy down."

"Sure, what do you need to do to him?"

"His feet are burned, but he won't let us touch them."

"Let me chat for a minute and see what I can do," I said, then asked the dog, *"How are you?"*

"My feet hurt really bad, and my tail hurts, and my stomach hurts, and my back hurts, and these people are nuts! I don't like my feet touched."

I relayed what he said to the doc. She rolled her eyes at me. "Really? I know that about his feet and tail. But good to know about the rest. I can check that out."

I continued to chat with our new friend. I said to Debra, "Is there some way to use a litter pan and put the solution in it? Then you can put one foot in it at a time, so that he sees it's cooling off the burn. I think he'll better understand you're trying to help him, and he'll calm down."

The doc looked at me. "That's a good idea. Why didn't I think of that?"

"You would have, I'm sure. I just beat you to it."

She had a vet tech get a litter pan—it was light yellow. I said to the dog, *"Look at this a pretty yellow dish. They are going to put some solution in there, like water, to cool off your feet. Then they will need to wrap them in bandages. Ok?"*

He looked at me, and all of a sudden, realized I could hear him. *"You can hear me?"*

"Yes, I can."

"Are they trying to help me?"

"Yes, they are."

"Everyone else has been chasing me for three days. They put me in a car and brought me here. I thought they were going to kill me."

"I'm sorry. They had to bring you here to get you out of all

the burning chemicals where you were. The humans have been told to get out of that area, and they're trying now to get all the animals out."

"Oh."

The vet tech had the cooling solution in the litter pan, so I looked at the dog and said, *"This pan has something in it to help stop the burning. I want you to put one foot in there, so you can see that it will quit burning. Ok?"*

I placed my hand all the way in the tub. The dog looked at it and saw I wasn't hurt. He looked me in the eyes and said, *"Ok."* Then, on his own, he lifted his right front paw and slowly began to place it in the litter pan. He stepped down on it, then looked at me and kissed my face.

"Feel better?" I asked him.

"Yes!" He put both front feet in and tried to get his back ones in too.

"Wait a minute," I told him and asked Doc Debra for a bigger pan so he could get all four feet in. She was already on it. She had gotten another litter pan and was now putting solution in it.

His back feet went in quickly. *"Ahhh. That feels good,"* he said, standing in the solution.

Debra said, "Talk to him about us touching his feet, before you go anywhere."

I looked at our friend and said, *"When you get finished soaking your feet, the docs are going to have to put some salve and bandages on them so they can heal, Ok?"*

He looked at me and smiled. Our boy was just enjoying the burning being gone. Then he realized what I had said. *"Oh! Tell them they have to go slow, my feet tickle."*

I relayed the message to the doc and she said to him, "Don't worry, my feet tickle too."

The dog said, *"Ok."* But it didn't look like he was going to get out of the solution anytime soon. I said to Debra, "You might want to let him soak a while before you finish.

Maybe work on someone else for a bit and let him enjoy his moment."

"Not a problem. We're backed up," she said and asked the vet tech to stay with the dog, who was now happily sitting in the solution.

I asked Debra about the beige dog I brought in. "He's over there. We put him on fluids. It looks like he'll be ok."

I headed to his kennel. When he saw me coming, he stood up and wagged his tail. We said hello to each other.

"You ok?" I asked.

"Yes. They put this thing in my arm and it makes me feel cool. I'm not so dizzy now."

"Good. These are fluids to help your body feel better. The doctors will make sure you have food and water, and you can rest here tonight."

"Thank you. I'm so glad you came for me."

"I am too." I began to get tears in my eyes again. It looked like he was too. I opened his kennel. He walked out and snuggled in between my legs, like he had done in the road. I held him for a long moment and said, *"You're going to be ok now."*

"I know. Thanks to you."

A tear fell from my face and got lost in his coat. His tear landed on my forearm. Time had stood still for a moment. No noise. No movement. Just us embracing.

When I put him back in his kennel, I said, *"These people will take very good care of you."*

"Thank you. I need to rest. I'm very tired."

"I'm sure you are, my friend. Sleep well and I'll check in on you in the morning."

I smiled and headed back over to Debra, who was working on the feet of yet another dog. She said, "That one hit your soft spot."

"You should've seen where I got him. He just walked up to me—he was done."

"Nice moment. We all had tears watching you two."

"Yes, he does that to most of us."

"Now, you have to tell the puppy to get out of the solution. He's not moving."

I laughed and headed to the dog. He didn't budge until the doc came back. Then I said aloud, "Ok you have to get out." He lifted his right paw and said, *"Ok. This one was first, so you can wrap it."*

I told Debra, "I think you have to do this in the order that the paws went in. That's how they're coming out."

She laughed. "Ok. As long as he keeps them out after they're wrapped."

I told our boy the deal, and this time, he kissed the doc. She wiped her face on her sleeve and kept working. "I think we have it," she said when she was done.

"I'll see you in the morning, early. I will want to check on my friend," I said, motioning to the beige dog.

"They are moving the animals out quicker now. He should still be here in the morning. But after that, they will probably move him."

"How about the two dogs with the neck wounds?"

"They are gone—doing well."

I smiled. "Good for them. I'll see you tomorrow."

"You got it. Oh, before you leave, take a look over there toward the front of the barn," she said, pointing at a kennel with a blanket in it. "Something special in there. It's going out in about an hour."

I peeked inside and saw a raccoon, sleeping all curled up. He had been given fluids and was resting quietly, so I left him alone. As I glanced to the right, I saw some snakes had also made their way to Barn One and were getting fluids.

I went back and asked Debra about the snakes. She said, "It was the funniest thing. When they came in, some of the vets almost ran away—they don't like snakes. But a couple were excited to help these little guys."

"I'm glad some of them will work with snakes!"

"They actually are very sensitive creatures. The fact that

they are getting rescued after all this time shows how sturdy they can be. They all needed fluids when they came in. But we have to transport them right away, because they can die without proper care. I prefer working on dogs, so I'm glad that young vet over there likes the snakes. We've had twelve come through and he's gotten them all."

I said goodbye to Debra and the techs and headed to the van. I wanted to get a shower before the meeting. When I arrived in the back near my tent, Kat and the Texas gang were sitting on lawn chairs. Kat waved me over. I sat and had some water with them as the others from our group showed up.

Kat decided to start our debriefing early. We talked about how the day went and some people shared their experiences. Jax said the Guardsmen we were with took a bit of time to warm up, but then everything was good. All the groups agreed that once the military men got used to things, we worked well with each other.

Kat said, "We had a very good day! We are going to try to get out of here tomorrow morning by six. So meet me here at five. If you can, load your trucks tonight. That way, we can get downtown early and leave town when the big rig is full. I'm getting longer lists now, so we have a lot to do. Get some sleep tonight. I will see you in the morning. Meeting adjourned."

Kat and I talked for a few minutes after the meeting. She told me she lived in New Orleans and still didn't know if her two cats were ok. They were in a neighborhood that should be fine, and she had left out food and water. But the authorities were not letting her into the area yet. She had someone who was going to sneak in and get them out tomorrow.

I asked their names, got quiet for a moment, and reached out telepathically to communicate with her cats. Then I said to Kat, "They're ok. Tomorrow would be a good day to get them, though."

"Thanks. I hope you're right."

I was glad I had waited to take my shower. I helped unload

the big rig, while Jax washed out the back of the van to get rid of any chemicals that might have come along with the animals we picked up during the day. Then we drove over and got the supplies we would need for tomorrow. We also stopped and picked up a case of red and blue Gatorade. I told her I'd come back in the morning and get ice.

I drove us back to the water tower and parked the van. Jax asked me to check on her in the morning because she had no alarm clock. She pointed out her tent, and I thought I could make out a big dome shape in the distance.

I headed to the showers. When I returned, I said good night to the Texans and crawled into my tent. I put on my headlamp, set out my clothes, and realized I was almost out of socks. I really needed to do laundry.

I wrote in my journal and set my alarm. It was 10:00 p.m. The Texans nearest to me had a generator going for the air conditioner in their camper. I put in my ear plugs and the quiet surrounded me, and I floated off to sleep.

CHAPTER SEVEN

Monday, September 19, 2005

My alarm went off at 4:15 a.m. I grabbed it quickly, trying not to disturb any of my neighbors who weren't getting up this early. I reached around in the dark, felt for my headlamp, and got dressed. Next I headed to the restrooms so I could blouse my pants, brush my teeth, and comb my hair in the light there. I had a perfect bed head, but no one was around to share it with.

With my headlamp on, I went back out into the dark to try and find Jax's tent. I whispered, "Jax, you up?" A little louder, "Jax, you up?" On the third try, I could hear her voice from a tent to my right—not the one I thought she was in—saying, "I'll be out in a minute."

I whispered, "I'll meet you at the meeting. I don't see anyone out there yet." I went back to my tent, put my headlamp away, and found a lounge chair to sit in. By this time, three of the four Texans were outside and we chatted quietly.

People slowly began to assemble. There were a couple of new faces. Kat had hit the HSUS group's night meeting and stolen Troy and Gary, who she had worked with the previous week. Jax came over and finished putting gear on her belt. It was just beginning to get light as the meeting began.

"I hope you're out there. It's still too dark to see you all," Kat said, and everyone laughed. "Thank you for being here. Today I hope we can get a lot of animals out and get back to camp earlier, so some of you can have a break.

"You should all have loaded up last night. Now we can get ready to go. I'll give you all until five forty-five to get in the lineup with your vehicles and we'll head into town. I'll see you all shortly. Let's get to work."

As we left on our one-hour ride to New Orleans, we could see there were more tents, campers, and fifth-wheels— additional volunteers had come to help.

We met the National Guard at 7:30 a.m. Before the commander turned his men over to Kat, there was some discussion about changing groups. Thomas went and spoke to him for a few minutes. Then the commander turned to us and said, "I agree with Sergeant Thomas. The groups should remain the same."

Thomas smiled right at me. I guessed he was now comfortable being deployed with an animal communicator.

We headed to our first address to pick up a large German shepherd. The dog was sitting inside the front door of the house, ready to go, but we had trouble getting the door open. Once we got the dog out, Thomas wanted to walk him to the kennel and give him food and water. He liked shepherds.

As he was taking care of the dog, Clark told me why Thomas changed his mind about working with me and Jax. "The three of us were getting razzed last night, and they were pretty tough on Sergeant Thomas. Even when it was announced how many animals each team brought in, they were still razzing the Sarge, because his name wasn't being called at all. But then the commander looked right at us and said, 'Gentlemen, I am pleased to report that Sergeant Thomas, Sergeant Porter, and Private Clark brought in the most animals with their team yesterday—more than all of you combined.' The room got really quiet. The Sarge just smiled and didn't say a word. Then the commander said, 'Good job, gentlemen,' and he left. No one razzed the Sarge again. I think he needed that."

"That's good to hear," I said. "But my team knew where

we were going. We had been feeding a lot of the animals, so we knew where they were and how to get them. The Texans had to get their bearings and had no help in using maps or directions. So I'm sure it took them some time to figure things out. I bet everyone does better today."

The German shepherd filled up the back of the van and looked like he could use some air conditioning, so we took him to the drop-off and made sure he got inside the cooled Texas big rig.

We headed to our second house, where we picked up a two-month-old black Lab puppy. The day was moving slowly and we were retrieving fewer animals than we had before. The number of animals on the streets had diminished, which meant that most of the pets would be inside of houses.

These rescues could be quite a time-consuming process. We first had to check the perimeter of the home to look for easy access, or the easiest way to break in with the least amount of damage. Then it was often slow-going to find animals that were hiding or blended in with all the mud—a black dog in the dark was nearly impossible to see. Usually, I felt an animal telepathically first, then would know where to look.

Our three Guardsmen were getting excited about helping Jax break into houses. So when we got to the next address and saw both a security door and a front door, they quickly went to work on them. I decided to look around the outside of house and see what I could find.

As I rounded the corner, I saw the whole side wall of the house was missing and figured the dog was probably gone. But I kept walking. When I got to the back, I turned the knob on the back door and it opened. I went in and closed it behind me. I was in the laundry room, and all of a sudden, I felt like I wasn't alone.

I turned and saw a white poodle sitting on the floor. Next to her was a month-old puppy—a tiny thing, and jet black to boot. The white poodle looked up at me and said, *"Look, I kept her safe! Look, I kept her safe!"*

"Yes, you did! Look at you two!"

The poodle beamed with pride that she had kept her friend safe. When I kneeled down, she looked at her little charge and said, *"It's ok, you can go to her. I think she is going to help us."*

"Indeed I am! Look at you two. You are just adorable."
Then I said to the poodle, *"You are a good big sister."*

We could hear the gang banging on the front door. The poodle asked, *"What are they doing?"*

"I think they're trying to get in here to get you out."

"Mommy left the door unlocked just in case someone came—and you did."

"I'm sorry it took me so long."

"It's ok. We're together and we're fine. Do you have food? She needs to eat."

I saw the remnants of kibble on the laundry room floor and a big dish of water that was now empty.

The poodle said, *"I had to make sure that we only ate a little each day, so we could wait for you to come."*

Tears welled up in my eyes. *"I'm glad you're ok. You are the best big sister ever. Now let's get you out of here and get some water and some food."*

I put down my catch pole, picked them both up in my arms, and we went out the back door.

As I walked toward the front, I yelled, "Hey, can someone help me with these two?"

Everyone stopped their work on the locked doors, saw me with the two little dogs, and sprang into action. Thomas took the puppy. Jax took the white poodle. Clark and Porter got out the kennel and some food and water.

"Where did you get these two?" they asked.

"They were in the back of the house, in the laundry room. The poodle is very happy she was able to take care of her new sister. So why don't you put them both in the same kennel. That way, they'll be sure to stay together."

Thomas asked me how I got in the house.

"Let me show you guys something—I have to go get my catch pole anyway," I said and motioned them to follow me.

Their jaws dropped when they saw the side of the house was totally gone. Then they looked a bit embarrassed when I showed them the back door was unlocked.

I smiled. "You saw front door and just focused on that. So I thought I would check the back. I figured the dogs had gotten out of the house, until I found these two just sitting on the floor, waiting to go."

Thomas took off his hat and scratched his head. "Well, I guess we learned our lesson here."

We headed to the next house. We all heard barking inside, so we knew we had to get this dog out. The front door gave us a hard time—both the dead bolt and doorknob were locked. All of the windows had bars on them, and there was no air conditioner to drop out.

Jax and the guys took turns trying to get the locks to give way. Finally, Thomas hit the upper half of the door and a panel fell out. He reached in, unlocked the knobs, and said, "I think you can go in now."

Suddenly, the dog's head popped up through the hole. He snarled and snapped at us, and then he disappeared.

Thomas got out of the way, and we all took a step back. I said, "Our work is cut out for us on this one. Make sure we have a kennel ready with food inside. If we need to, we can walk him in and then add water from the outside. Jax, why don't you get a catch pole and join me, just in case."

I opened the door. There was no sign of our snarling dog, so I went in the house. Jax came in behind me and shut the door. I looked at her and she looked at me. It was quiet. I whispered to her, "Let's go slow. Keep your catch pole in front of you."

We stood in a small, but nice, living room. There was a short sofa and an older TV with rabbit ears. The coffee table had floated over and was blocking the kitchen door. Straight ahead of us was the hallway back to the rest of the house. I said to Jax, "You want to look in the kitchen and see if you see anything. I'll keep watch here, just in case he darts back out."

She moved toward the coffee table and looked into the kitchen. "No, not in there. It's clear."

We slowly walked down the hallway. On our right was a small bathroom. No dog in there either. I said, "He must be in the back bedroom. So let's go slow and let me talk to him first."

The door was open about a foot. I tried to push it further, but it was blocked. Something must have floated up against it. It was pitch black inside the bedroom. "Great," I thought. "This might be a problem."

At that moment, the dog jumped at the door, pushing it toward us. One of his paws hit the wall next to the door, and I could see he was a white-and-brown pit bull. We backed up a step.

"Found him!" I said.

"Ya think!" Jax replied.

I talked aloud to the dog, so Jax would be able to hear my side of the conversation. "Hi there. Are you ok? We have come to get you out of here. Can I come in and talk to you?"

I didn't hear anything. I paused for a few moments and again said, "Hello. Can I come in and talk to you?"

I waited. Then I heard the dog say in a very slight voice, *"Move slow."*

"Jax, I'm going in. You stay here and don't let him run past you."

I put my catch pole slowly through the door. Then I bent forward and put my head inside, just far enough so I could see where our pit might be.

He was lying on the bed, on top of a big pile of stuff that had settled there from the flood.

"That's good, you just sit there. I'll come in slow and we can chat. Ok?" I said, as I squeezed through the door. I stood along the side wall and stopped to take a breath, then I suddenly saw the situation.

There were two dogs in the room. I said, "Jax, there are two dogs!"

"You coming out?"

"No, I think I have it. Just wait."

I started to speak to the pit that hit the door and snarled at us—I knew that he had to give permission. *"My friend and I have come to get you out of here. I would like to get you some good food and water and take you to a place that has really fresh air. Do you think it would be ok? I want you both to go with me. Would that be ok? You two can stay together. What do you think?"*

I waited for what seemed like a long, long pause. I could tell he was thinking things through. All of a sudden, he sat up on the bed. I raised the catch pole just in case.

"What is that for?"

"That's for you and me to walk together—like a leash—so we can get you to the safe spot. I want to make sure I keep you safe, once we step outside."

"And my friend?"

"My friend Jax can come and take him outside too. Would that be ok with you?"

He thought for a long time. *"Is the water going to come back? I don't think I can do that again. It was hard to keep my friend safe for three days, I think. It was lots of swimming, and we had to stand on the refrigerator in the kitchen just to breathe."*

"Wow! You're very smart to do that. I'm very sorry that you had to be here for the flood."

"Mom will be upset. She likes this house a lot."

"I can tell by the way she keeps it that she likes the house, and you two, a lot."

My white-and-brown pit bull smiled, tongue panting.

"So how about it? Do you think we could go, you and me? And Jax will get your friend."

"Ok, but move slow. I don't like things like that," he said, looking at the catch pole.

"I'll be real careful."

I slowly picked up the front of the catch pole and moved it toward his head. *"We need to put this on like a necklace. Then I will tighten it just enough so we can go out together. Ok?"*

He sat waiting, while I got the loop over his head. I took a small step toward him so I could tighten it, and the other dog moved.

"It's ok. You're going too. Just wait a minute for Jax, ok?" I said and the dog sat back down.

I slowly tightened the catch pole on my pit. *"Ok, you ready to go?"*

"Yes. You're sure that my friend is coming, right?"

"He'll be right behind us. Right, Jax?"

"Yes, right behind you."

"Jax, just in case, why don't you go back over by the coffee table. I'll head out with him, and then you can come and get the other dog. I think you'll be ok."

"Gimme a minute to get out of the way. This mud is slippery."

"Tell the guys we are coming out. I'm not sure what he'll do, so they should give us some space."

I said to my pit, *"Just a second and we will head out."* He was ready to go and getting anxious. Soon we heard Jax give the ok.

I looked him in the eyes and said, *"Let's go."* Then I looked the other dog in the eyes and said, *"Jax will be right in for you."* He sat back down on the bed.

I stepped to the right, allowing the catch pole to swing around so the pit could go out first. He slipped through the crack of the door and bolted out to the living room. I got stuck getting out of the room, but I had a good hold on him. I pushed through the gap in the door and we headed out.

I saw Jax off to my left as we zoomed by. "Don't let the other one get loose," I said.

When I got outside, Porter was standing by. "Close the door behind me. There's another dog we still have to get."

My white-and-brown pit was delighted to be outside! He headed right for the water dish and took a big drink. He looked in the direction of the door, and I said, *"They will be coming soon. Jax is getting your friend."*

He had more water and I took him for a few yards down the street, where he decided to pee. I finally had a chance to take a good look at him and saw he was thick in the middle. Then it dawned on me: he was a she—and she was pregnant! No wonder she was protective of the other dog.

"You have babies coming, don't you?"

She looked up at me and smiled. *"Yes!"*

"Let me put you in the kennel, and I will go help Jax bring out your friend."

When I headed toward the house again, Jax emerged with her catch pole and a little black puppy about three months old. Jax said, "This one was hard to see in the dark. I had to move the dresser to get back out. You're thinner than I am."

I told Thomas, "Let's put the puppy in its own kennel. But mark them together so the pit won't be labeled 'aggressive' at camp."

We took our rescues back to the drop-off point. When we headed out again, we decided to stop for lunch—in the middle of an intersection. Porter and Clark thought it was fun, because they couldn't do that anywhere else.

Our next house was a bit complicated. The yard had a chain-link fence around it. The house was up on cinder blocks, but one corner of it had fallen off of the blocks. The dog was under the house and was poking his head out one side then the other.

I said, "We might need everyone for this. Jax, get your pole and head to the far side. I'll stay on this side. If you get him on your catch pole, let me know. You guys might need to stand at different points around the house and send the dog our way so we can catch him. He doesn't look vicious, but it doesn't look like he wants to go yet. I'll chat with him and see."

I went to the van, got our extension catch pole, and gave mine to Porter. I then spent some time talking with the dog, a grey-and-white pit bull. He was uncertain at first, and he shied away when any of us came near him. So I asked Clark to get me a can of cat food.

I opened the loop on my catch pole and placed it on the ground next to the house. Next I opened the can and plopped the cat food in the center of the loop. I said to Porter, who was a few feet down from me, "Don't move. Let him see you, but don't move."

I walked to the other end of the extension catch pole, and we all waited. About a minute later—less time than I thought this boy would take to smell the food—he poked his head out from under the house, looked at us, and ate the pile of cat food. I slowly moved the loop up around his head and tightened it just enough so I knew I had him. I let him finish his food and said, "Ok, everyone can move."

The dog looked at me and said, *"You got me."*

"Yes, I got you, and you got me. Want some water?"

"Yes, please."

I was a bit surprised that he said "please."

I shouted to Clark at the van, "Would you get this boy some water?"

"I'll have it ready when you get out here," he said.

I slowly shortened the catch pole and asked my new grey-and-white friend to head to the street with me.

He stopped, looked at me, and said, *"I never go out of the yard."*

"Have you ever wanted to go out of the yard?"

"Yes, but I haven't."

"Well, to go find your parents, we need to go out of the yard."

"Really? I can go out of the yard?"

"Yes, I'll be right there with you. We're attached, so you should be ok."

When we got to the front gate, he stopped for a moment, sniffed it, and stood up very straight. Then he walked, quite regally, right out of the gate.

The guys asked me, "What did you do to him?"

I smiled. "He's never been outside the gate."

They looked at him and smiled. Thomas said, "That-a-boy. Look at you! Good job!"

Hearing that, our grey-and-white pit bull seemed to stand even taller—and he went right into the kennel!

When we pulled up to our next address, we found the same type of house on cinder blocks, with a fenced-in yard. This house was still intact. We saw a grey pit bull as he poked his head out from under the front steps.

I said, "Let's try the same plan and see what we can get."

This time, Jax, Porter, and I each took a can of cat food. I said, "Whoever gets close to him is the one who drops the food."

We all headed to different sides of the house. Jax was closest to our grey pit, so she put the food on the ground, placed the loop around it, and backed off a bit. We waited.

This dog took more time than the last one to come out. He grabbed a big bite of food and darted back under the house before Jax could loop him.

"Shoot!" I said.

Jax uttered a few cuss words. She looked at the guys and said, "Sorry." They laughed and assured her, "You were just saying what we were thinking."

The pit decided to lie down in between some support blocks underneath the house. I said to everyone, "I'll use the extension to see what I can do. If he heads your way, loop him."

Even with the extension pulled all the way out, I had to crawl under the house. As I got close to our grey pit, he edged out of the way and didn't look at me. Next I got on my hands and knees and headed directly for him. He went out on the side where Jax and Thomas were waiting. When they stepped toward him, he darted back under the house.

I talked to him constantly, but this dog wasn't giving us a break. He knew his job, and he was staying—food or no food. He headed back to the center where I was, but my catch pole was too extended for me to nab him. I told Porter that he was headed his way.

We didn't hear anything for a minute, then Porter said, "I got him!" When I came out from under the house, I saw he had the dog eating kibble and drinking water. I asked Porter, "How did you get him?"

"By accident. I had put the loop of the catch pole at the base of the house, so the loop hung under the side. He walked right into it. I almost lost him, because it took me a second to realize I had him and tighten the loop."

"Good job! You are now an officially trained, animal search-and-rescue responder."

Porter smiled most of the day after that.

Our next two addresses were both in badly flooded areas. As we looked around, we found each had a dog that, unfortunately, had passed. So we completed the documentation and continued on down our list.

We pulled up to a grey house with white trim and saw most of its chain-link fence was washed away. I said, "If there was a dog in the yard, it's probably gone. But let's look around anyway."

We walked down the side of the house, and all of a sudden, I stopped. "Shhh!" I said, "Did you hear that?"

Everyone shook their heads. I listened harder, then realized I was hearing a voice in my head. *"Look for me! I'm down here. Everyone keeps missing me. Please help. Please help!"*

I held up my hands about waist high and turned my palms toward the ground—I wanted to let everyone know I was doing something so they would be quiet. I bent down and looked to my left. Way back under the house, I could see an eye looking directly at me.

I stood up and smiled. "I found him."

Everyone kneeled down to look, but no one saw him between the blocks that were holding up the house. Then Jax said, "I see him. Wow, Terri. Good eye."

The Guardsmen were still having trouble seeing the dog. Thomas said, "I'll take your word for it. What do you need?"

"Jax will come with me. You guys go around the other side to make sure he doesn't get out. I have a feeling this one is stuck and can't move. So Jax and I will go check it out. Stay within shouting distance and we'll let you know what we need."

I turned to Jax. "I'm going to crawl under and go to the left side. You go to the right, and let's see what we have there. I'm thinking it's a bigger dog, but from just his eye, it's hard to tell."

We both headed under the house—to what we weren't sure. Jax got around her side first and said, "It looks like he's tied to the blocks."

"I'll be there in a minute," I said as I maneuvered around a mud puddle. I poked my head around the corner and said out loud, "Really?"

The poor guy was tied up with a three-quarter-inch chain, and his head was right up against the cinder block!

"Let me chat with him. We are going to need a hacksaw or big bolt cutters. Do you have any?"

"I'll go see what I can find. Are you sure it's three-quarter-inch?"

"Oh yes, it's at least that thick."

"Can he move?"

"No. He is chained right up to the cinder blocks. I'll see what I can find out."

I looked at dog. He could barely turn his head. *"Are you ok?"* I asked.

"No, my dad is mad at me and he left me here. I could die,

he didn't care."

"I'm so sorry. Why did he do that?"

"I'm not mean enough. I wouldn't fight like he wanted me to. He wanted me to kill another dog, so he could win some money. Just money. Why would he want me to do that?"

"Oh my!"

"I went with him to a ring. They put us in there together and neither one of us would fight. The other owner shot his dog right there and left him in the ring. I was waiting for him to shoot me too. Then my owner said, 'Don't waste a bullet on him. I have a better idea.' So then he yanked my neck, held me in the air, and I passed out. I woke up here. I was here for two days, and then the water came. It was fast and moving. I was lucky, because these bricks made the water go around and I could still breathe. I thought I was going to die. Then it went away as fast as it came, and I was standing in mud. It has been days and I just stand here waiting—and then you heard me."

He looked in my direction, when he realized what he had just said. *"You h-e-a-r-d me! That's why you looked for me."*

"Yes, I did. I heard you in my head. I can understand everything you're saying. I'm sorry your dad did that."

"You can hear me?"

"Yes, I can."

"Can they?"

"No, just me."

"Can you help me?"

"Yes, that's why Jax, the other lady, went to get something to get you out of here. Then we can take you outside, feed you, and give you some good water."

"Really? I'm no good, you know. My dad says I don't deserve food or water, and I should just die."

"Well, looks to me like you're doing really well. That water was a hurricane. Then the levees broke and more water came. But you're still here. So I think you are going to be just fine."

He looked at me through the corner of his eye again.

"Really?"

"Yes. As a matter of fact, I'm very proud of you for NOT fighting. And I'm very proud of the other dog for not fighting too. There is a whole world outside that thinks the fighting is wrong. I'm going to see that you get to a new place, where there are other dogs. And I think you will find a new home. You have to be nice, though."

"I can do that! I can be very nice!"

"I was just thinking that you could."

"You mean people don't want me to fight?"

"No, people don't want you to fight. They want to hug you and pet you and take you for walks and just let you be you. And, of course, they will have food and water too."

"Really? Or are you just kidding me?"

"No, I always tell the truth—especially now with you. We just have to get you out of here. Can I come closer and look at your chain?"

"Yes. I am really getting tired of standing here. When I try to sit down, it chokes me."

"I can see that. When we get you out of here, I have a nice kennel for you to actually lie down in and take a nap. But that would be after some food and water, of course."

He glanced at me again. *"Really? I can eat?"*

"Yes, you can eat for the rest of your life."

"I would like that!"

I began to wonder where Jax was, when Porter came around the other side of the blocks. He looked at me and said, "Wow, he is stuck."

I said, "Yes, this is my new friend." I couldn't tell what color he was, because he was so full of dirt. But it looked like he was black underneath. *"What is your name?"* I asked the dog.

"I don't have a name. I don't deserve one."

"Oh yes, you do!" I said out loud.

Porter looked at me. "What?"

"Sorry, I'm talking to the dog. Where's Jax?"

"She's trying to find bolt cutters. Sarge is going back to base to get a hacksaw."

"Good. I think we're going to need the hacksaw. This is too big for bolt cutters. Come over this way and you can see."

I told the dog, *"My friend Porter is going to come around behind you. He just wants to look at your chain, so he can help. Ok?"*

"Ok."

I said to Porter, "The owner put him here because he wouldn't fight."

"Aw, no!"

"And he doesn't have a name because his owner said he didn't deserve one."

Porter got tears in his eyes.

"I think we should call him King. What do you think, Porter?"

"King is a good strong name."

I looked at the dog. "What do you think? Is it ok if we call you King?"

"King. Really? That is a strong and powerful name?"

"Yes, it is. You deserve it, because you have been tied here for twenty-four days. Did you know that?"

"That long?"

"Yes."

Porter looked at me. "That is disgusting! I hope that owner drives up while we're here. I think we should put him in these chains, and see how he likes it."

We exchanged glances and he said, "Well, you know what I mean."

"I do. But I think King here doesn't ever need to see his owner again. I think King might like not having to see him again. What do you think, King?"

"Yes! Can you do that?"

"Yes. I'm going to the woman in charge of helping the animals. I'm going to tell her what you told me, and I think

she'll make certain that you're ok. Is that ok with you?"

"Yes! Yes! Yes!"

Jax came under the house and said, "I have these bolt cutters we can try until the Sarge gets back with a hacksaw."

I looked at the dog. "King, Jax and I are going to get closer to you and see if we can get you loose, ok?"

"Ok."

"Now I'm going to touch you on your back, ok?"

"Ok," he said. But when I touched him, he jerked a bit.

"Easy now. That was me. It's ok." I slowly moved my hand up from his behind to his shoulders so he would know where I was.

I said to Jax, "I think I should get the catch pole on him first, so when you get him lose, we can just head out."

I explained to King what I was going to do. I wasn't sure how he would respond with another thing around his neck. Luckily, he said, *"Ok."*

When King saw the size of the cord on the catch pole, he said, *"That isn't much."*

I laughed. *"No, it's just enough so you and I can stay together, ok?"*

"Ok."

I told Jax we wanted to be extra careful, even though he wasn't a fighter. I held the catch pole while she tried to cut the chain. Unfortunately, it was as I thought: the bolt cutters weren't big enough to cut it.

Porter wanted to give it a go, so we all switched positions. I kept my eyes where King could see them and told him what Jax and Porter were trying to do. Once while they tried to cut the chain, it got twisted, cut off King's air, and he yelped.

I said, "That's enough. Let's give King a break and wait for a hacksaw. He's been through so much, and when Sarge comes, he is going to have to be very still so you can get close enough to saw."

Thomas arrived about 20 minutes later with a hacksaw.

He crawled under the house and looked at the situation. We discussed our options and decided that the chain would have to be cut right by the dog's head.

I said, "I'll tell King to stay still. Let's put some cardboard between him and the saw so the shavings don't go in his eyes or his mouth or his throat while you're cutting. This could take a while."

Porter sawed for a bit, then Thomas, and then back to Porter. When Thomas asked to relieve him a second time, he said, "No. I'm going for it."

The man was on a mission. The saw kept going, little small cuts with each small stroke. There wasn't much space. Faster and faster and faster. Porter turned red, but he didn't give up.

"Give it a break, Porter," Thomas said. But he kept going and going and going.

Finally, the chain gave way. Nothing budged.

Porter had cut through the chain, but it was too thick to pry open. He said, "We have to make another cut, so we can get it open."

Thomas took over the sawing. He got the cut about halfway through and had to take a breather too.

This rescue was no easy feat. We were all on our hands and knees—and sometimes, our butts—getting mud all over us. We were trying to keep our hands dry, so we could get a good grip on the saw and cut at the right angle. Meanwhile I was talking to a piece of cardboard, because King's face was covered to keep him from being cut and getting shavings all over him.

When Porter had to get out for a break and stand up, Jax took a turn. She went at it, also not wanting to give up. But finally, she had to give it a rest too. I told Thomas I would take a turn.

"No, we need you to get him out of here when we get him free," he said as he grabbed the hacksaw and started cutting again.

I said to King, *"They're working hard to get you out of*

here. We're getting closer. Just hang in there. Think about the food you're going to eat and the water you're going to drink. Ok?"

"Uh huh."

The cardboard against his face was taking a toll on the dog. I said, "Sarge, let's give King a breather."

He stopped sawing and Jax pulled the cardboard away from King's head. Then Thomas grabbed the chain and said, "I just want it to break!"

He yanked the chain toward King and it pulled apart! As he fell backwards into the mud, I pulled King over the top of him and away, just to make sure he wasn't going to bite anyone.

King looked right at me. I said aloud, "Look at you, handsome! Let's go get that food!"

King smiled. He moved slowly and was very stiff from standing for so long. I said to the dog, *"Let's take it easy, though, because I'm stiff and I have to crawl."*

King looked at me. *"Thank you!"*

He stopped, turned his head to the right, and looked directly at Thomas, and then Jax. *"I won't forget what you did for me."*

I told them what he said. Tears welled up in Jax's eyes. Then Thomas started crying. I thought, "I better get out of here before I lose it too."

King looked at me and said, *"Would you take me to the other man who saved me? I need to thank him too."*

"Sure, I'd be happy to."

I shouted out to Porter and Clark that the dog was free. (Clark had watched the vehicles the hour and a half we were under the house.)

Porter popped his head under the side of the house. I said, "King said he wants to thank you, but let us get out first."

"No thanks necessary. I'll make sure there's food out for him."

As we got out from under the house, I stood up and was quite stiff. I looked at King and asked, *"You ok?"*

"I'm very tired. Everything feels very heavy."
"Let's just rest here for a second."

King swayed and I saw he was about to fall. I quickly went up the catch pole and grabbed him around the waist and chest. I dropped the catch pole, pulled him to me, and picked him up. *"Maybe I should give you a lift. Ok, big guy?"*

The dog drooped down, and I picked him up higher so I could get a better grip. I yelled toward Porter, "He's down. I got him. On my way out." I moved as fast as I could with the catch pole dragging behind us. I was worried about whether he'd be able to drink water and if we'd need to get him to base quickly.

I rounded the corner with King in my arms and Porter was there. "Let me take him."

Porter started to lift King's head, when our boy put both paws around his neck and pulled the Guardsman right up to him. King looked him in the eyes, then hugged him and put his head along the side of Porter's. He was holding on tight.

I said, "You take the front and I'll take the back."

We walked out of the yard and into the street, where Clark had water, food, and a kennel waiting for us. We gently put King on the ground. He dove for the water, spilling it everywhere.

"It's ok. Easy, big boy. We have more," Clark said, while King drank the little bit in the bowl. He waited for Clark to open more water and started drinking as the bowl was being refilled.

I said, "Not too much. His stomach hasn't had anything for a while. A little at a time."

King drank a whole bowl of water and asked for more. He drank about three-quarters of the next bowl and ate a full bowl of food. He popped up his head when he was done and I thought, "Oh no! He ate too fast and he's going to barf it all up."

King stretched his neck a little, pushed his head forward,

and let out a great big belch. "Burrrrrp."

Clark, Porter, and I looked at each other—we were surprised, relieved, and happy.

King started panting and a big smile came over his face. I saw his neck was stiff and he couldn't move it much to the left, but he kept smiling. He took a deep breath, looked at me, and then tried to get up. I kneeled down and held him again. He stepped on my knee, climbed up, and put his paws around my neck. He put his head along the side of mine and held on tight. I hugged him tightly too.

He started to moan, louder and louder. I said, *"It's ok. You're ok now. You're ok now."*

"I know. I know." "Owwwhhhh! Oowwwhh!" he yelled with joy.

Thomas and Jax came to the street, wondering what was wrong, when they saw King hugging me and making a racket.

Jax said, "Ok, you guys. I just thought I was getting ahold of myself. Now you're making me cry again."

I let King hold me for what seemed like a long time. I could feel his head was spinning from the dehydration. I said, *"I think we should take you to see a doctor and get you some fluids so you can feel better. It's ok. We're all going to go with you to meet the lady in charge, ok?"*

He started to release his grip, then hugged me tightly again. He kept thanking me for hearing him. I took a deep breath and my tears came. *"I'm glad I heard you too, my friend. I'm so glad I heard you."*

King pulled back and looked me right in the eyes. His look went deep into my soul. I knew I would never forget his face.

We helped him into the kennel. With his muscles so stiff, it took him a minute to lie down. We gently picked up his kennel and I said, "We are taking him back now."

When we arrived at our base, I took King's paperwork to Kat. I told her how we found him, what we had to do to get him out, and what his life had been like—and that he never wanted to see his owner again.

"What was that address?" Kat asked. I showed her the paperwork. "I know that man," she said with a disgusted look on her face. "What did you say you're calling the dog?"

"We all decided his name would be King."

"King. That's a great name. If I have anything to say about it, his owner will go to jail. But right now, I think King needs to see the doctor when we get him back to the shelter."

"You're reading my mind."

Our group total for the day was seventy-seven dogs, ten cats, and three roosters. Thomas, Porter, Clark, Jax, and I brought in only eight dogs—two underneath and six inside of houses. We had a few more days to work with the National Guard, and we were all hoping to get out more and more pets each day.

There were hugs all around when Jax and I said goodbye to our military men. We met Cindy, Anthony, Sharon, and Glen, then headed off to get gas and dinner from the Navy. During dinner, I found out that Cindy, Anthony, and Sharon had just two more days with me. They were heading home on Thursday.

We arrived back at camp at 7:00 p.m. as the big rig was just pulling away from the front gate. I headed to get supplies and also went to the food tent for drinks and ice. Then I stopped by to check on King, who I figured was at the vets' station by now. I said hello to Doc Debra, and she pointed me to where he was resting and hooked up with fluids.

She said, "I knew it was probably one of yours because he had a name and no collar."

I told her King's story, how we found him and how we got him out.

"I'll make sure he's taken care of. I'll watch him for a while, then see if we can get his neck moving better."

I told King what she said. He looked me right in the eyes. *"I heard her."*

I looked at Debra. "He heard you."

She smiled. "We're going to get along just fine."

"When are you leaving?" I asked.

"Wednesday. I have to get back to my practice."

"I'm glad you've been here."

"And I'm glad that you know how to pick up gauze and put it in an ambulance. Because if you had just walked by, we never would have worked together. It's been a pleasure!"

We shook hands. "Doc, thank you for being open to someone like me."

"Are you kidding? You saved me a lot of time. I could do procedures the other vets couldn't because of your help. I'm sure the animals are all talking about you."

I looked at King again and he said, *"I'm going to tell everyone I meet about you, and how you saved me."*

"King, there were five of us."

"You heard me. You saved me."

"Thank you, King. I will always remember you. You're very special. Don't you forget that!"

I turned to Debra. "I'm going to head into Gonzales and find a laundromat. Got a little muddy today with King. He likes to hug," I said and winked at him.

I went back to my tent to get my laundry, when I heard Kat tell everyone it was time to have a debriefing.

"Things are changing by the minute," she told us. "So I want to leave even earlier tomorrow. Let's head out at five. We'll meet here at four forty-five. Go get your vehicles stocked tonight, so all we have to do is line up and get going."

When the meeting ended, I grabbed my clothes, some soap, a roll of quarters, and my journal, then headed into town. There was no one else in the laundromat, and I wrote about my day while I waited for my laundry to finish. I looked at my notes and thought, "I know I'm keeping this for something. One day I'll know what to do with it. If not, I'll have it as memories of a time when I could do some real good."

I got back to Lamar-Dixon as fast as I could. I knew I had

to get up at 4:00 a.m. to wake up Jax. I put away my clean clothes, laid out one outfit, and set the alarm. Then I put in my ear plugs and let the quiet engulf me.

CHAPTER EIGHT

Tuesday, September 20, 2005

I reached to shut off the alarm and thought, "This can't be right. I just shut my eyes." I remembered I went to bed at 10:30 p.m. It was now 4:00 a.m. No wonder it felt like I had just closed my eyes.

I sat up so I wouldn't fall back asleep and started my process of getting dressed. I kept telling myself to stay awake. I stepped out of my tent and drank in the warm, early-morning air. It felt good. I headed to the restrooms and tapped on Jax's tent. "I'm up," she said.

"I'll see you at the meeting."

Kat's meeting was short—and funny. She used a flashlight to see who was present. When she asked about a couple of people, someone scurried off to make sure they were awake. Then we actually loaded up and headed out at 5:15 a.m.

Kat asked Jax and me to take some paperwork to the EOC and then meet up with the rest of our group at the National Guard base. Jax slept on the way downtown, and I enjoyed the quiet.

I went inside the EOC to drop off the documents while Jax waited in the van. When I returned, she was talking to two men. They said there were two pit bulls in the ten-story parking garage that had been there for almost a week. The dogs were tied up to a cement pillar, but they were mean and no one could get near them.

I told Jax we were supposed to head directly to the base and meet Kat. She just gave me a look.

"Are you feeding them?" I asked the men.

They looked me in the eyes and said, "No. They're not our dogs."

"Seriously?" I thought. I looked at Jax and then back at the men. "Can you show us where they are?"

The dogs were in the garage, not far from the entrance to a mall where the men's store was located. The garage was totally enclosed and there was no fresh air. It was dark, except for the lights that I assumed were on 24/7. I looked at the pit bulls and said to Jax, "We have to be careful here. Let's get the kennels out."

The men asked, "Can we help you?"

"You could have helped them. You could have fed them. I think you might want to go in your store before I put my catch pole on you and drag you around!"

Jax looked at me and then at them. "Maybe you should go. We'll take it from here." They left and she said to me, "One of us had to be calm—and I already exploded at them before you got back to the van."

I smiled. "Well, we know the dogs need to eat. Let me chat with them and see what we have."

They had been dropped off a week ago, and no one who walked by gave them any food. I looked at the dogs and said, *"Really? I'm sorry."*

One of them continued to tell me their story. *"Those men tried to poke at us, so we decided to growl at everyone who went by. No one was helping. One woman gave us water. She came the last two days. She said she was sorry she had no food for herself, or she would give it to us. She sat over there and slept with us. Then left."*

I looked over at the cement wall where the woman must have slept at night and figured she was probably homeless.

I said, *"My friend Jax and I are going to take you to a place*

*where you can get food and water and be taken for walks.
Would that be ok?"*

"Ok."

"Are you two brothers?"

"Yes, I'm the smart one and he's the strong one."

*"I see. How about I take you first, then we can get your
brother there. Would that be ok?"*

"Sure."

The pit told his brother they were going to go with us and
that they would be safe. He looked back and me and asked,
"Right? We will be safe?"

*"Yes, you'll be safe. I'll even put on your kennels that you
are brothers."*

Just then a car door slammed, and the dogs reacted by
snarling again. One of the store owners had come out to get
something out of their car. I glared at him. He shrugged his
shoulders and mouthed, "Oops."

I said, "If you come out here one more time while we are
doing this, I will leave them here for you to deal with."

"Oh, sorry, lady. So sorry. We'll wait," he replied and went
back into the mall.

Jax looked at me. "I think he thought you were serious."

I smiled. "I knew that would make him leave us alone."

I said to the dogs, *"Ok, you two. Jax and I are going to get
you out of this noisy garage."*

They kept snarling, so Jax decided to go around to the back
side of the pillar and cut the first dog loose. She said, "Just take
him. I'll wait for you, and we'll get the second one together."

I headed with the dog to the food we had sitting out. Next thing
I knew, Jax arrived with the second dog. I looked up and smiled.

"He was ready to go," she explained.

"Good. Let's get them fed, loaded, and out of here! This
garage doesn't have anything but fumes. I'm sure our boys
would like some fresh air—and I'm sure Kat is wondering
where we are."

We lifted the two kennels into the back of the van.

"Ok, boys. Let's get you some fresh air!"

As we drove out of the garage, I stopped off to the side of the road and looked back at them. Both of our pits were sniffing the air.

One said, *"Yes, fresh air. That's nice."*

"Yes," his brother said. *"I thought they were going to kill us. The men were talking about bringing guns to shoot us, but couldn't because there was always people around. We're very glad you two came to get us."*

"I'm glad too."

I told Jax what they said about the guns.

"Maybe we should come back with guns and see how they like it," she said.

"Down girl," I said, and she smiled.

When we arrived at the base, I explained to Kat what had happened and why we had two pits bulls in the back of our van.

"I'm glad you got them. There are some people who are just shooting animals. It's really sad. Some of the dogs have been making packs to hunt—and the police were told to shoot them."

Kat told us the National Guard would no longer be going with our team. They had other, more important, work to do. She gave us our addresses and said we should be able to get the animals because the DEA had been through the area and left signs on the houses. She told us to be back by 2:30 p.m., because she needed to have a meeting at 3:00 p.m.

We pulled up to the first address and saw the markings on the front of the house: "1 DOG BACK BEDROOM." We went in the front door and headed through the house to find the dog and get him out. We looked everywhere, but didn't see a dog. Then we looked again, slowly, just in case the dog had passed. There was no dog anywhere. We had to assume he had either gotten out, or someone took him and didn't put an "X" across the sign on the front of the house.

We went into six different homes and all of the animals had been taken—there were no X-ed off marks on any of them. We had completely wasted our time.

We drove around a corner and saw a golden retriever walking down the road. I said, "Jax, let's get him. He should be easy."

She smiled. "Yeah, piece of cake."

I stopped the van and Jax went around back to get out the kennel. When she returned, I was chatting with the golden, who was just standing there wagging her tail.

All of a sudden, there were three pit bulls around us, one on each side, snarling and snapping. I grabbed Jax and told her to put her back against mine, so we could keep our eyes on all of them. I told her to stay with me while I moved toward the pit who was telling the other two what to do.

Luckily, Jax also had her catch pole and could use it to defend herself if needed. "What are we going to do?" she asked.

"We are going to get this beige one here."

As I looked at him, I said, *"You hungry? I have food, and you can have it."*

"Where is it?"

"It's in the van. I'll get it for you. But you have to let me put on this necklace, and you can go with me to get out of here."

He snarled again. Jax whispered, "Don't piss them off!"

"I'm trying not to."

The beige pit looked at me again and said, *"You have food?"*

"Yes."

When he looked over at the van, I was able to get the loop of the catch pole around his neck. I tightened it quickly, just as he jerked back. Whew! I had him.

He stopped in his tracks and looked at me. I stood my ground and took a deep breath to release my extra energy. I kept my back against Jax and said to her, "We have to get that one in front of you."

"You want to get him?"

"No. I have to hold this one. He's very strong. I'll talk you through it."

I said aloud to her dog, "I have your friend. He wants to eat. If you get a leash on you, you can eat too."

He looked at Jax and snarled some more. He backed up a little and turned like he was going to run.

"Jax, now!"

She looped the catch pole around his neck. The pit jerked back, but stayed in the loop. Jax quickly tightened it. She had him.

"What about the other two?" she said. "We're stuck."

"Let's go for a walk with our friends and see what they do."

Neither of us had another catch pole or anything we could use if we were attacked. We turned to walk down the road, keeping our two dogs a good distance away from us. My grey pit said, *"You're walking me away from the food. Did you lie to me?"*

"No. I'm just making sure the other two are going to be nice while I get you settled."

"I'll tell 'em."

"Ok," I said and started to turn around to head back to the van. I told Jax, "Turn and walk with me. Keep your dog on the other side of you. When we get to the kennel, I'll put mine in and you keep walking. I'll get another kennel down for you, and then you circle back and put yours in."

"What about the other two?"

"Let's just see what they do. I think they want food too."

I walked my dog right into the kennel. I used my foot to hold the door, released the catch pole, and latched the lock. As I pulled out a second kennel, I saw the other dogs were standing at a distance, watching me.

I took a bag of kibble out of the van. I poured some for my dog through the wire mesh on top of his kennel and he started to eat. Jax walked her dog up and guided him into the other kennel as I poured food through the top. She released the catch pole and shut the door.

We pulled out two more kennels and grabbed the dishes.

"How are we going to get the other two?" she asked me.

I put the food in the kennels, opened the doors toward the dogs, and yelled, "Come on! It's time to eat!"

To our surprise, both dogs walked into the kennels and went for the food!

As we shut and locked the doors behind them, Jax said, "That was a close one—and I still have my arms and legs."

"Good thing we got them. Let's pour some water on the floor of their kennels so they can get a drink. After they get full, we'll figure out how to load them into the van." The four of them drank two gallons of water. The golden was relieved to be in a kennel. Jax and I tried not to think much about what had just happened. We concentrated instead on lifting them into the van and heading back to the drop-off site.

We arrived back there at 2:00 p.m. After we unloaded our four rescues, Jax and I sat in the van, enjoying some snacks and a cold Gatorade.

Kat popped her head around the door and asked, "Did you bring in those four dogs over there?"

"Yes, Jax and I did. Why?"

"I'll be," Kat said, shaking her head as she walked away.

I looked at Jax. "What was that about?"

"Maybe we're in trouble."

We both hoped we weren't in trouble, because we didn't want to be sent home. We waited for the meeting. Now we really wanted to hear what Kat was going to say!

"I want you all to know there is another hurricane headed our way," Kat said, surprising everyone in our group. "It's about three days out. But it appears to be building and headed for us or the Gulf Coast of Texas."

We all looked at the folks from Texas. "We're staying," they said.

Kat said, "Thank you, we really need your big truck. The Guardsmen who were helping us are now evacuating the people still left in town, if they can get them out. Then they will be moving their command to a safer location. The Navy will be leaving soon to get to safe water as well. So we are done for today. We will go day by day to see if we can come back in and continue our search and rescue. Oh, and by the way, I want you all to know that we caught one of the packs today."

Everyone cheered and someone asked, "Who got them?"

"Jax and Terri, the animal communicator. I hear two of the dogs just walked into their kennels when Terri asked them to."

Jax nodded and said, "I saw her. She told them to get in to eat and let's go—and they did."

Everyone laughed. I think they were surprised, because they expected to hear that two animal control officers got the pack dogs. Our group was delighted—Jax and I were just glad we weren't in trouble.

Kat said, "From now on, you both are getting all the tough ones. After we empty the big rig, we'll have another meeting tonight at eight o'clock. I'll let you know where we stand at that time. Let's go."

My group looked tired. I said, "You guys need gas, right?" They smiled at me and nodded. I told Kat we were going for gas and would see her at the meeting.

After we hit the gas station, it was time for some dinner with the Navy.

When we arrived, we saw all their canopies, tables, and buffet equipment had been packed up. The ship was leaving the next morning, they told us. Now we were on our own for dinner. We decided to go back to Lamar-Dixon to see what food had been delivered to camp.

A small, older woman stopped Jax and me as we got to our van. She was walking three dogs on leashes. "Do you have any dog food?" she asked.

"Yes, we do. Would you like some?"

"I need it for them, if it's ok?"

Jax opened the van and said, "Sure, we can give you a big bag."

"No, just a small one, please. I'm on my own and I can't carry a big one."

"Are you ok?"

"Yes, I'm getting along. You know, when this whole thing started, they wouldn't take me and my dogs. I couldn't leave them, so we all stayed together. We've been getting by ever since."

I smiled at her and said, "How about some water for them too?"

She said she could take a gallon but couldn't carry anything bigger. I said, "How about a Gatorade for you?" It was all I had to offer her.

"Do you have any of the blue ones? I like them best."

Jax was on it and handed the lady a Gatorade.

She talked about how nice the world was. "Those of you in the blue shirts, with those letters H-S-U-S, you are good people. Thank you for coming down here to help us. Let me hug you proper."

She stretched out her arms around each of us, then took the food and put it in her rolling cart. She waved goodbye and walked on, with her three dogs following along.

When we returned to Lamar-Dixon, I parked the van in front of the Texas campers. As we grabbed dinner, we found out that HSUS had called a meeting with everyone at 7:00 p.m., before the Louisiana SPCA meeting with Kat at 8:00 p.m.

Eric Sakach, who handles law enforcement cases for HSUS, stood in the back of a truck near the front of Barn Five. He was now going to be holding the briefings. At 6 feet, 5 inches, he is the type of guy who easily commands attention, but he used the bullhorn anyway.

The crowd of volunteers, who had come to help from around the country, had gotten bigger. He said, "I'm very pleased to see many more people here. We need you and we thank you. Wayne Pacelle is going back to Washington, D.C., to continue to get funding for the outstanding work you're doing."

Next Eric wanted to make sure everyone understood that another hurricane could be coming our way in three days. "Here's how it looks with the possibility of Hurricane Rita heading our direction: if it hits us, we're screwed."

He paused and let that thought sink in with everyone.

"If it hits Texas, we'll be on the eastern side of the storm, so we'll be better. But maybe not, because the right side of a hurricane always has the most rain and water. We'll just have to wait and see where we are tomorrow, and we'll go from there. All of you doing search and rescue will meet in the morning behind the incident command motorhome, except the group with Kat from the LASPCA that has another meeting spot. In the evening, we'll all meet here again at seven and I will give you the latest on what's going on."

When Eric adjourned the meeting, I walked over to him and we gave each other a hug. We had worked together on animal cruelty cases in California. He had been at Lamar-Dixon for a couple of days, but the search and rescue I was doing downtown kept us from catching up with each other.

We talked for a few minutes, and I could tell he had a lot on his mind so I didn't linger. I went to Barn One to check on King. Debra said she had him taken to the hospital so he could be monitored, but she thought all he really needed was sleep.

"I'm sure he does. He was standing with his head stuck for twenty-four days. I wouldn't be surprised if he sleeps for a week."

"I wanted them to take care of him because I'm leaving tomorrow." There were tears in her eyes when we hugged goodbye. "How long are you here for?" she asked.

"Until next Tuesday."

"I've been here three weeks. It's the right time to go, because I'm getting cranky. But if you talk to these guys," she laughed, waving at the other vets, "they think I just came here that way. Kept them out of my hair."

I laughed too. "Take care of yourself."

I had just enough time to get a quick shower before our 8:00 p.m. meeting. I laid my clothes out for Wednesday and went to the meeting. I hoped it would be short so I could get to bed early. I needed some rest.

Kat began the meeting by looking at me and asking, "Terri, do you know Dr. Lois Abrams? She wants to address our group."

"I do. She came in with some other animal response volunteers I've worked with in California. Lois is a psychologist. She probably wants to make sure everyone is ok with what they are seeing in town. If you need to have a chat, she'd be good."

Everyone looked around, pointed to the next person, and said, "You need to see the shrink."

We all laughed. Kat said, "Well, she'll be here in about 10 minutes. So you all be on your best behavior or I'll lose my whole group—because I know we're all nuts. We don't need a shrink to tell us that."

Kat said there was talk about closing down New Orleans because of Hurricane Rita. "We're also beginning to hear that the big sand mounds being used to stop the levees from leaking are beginning to seep. So here's what I'm proposing: I'm going to lead whoever is up with me in the morning to town, so we can drop food and leave water for the animals, in case we can't get into town for a couple of days. We'll bring back all the animals we find. If we have addresses when I leave here in the morning, fine. If not, we'll find whatever we can and get it safe. If we get turned back, we get turned back. I want to leave here at four forty-five."

Lois arrived and I introduced her to Kat and the rest of the group. It seemed to surprise everyone that she was in her 70s. But her age and her presence at a disaster gave her instant respect. She addressed the group and was very funny.

"If anyone would like to talk with me about anything—even what you had for breakfast—I'm available. I understand you all do a debriefing at night. I think that's good, so keep it up.

You all look to me like you're handling everything very well. Kat will have my cell number. Feel free to call anytime, no matter what time of day. I'll be here."

Everyone applauded and Kat added, jokingly, "Now children, get to bed!"

"Yes, mom," we said and laughed.

I was pooped and went right to bed. I took a few minutes to write in my journal, then set the alarm. With my ear plugs in to block out the generator noise, I immediately fell asleep.

CHAPTER NINE

Wednesday, September 21, 2005

This morning I caught the alarm on the first buzz. "Whew," I thought. "Now I need to get Jax up."

With flashlights in hand, we met up with Kat, who gave us what looked like black t-shirts with "LASPCA" in white. She said, "Put these on before we leave. It will make you all look like you work for me, and you do. I'm hoping this will help get us into town. So go change and be back here in 10 minutes. Hopefully we can beat the closure of town—it will be harder to find us if we're already in."

I changed and when I got to the van, Jax was sitting in her seat, ready to go. "How did you beat me back here?" I asked.

"I changed t-shirts right here. I'm not missing my ride today. This is going to be exciting!"

We arrived at our drop-off site and everyone got out of their vehicles. Kat, who had been on the phone all the way into town, told us our orders had changed. "We can't go into our areas until they are checked. There's leakage there from the sand mounds at the levees. So we are headed to Lakeview, which has not been checked since the disaster struck. The word they've gotten is that nothing is alive over there. But today, we're going to go check it out."

Kat split us into four groups. Cindy, Anthony, Sharon, Glen, Jax, and I were all on her team. It was Cindy, Anthony, and Sharon's last day before they would be heading home.

Then Kat led everyone in a caravan to a new drop-off site about 30 minutes away. The big rig stayed there, while our four groups headed into Lakeview to see what we could find.

Jax looked at the map, trying to figure out where we were. Suddenly she said, "We are headed right in front of the levees—and they're supposedly seeping!"

As we got closer, the air started burning our eyes and noses, and we had to roll up our windows so we could breathe. Kat pulled to a stop in the middle of the road and walked back to our van. "If you have face masks, get them out. If not, I have some. We need to keep the air conditioning off and the windows down, so we can hear any animals that are still alive. If I roll up the windows on my truck, then you do the same. Keep your masks on no matter what—even if your windows are closed. We're going to split up. You two will follow me, and I'm going to send the other two vehicles one street away from us. We can cover ground quicker that way. It's hard to breathe here, so I want to do this fast."

"That big thing there is the levee, right?" I asked, pointing.

"Yes, it leaked on the other side. This side was flooded with toxic waste from the oil spill and the levees. We should be ok. If we have another hurricane, I want to check and see if there's anything to get out now," she said and walked on.

I looked at Jax, who was already adjusting her mask. I pulled mine out of my bag and said, "I don't think we are going to find anything. The animals wouldn't stay here, they would leave."

"You're right about that—unless they are stuck."

"True. I just hope we can tell where they are."

Lakeview was a very nice, high-class neighborhood, but was now totally ruined. In some places, the water marks on the homes were as high as one-and-a-half floors. We drove and drove, and there was no sound to be heard. The whole area just felt dead. There were no birds, no seagulls, nothing.

After an hour and a half, Kat stopped in the center of the

road and came back to us. "We are getting out of here before we all get burnt lungs. I don't even think there are mosquitoes here. Animals are smarter than to stay in this area. They all know better and left. If we would have found anything here, it would have been human."

We rolled up our windows and headed out of Lakeview. It was a good distance before Kat rolled down her windows. We all followed suit. It was nice to breathe fresh, humid air again.

We reached the big rig about 11:00 a.m. Kat had to check all the animals that had been brought in by the other teams, so she told Jax and me we'd be going out with two new pairs. She said they had to go get a very mean dog, and she was hoping I could help with it.

I looked at the four men we were now being partnered with. I could tell they were not like Sergeant Thomas and his guys. I didn't think they were the type who would pay me any mind. "I'll go, as long as they listen to me," I said.

Kat looked at one of the men and pointed to me, "Greg, Terri is in charge. If you don't do what she says, I will send you all home. And Greg, if you don't mind her, I will put you on shit duty here with me."

He looked at her and nodded.

"Greg works for me, so he better cooperate. They'll show you where the dog is. Then you guys let her tell you what she needs. Understand? Now, go!"

We drove into an older neighborhood with nice houses. As we pulled to a stop, I could see the guys getting out with their catch poles. They looked like they were headed to hunt and started toward the house—ignoring what they had been told.

I said in a loud voice, "Where are you all going? Do you guys want to catch this dog? You need to move slowly and take your time. We're going into the yard, and the last one in will shut the gate so the dog will stay inside the yard."

These men didn't want to listen, but I kept talking. "Then we'll move slowly around the house, looking underneath, and around the cinder blocks, for the dog. When it is sighted, you will stop and take a deep breath. Don't move. Let me know where you are and I will walk you through it. Ok?"

"Ok," they said.

As soon as we got into the yard, one of the guys saw the dog go under the front porch. They all scattered, each hunting game with his catch pole. They stuck their poles in this hole and that hole, trying to get the dog. I couldn't believe what I was seeing. This was not search and rescue. It was hunt and terrorize!

I waved at Jax. "Get some cat food and meet me on the side."

While the guys were scaring the poor dog to death, I walked down the side of the house. Jax handed me the cat food over the chain-link fence. I put the food on the sidewalk next to the side of the house, then put the loop of the catch pole around the food.

Jax and I waited. We could hear the guys at the front of the house, still yelling at the poor dog.

"He's here!"

"No, now he is over there!"

"Oh no, you missed him!"

Then they got quiet. "Good," I thought. "The dog smells the food. I have one chance, and that will be it."

He poked his head out from under the house and looked at me. I looked away from him and stood still. He went for the food, trying to grab it in one gulp. I looped the catch pole over his head and got him.

"Thank God!" I said.

"Thank God, indeed," Jax said.

"Can I have some more cat food? I think our friend needs more to eat. While I'm feeding him, get those knuckleheads out of here."

"I'll get the kennel out too."

I kneeled down with my little friend and plopped another can of cat food on the ground. *"Here you go. My friend is getting rid of the hyenas. Then we will get you some water and get you out of here."*

"Thanks. They're trying to kill me."

"I've got you now. You are coming with me. Ok?"

"Ok. Thanks for the food. I haven't eaten in days."

It was quiet up front. Jax came down the side of the house with Ole Faithful, her ball-peen hammer. I smiled. "Any trouble?"

"No, not now. I can look pretty crazy when I want to. I told them to get in their vehicles and head back. If they wanted to go home, I didn't care. And if I saw one of them when you brought out this animal, I would make damn sure they never made it home."

"I see. Ready to escort us out?"

"Yes, boss. I'm going first, just in case."

"Lead the way. My new friend here will follow you at a safe distance, and I'll take up the rear."

When we got to the front yard, I saw two of the men pulling away in a jeep. (I never did see them again.) But Greg and his partner were still there.

I put the dog in the kennel and fed him some more food. Jax had put a water bowl inside the kennel and refilled it so he could have a good drink before we lifted him into the van. Greg walked up to the kennel, started to pound on the top of it, and said, "Why didn't you come when I told you to? You stupid dog! Stupid dog!"

I yelled at Greg, "What the hell do you think you're doing! That dog is defenseless in that kennel. He's ready to go, and you're going to make him mean."

Greg actually glared at the dog and then at me. He walked to his van and they left.

"Thank God. What the hell was that about?" Jax asked.

"I don't know. Greg might've been down here too long. He works with Kat, and they haven't had a break. Let's just hope that's it. When we get back, I want to let her know who she has helping her. The sooner the better, or all the dogs will be packing up—and with good reason."

I looked at our new friend and said, *"Are you ok?"*

"Yes. What did I do?"

"Nothing. Absolutely nothing. We're going to see that you are well taken care of from now on. Let's get you out of here. Ok?"

"Ok!"

When we returned, Kat came over to our truck and asked if everything was ok.

I said, "Jax, the dog, and I are ok. But the rest of the guys are nuts. This poor dog felt like they were trying to kill him. It was a dang free-for-all with that bunch. I'm not going out with them again."

"Tell me what happened."

I saw Greg back near the truck and said, "I wouldn't let that guy near any animals." Then I told her the story.

She said, "I know he's exhausted like the rest of us, but that's no reason for him to do what he did. I'll keep him here with me and I'll watch him. We'll put the dog in the front part of the truck to keep him calmed down, and I'll keep Greg working in the back."

Jax and I loaded up and headed out to get more animals.

Our last rescue of the day ended up being a memorable one. We pulled up to a house in a nice neighborhood where there had been some flooding, but not as bad as in other areas. When we got inside, it was dark. We saw the water had come up to about 3 feet and the walls were getting moldy. It was smelly and there was mud and clutter all around on the floor, most of it still damp.

Lying on top of a stack of papers on the kitchen table was our catch: a big cream-colored cat with beautiful green eyes. She looked to me like she was ready to go.

When she saw us, she got up and jumped over to the kitchen counter, which was a mess with dishes, cereal boxes, and cans. *"Look what I've been eating! These are mine!"* she said proudly.

She stood next to three boxes of strawberry Pop-Tarts that had been clawed opened and eaten through. There was a fourth box in the cupboard above her.

This 22-pound cat had a huge belly and was in no danger of starvation! It was a shock for us, since we had been seeing so many emaciated animals. She told me she had gotten into the cupboard, pulled down the boxes of Pop-Tarts, and been able to feed herself when she needed to eat. She had used the good water left in the sink as her "drinking fountain."

I relayed her story to Jax, who smiled and said, "She won't fit into this carrier. I'll go get a kennel."

"*What's your name?*" I asked, as I walked over to our new friend.

"*Jasmine.*"

"*Well, Jasmine. I'd like to take you someplace safe and dry, where your mom and dad can find you.*"

"*Ok. Can I take my food with me?*"

"*Yes. But we have some nice canned cat food for you instead.*"

"*Really? I haven't had that in a long time. Can I have some?*"

"*Of course,*" I said to our big girl and yelled out to Jax to bring a can of food with her.

Jasmine wouldn't let me put her in the kennel until Jax had gotten the can inside—and she wanted one last drink of water from the sink. She also asked me to carry her outside, which was a good idea because I am taller than Jax and could lift her just that much higher off of the dirty, stinky floor.

On the way out, she told me she was happy to be a big cat. "*I like to eat so I can stay healthy,*" she said.

We took Jasmine to the drop-off site and headed back with the team to Lamar-Dixon.

When we arrived, things looked very different—and ready for the arrival of more volunteers. There was a big white tent about 100 yards from the area where the Texans and my group were camped. It was huge inside and looked like it could hold 150 people. There were fold-up cots stacked on one side so that people could help themselves and set up a spot to sleep. A couple of folks had actually moved their tents inside the big tent.

There was now a 10-foot chain-link fence running from the intake area all around the barns. The fence had an entrance at the intake area, another in the back by the food tent, and one by the front of Barn One, not far from the restrooms. There were security guards at each of the three entrances. All animals being removed needed special paperwork to leave the fenced-in area, and it was checked again at the front gate. I knew the animals were even safer now.

At the 7:00 p.m. meeting, Eric told the group about all of the improvements. He said volunteers would need name tags to get in and out of the security gates and told us the big white tent was available for everyone's use. "We've been told Hurricane Rita is dissipating, so we'll resume search and rescue tomorrow."

I gathered they had stopped other groups from heading into town today. Fortunately, our Louisiana SPCA team had brought a full load of animals back to camp.

I had to hurry to Kat's meeting and arrived in the middle of it. Everyone had been sharing stories of their day, and Jax was describing how our Pop-Tart kitty had found and rationed her toaster pastries. Then Richard, a new addition to the group, told us what had happened to him.

"We were sent to a house to get a fish—and not just any fish, mind you. It was a piranha. I guess the people had paid a lot of money for it. We were looking in the tank and trying to figure out how to get it out without it nibbling on us, because it was still alive and hungry. While we were standing there thinking, I heard a small scratching noise coming from the kitchen. I went to check it out and didn't see anything. Just as I was about to leave the kitchen, I heard the scratching again, ever so faint. There was a doorway to the laundry room, so I thought I'll just peak my head in there and see. As I looked around the corner, I saw the washing machine was propped up on top of a grey plastic kennel. I looked in the side of the kennel and there was a beagle looking back at me. I opened the door to the kennel and he came right into my arms."

Richard paused as the tears welled up in his eyes. "I just couldn't believe he was still alive. The water must have floated everything in the room, and when it all came back down, the washer was on the kennel, pinning it to the floor. If we hadn't been trying to figure out what to do with the piranha, we would've never thought to look for anything else. I thanked God for the piranha, because today he was the hero. If it wasn't for him, we wouldn't have rescued the beagle."

Everyone applauded and several people had tears in their eyes. He said, "It also taught me to look in the whole house, instead of what's just on my list. That way, I make sure I only have to take one trip and get everything out of the house."

We all applauded Richard again, then had a toast to the piranha with our water and Gatorade.

Kat told us we would be leaving at 5:00 a.m. and we should get some rest, because tomorrow would be another big day. She asked me to come chat with her and we walked away from the group. She said, "Thank you for letting me know about those guys. I've sent them home. I also had a talk with Greg, and I've given him the next four days off. I think he needs to de-stress. None of us who live here have had any breaks, and I think it's all gotten to him. He lost his home and his dog."

"I'm sorry to hear that."

"Me too. Some of us just rented a house in Gonzales, not too far from here. We are staying together until we can figure out what to do. A lot of them lost their homes. Mine is ok. And my cats are ok, so we moved them to the house here. I'm going to start a rotating shift, so some of my guys can rest while we have volunteers like you to help."

"That's a good idea, Kat. We'll all eventually go home, but you will still be here fighting the fight."

"I just wanted you to know I took care of the problem. If you see any others, let me know."

"Ok. Did you find out what happened with all the houses not being marked that the animals were removed? That was a huge waste of time."

"Yes, the other group with HSUS doing search and rescue forgot to tell people about marking the houses with spray paint. Now they are trying to backtrack with the paperwork to see what has been brought in and what still needs to be picked up. I'm just glad I don't have to do that paperwork."

"You and me both. What a mess. See you in the morning."

I walked over to the showers and had to wait for three people in front of me. I realized that folks were beginning to figure out the best times to grab a shower. I went to my tent, put out my clothes, and set my alarm for 4:15 a.m.

I wrote in my journal: "I'm glad Hurricane Rita has dissipated—that would be a big mess."

CHAPTER TEN

Thursday, September 22, 2005

I heard a slight buzzing noise as I rescued a dog from underneath a house. Jax was smiling at me.

That buzz was my alarm, I realized, and I tapped the top to turn it off. I sat up, dazed and groggy from my sudden awakening. "Well, at least I finished catching the dog before I woke up," I thought and smiled.

I hoped I hadn't let the alarm go on for a long time. It showed 4:16 a.m., so it had buzzed less than a minute.

I turned on my headlamp to see where my clothes were. I knew I could probably do everything in the dark by now, but I figured the light would help me wake up more. I dressed, went to the restrooms, and headed over to wake up Jax.

I tapped on her tent and it took a bit to roust her, so I didn't feel too bad about my alarm. We were all showing some signs of wear and tear. "I'm up!" she finally said in a loud voice.

We met at the meeting and were surprised to see Cindy, Anthony, Sharon, and Glen. We thought they were headed home.

Cindy said, "We all decided we didn't get the messages from our command telling us to head back. With the new hurricane, we'll say we lost signal. But today will definitely be our last day."

As we drove to New Orleans, the sun was rising and the whole sky was red. It was a beautiful morning!

The big rig was just pulling in when we arrived at the

drop-off site. Kat got out of her truck, still on the phone, and signaled to everyone to stay put. When we waited like this, it usually meant things were changing. We needed to be flexible and go with the flow.

She was on the phone for about 10 minutes and our group was getting restless. We looked out to the road and saw four fire trucks. I was wondering where the fire was, thinking they would pass by us. But they slowed down and turned into our lot.

"They're here!" Kat said and hung up her phone. "Everyone, listen up. We're going with the firemen today. They are looking for cadavers—human cadavers. They will be breaking into homes where people are considered missing. We'll be on hand to bring out any animals they find.

"I also have some new addresses and I'll give those to a couple of groups. The rest of you will accompany the firemen. We have some new people from California to add to our group today. And we have a vet and a vet tech with us. They'll help as the animals arrive and can give fluids right here. The animals we are going to get out now are probably going to need fluids immediately, and we don't want them to wait all day."

Kat introduced the new people. She assigned four California gals, Sharon, and Glen to follow the fire rigs. Richard, who was by himself, was also assigned to a rig. That left Cindy, Anthony, Jax, and me to go to the addresses and get more animals out.

Jax and I went to the Lower Ninth Ward again, my old stomping ground. We headed for our addresses and one, two, three, the animals came out pretty easily. At two addresses, there were no homes—the houses were totally missing. I silently wished that the animals got out safely.

We turned a corner and came face to face with Cindy and Anthony. We had addresses on the same street and were able to quickly get our catches. When we were ready to move on, I heard a dog in my head say, *"Please don't leave me again. Please! I'm over here!"*

I said to Jax, "We aren't leaving yet."

Then I heard another voice, weaker than the first. *"Please, help me. Please."*

I said to Cindy and Anthony, "And you guys aren't leaving either. I'm hearing some animals. We need to get them. Let me focus for a minute. I think one's in the house two down from ours. Hold on."

I walked along the street and told Jax to follow me in the van. I wanted to focus on the voices. Cindy and Anthony turned around and followed Jax.

When I got a little closer, I waved and they turned off their motors. I closed my eyes. *"Ok, I hear two of you. I think you're in different houses, but I need to know where you are. One at a time. The deep voice: talk to me so I know where you are. Tell me what room you're in."*

There was silence. I debated if I was hearing things.

Then I heard the voice again. *"I'm here. I'm here."*

"Keep talking to me. I'm headed your way. Keep talking. Just say anything."

"I'm here! I'm here!"

I turned to face a white house. *"Can you hear me?"*

"Yes!"

"Ok. I'm going to use my human voice and you tell me if I'm in front of your house, ok?"

"Ok."

"Hello. Are you in the white house with the white fence?"

"Yes," I heard in my head.

"What room are you in?"

"I'm in the back bedroom. I can't get out. There's something in front of the door."

"Can you see light?"

"Yes, there is a window at the back of the house."

"I'm going to send someone to get you, ok?"

"Yes, please! I'm right here."

I pointed to the house and told Cindy and Anthony to go to

the back, break in, and get the dog out.

"You sure?" Cindy said.

Jax replied, "Just do it. She knows what she's doing."

They took off toward the back of the house.

I said, *"Ok, the small voice: where are you?"*

I could hardly hear the voice earlier, so I figured I'd be closer in the street and started walking back the direction we had come. I told Jax to stay put until I knew for sure where the dog was.

I got back to where I had first heard it. *"Talk to me again. Am I closer?"*

"I'm here." The voice was still faint, but it sounded slightly louder.

"Just keep talking to me."

"I'm here. I'm here. I'm here."

I kept walking, then turned to my left. "Are you in a pink house?" I said aloud.

"Yes, Yes! That's my house. I'm stuck in the kitchen. I'm on the top of the thing they keep the food in. I can't get down."

"We're coming to get you!"

I waved to Jax. "It's in the kitchen on top of the fridge. Pink house!"

"I'm on my way," she yelled, then got in the van and drove over.

As I walked around the house, I saw that all of the doors and windows had locked bars on them. I yelled for Jax to bring Ole Faithful.

There was a wooden porch in back, which made it easier to get to the door and window. I looked in the window and saw a white poodle on top of the refrigerator. When she saw my face in the window, she started wagging her tail.

I said, *"We'll get you out, just hang on. We need to make some noise, so we can get the door open. Just hang tight."*

She was wiggling so much I thought she might fall off the refrigerator. *"Hold on. We'll get you out."*

Jax rounded the corner of the house and I showed her the dog through the window. She looked surprised, then said, smiling, "Let me see what I can do about this door."

Jax actually ended up pulling off the door frame. The metal security door was tightly attached and wasn't coming off, but the wood frame was rotted by the flooding. It took her about five minutes to demo the frame and pull open the door. When I asked to help, she said firmly, "This is my job."

She opened the door and said, "You want to get her?"

"You go ahead. You did all the work on the door."

Jax walked in and over to the refrigerator. "I'm not tall enough."

I wasn't that much taller, but I lifted Jax up so she could reach the poodle, who was very ready to leave her house. She jumped in Jax's arms and we swayed under her weight. I tried hard not to lose my grip or we all would have gone down. When I did let Jax go, she landed on the kitchen floor with the white poodle in her arms, kissing her face.

"Looks like our little friend is anxious to go," I said. "I'll go get a kennel."

"I already have one out. You go back in the street and see if you can pick up voices from any other animals. I'll take care of this one."

"Ok, but I only heard two. I'll walk a little and see what I get."

"I'll follow in a few minutes."

I headed back out to the front of the house. Cindy and Anthony had just pulled up. She still had a shocked look on her face and asked me, "How did you know the dog was in there?"

"I heard it. Did you get him?"

"Yes," Anthony replied. "He was big. Took both of us to get him out the window."

"Let me walk some more and see if I hear anything else. I'll go back the way you guys came."

As I headed out, I could hear Jax telling Cindy and Anthony about the poodle. "This little girl was on top of the refrigerator.

She must have swam up there in the flood, and when the water receded, there she was, stuck."

I heard the white poodle say, *"I woke up one morning and the water was gone."*

I yelled back what she said. Jax looked over at me and said, "That makes sense." Then she went to the kennel to feed our newest rescue.

I walked to the end of the block. I calmed myself, got real quiet in my head, and said, *"Whoever is out there: if you can hear me, say something so I can come and get you out."*

It stayed quiet, but I felt something pulling me to my right. I waved to Cindy and Anthony that I was going to go down a different street. They nodded and kept their distance behind me.

I walked past one house, two houses, three houses. *"Anyone here? I can feel you, but I can't hear you."*

"I'm here," I heard in my head. It sounded directly to my right.

I stopped and looked over at the house. *"Are you in the yellow house with the black trim?"*

"Yes."

"Where in the house are you?"

"If you go in the front door, I'm in the bedroom on the right side. The door is stuck. I can't get out."

"I'm going to send my friends Cindy and Anthony to come get you. Ok?"

"Ok."

I waved for Cindy and Anthony to come my direction. When they pulled up, I pointed to the yellow house.

"In the front door, down the hallway, and in a bedroom on the right. I would try the side first. Looks like there's an air conditioner. You might just be able to drop it out. If we're lucky, it will be in that room. If not, the animal says the door is blocked and it can't get out. I'll go look for some more animals."

I walked further down this street. I got quiet again and asked, *"Is there anyone here who I can help out?"*

I waited. I didn't hear anything and I didn't feel anything. So I continued on.

I reached another intersection and I turned around to look behind me. Jax was in our van, just passing Cindy and Anthony's van. I waved her over and said, "Let me get a catch pole. I'll keep looking for a bit. If we don't find any more, then we should take these guys back."

I walked through the intersection and halfway down the next block. I was about to turn, when I saw a very thin man to my right, standing in the driveway of a home. I looked at him and said, "Are you all right?"

"Yes, but can you help get my dog out of the house?"

"Sure." I waved back at Jax and told her I was going to go help the man get his dog out. She waved at me and nodded.

"Are you sure you're ok?" I asked him.

"Yes, I'm fine. But I'm really worried about Buster. He's in the kitchen there and the door is unlocked. Can you get him out?"

I was puzzled and thought, "Why don't you go and get him out?" Then I figured I'd just go get the dog.

I went to the back door, opened it, and saw a black Lab lying on the floor, waiting. When I went in, he tried to get up.

"I've got you, Buster!" I said and went to the dog.

He looked up at me. *"You know my name."*

"Yes, your daddy asked me to come and get you. Let's go outside and see him."

"Ok. I'm a little tired."

"Yes, I can see that. Let me help you."

I did the best I could to get him up. When he got outside and into the fresh air, he was able to stand a bit better. I had the catch pole on him just in case, and I saw Jax pulling out a kennel. I looked at her and said, "This one is really weak. We should get him back soon."

She nodded, pulled a kennel out of the van, and dropped it on the ground. Then she grabbed a towel and came over. I introduced her to Buster. We put the towel under his waist to help support him, and by the time we got to the street, he was doing better.

I looked around and asked, "Where did his dad go?"

"I saw you talking to someone, but there was no one there."

"Really? I could have sworn he was right there."

Then I realized the man had appeared to me telepathically. I had been able to see an extra glow around him. So he was a man "in spirit," who had probably died in the flood. He wanted my help to make sure that his dog would be ok.

Cindy and Anthony pulled up at that moment. I looked at them and said, "This one needs to go back right now. How about if we load you up with all three, and Jax and I will keep at it."

We helped put the dogs into their truck, and Jax said, "I'm not sure you should leave me here with Terri. She's talking to dead people now."

Anthony looked stricken. Cindy cocked her head at me. I said, "I think the man who told me where his dog was is probably back in his house. So let Kat know this address and tell the firemen to come check it out."

Cindy laughed and said, "Anthony, they are messing with you."

I wanted to leave well enough alone on the subject of dead people. So I told them Jax and I would stay in the area for a few more blocks. "If we don't find any animals, we'll call you and meet you back at the drop-off."

After they left, I said to Jax, "I'm going keep going this direction to see what I can do."

"Ok. I'll follow—at a distance," she said, chuckling.

I started walking down the road and wasn't picking up anything. I looked around to the left and to the right. When I looked ahead of me again, I saw water on the road. I didn't think I had seen it there before. I looked back at Jax and pointed to the water. She shrugged her shoulders, so I walked on.

At the next intersection, I turned to the right. As I passed a white house with yellow trim, I felt something on my left. I stopped, and it was gone. So I continued walking. All of a sudden, I got this feeling that said, "Turn around."

I turned and saw that Jax had gotten out of the van. It looked like she was talking to someone at the white house. I stood still—I knew what was happening.

As Jax headed down the side of the house, I walked back her direction so I could keep an eye on things. I saw her go around the corner of the house to the left. I decided to wait a couple of minutes. If she didn't come back soon, I would follow and see if she needed any help.

I made myself useful and pulled out a small kennel, just in case. I put a bowl of dog food and a water dish inside. I had a gallon of water in my hand and was heading to the kennel when I saw Jax coming around the house with a small Shih Tzu in her arms.

Jax looked around and asked, "Where's the lady?"

I shook my head. "There is no lady!"

Jax stopped dead in her tracks. She looked surprised and asked, "Did you see the lady?"

"No, she came for you."

Jax started cussing at me. "F**k you! I told you not to do that to me. Scares me to death."

I laughed and said, "Now, don't scare the dog."

She remembered she was holding the dog and headed back to the kennel for the food and water. After she put the Shih Tzu in the kennel, she stood up and shook her whole body, like she was shaking something off of her.

"Don't you do that to me again!"

"I didn't do that—and besides, she was a nice old lady."

"You saw her?"

"I saw her when you were walking to the back of the house with her, but not before."

"But you stopped right here by the house!"

"Yes, I felt something. But then it went away. It was your turn," I said. "Good job!"

Jax shook again. "Don't tell Anthony and Cindy."

"Don't worry. We can keep it between you and me."

She shook again.

I said, "I think this dog needs to go back too. I can't pick up any others near us. I'm not feeling anything. So let's go."

My phone rang. Kat wanted us back at the drop site. She got a call from the California girls. One of them wasn't feeling well, so we needed to take their place.

We took the Shih Tzu to the drop-off and then went to relieve them. One of the gals looked like she had heat stroke. I said to her partner, "Don't let her drive, she's about to faint. Get her back to the big rig. Get some Gatorade in her and let her sit in the air conditioning at the back of the rig. We'll take over here."

I walked to where the firemen were working and asked one of them, "Have you found any animals yet?"

"No, but we'll let you know."

"Ok. Were those girls sitting here for two hours, just waiting?"

"Yes."

"How about we go get the three animals on our address list. If you find something, you call us and we'll head right back. Would that be ok?"

"Sure. We haven't found anything, so you might as well."

I gave him my cell number, then Jax and I went to the first of the addresses we had left on our list. When we arrived at the house, we saw the front door was open. I said, "We better look, just in case. I'm hoping he already got out."

We went into the house and did our search. We saw the back bedroom door was shut. When I tapped on the door, we heard a growl. "I think we have something here," I said.

I tried to turn the doorknob and it worked just fine. I pushed on the door, but it wouldn't budge. "Let's look outside and see if there is another way in."

Jax said, "I'll go. You keep trying."

I pushed harder on the door and it moved just a little. "It's moving. Looks like a dresser floated in front of it."

It was dark in the room. I couldn't see the dog, but it growled again. I said, *"Hang in there. We're going to get you out."*

I pushed again and made a little more progress with the door. One more push and there was just enough of a space for me to slip through. Slowly, I put the catch pole into the room. I didn't hear anything. I poked my head in so I could see where the dog was. I let my eyes adjust to the darkness. There was a window to the left with a little bit light coming in through a slit in the drapes. I scanned the room, looking for the dog.

Then I saw him—a big black dog lying on the bed with his head in his paws. I said, *"Hi there. How about we get you out of here?"*

"Really? I can go? How? Can't get out."

"We'll find a way."

As I squeezed into the room, I saw the furniture had floated toward the door. There was a dresser, then an armoire, and then another dresser, all lined up. It seemed hopeless.

I looked out the window at Jax, who was smiling in at me. "I think we have to come out the window," I said.

"Ok, let me get Ole Faithful. I'm going to put duct tape on the window before I hit it. But look for something to cover you two up, just in case the glass shatters your way."

I turned to the dog on the bed. *"It's going to be ok. Jax is really good at breaking things."*

The dog actually started panting, like he was smiling.

"You are a big boy, aren't you?"

"Yes," he said. He looked to me like a long-haired bull mastiff.

"Do you think you can walk?"

"I don't know. I haven't gotten up in days. I just thought I would lie here until I stepped out."

I didn't want him thinking any more about dying. *"Well now, we can't have that. Jax and I are going to make sure you get outside. I think fresh air is just what you need. Don't you?"*

"Fresh air. Yes, that would be nice."

"Ok, fresh air it is."

Jax was back at the window. "I'm going to tape the whole window, so it will get dark. I will let you know when I'm going to break it. Did you find something to cover up with?"

I had totally forgotten to look, and then spotted the drapes. I said to my friend, *"Do you think your parents would mind if we used the drapes to keep the glass off of us?"*

"No. They are ruined. Mom will get new."

I looked at Jax and said, "I'll use the drapes."

She gave me the thumbs up and I pulled on the drapes. The wood was so rotten that the brackets, screws, and rod all came out of the wall as well.

"See what I mean?" the dog said.

I took the drapes off the rod. Then I told my friend I would have to come over by him and cover us up when Jax broke the window.

"Yes, I thought so."

I noticed the dog wasn't moving—and he hadn't moved since I came in. I hoped we could get him up and out through the window when the time came.

Jax finished taping the window and said, "Ok, cover up and I will count to three."

"Ok," I said to her. I looked at my friend. *"Here we go!"*

I pulled the drapes up in the air between us and the window, hoping that if anything hit the drapes, it would fall on the floor, the bed, or the dresser.

"Bang, bang, bang, thunk," went Old Faithful!

"Done," Jax said, and I let the drape down so I could see. The whole window had popped into the house in one piece.

"Awesome! Let me get that out of the way and we'll see what we can do."

"Hand the glass to me and I'll put it out here."

"Ok. I'm hoping my friend will get up."

"I noticed he isn't moving."

"Let's see what the fresher outside air does for him."

I looked over my shoulder and saw the dog start to move. He stood up and stretched his whole body.

"I have to put my leash on you."

"Ok, but I'm not moving very fast. Stiff."

"Yes, I can see that."

I put the catch pole on him. *"How do you feel?"*

"Tired. But I think I can move."

"It's a bit of a drop out the window."

I heard something outside. I looked out and saw Jax dragging a big wooden box under the window. She stood on the box and said, "Let's see if this will help."

"Looks good. I'm thinking butt first with this guy."

"Ok. I'll try to hold him."

I told the dog how we were going to get him out. He walked across the bed to the top of the dresser and put his head out the window.

"Fresh air," he said, as he took a deep breath.

"Yes, fresh air."

He licked Jax's face, then said, *"Tell her to move."*

I did, and she stepped aside, just as the dog and the catch pole went out the window.

She said, "I got him. We are headed to the front. Can you get out?"

"I think so. I'll see you up front."

I sat on the window ledge and jumped down on the box, then stepped to the ground. It was nice to be outside again. It was very hot inside with everything shut up. I walked to the van, where I saw that our boy was still standing and eating out of a dish, tail wagging. He glanced my way, but kept eating.

Jax said, "He looks good, considering."

"Yes, he does. He looks great."

He headed over to the water bowl, and I said, "I hate to put him in a kennel."

"How about if I just put a leash on him and tie him to the inside of the van. That way, he can stand up. We don't really have a kennel big enough for him anyway."

"Sounds good. I think he needs to go back right away, don't you?"

Jax agreed, so I called the fireman and asked if they had found anything.

He said, "People, yes. And two dogs, both deceased. So nothing for you yet."

"We're going to take a dog back to the drop-off. Then I'll check in again."

As we pulled in, we saw the gal from California sitting in the shade and drinking a Gatorade. Her partner was helping the vet and the vet tech, who looked like they had their hands full. Kat came over as I got out of the van and said, "I thought you two were with the firemen."

"We were, but we didn't want to just wait around. I gave them my number and they'll call if they find anything. So we went to our addresses. I just checked and they have only found deceased animals."

"So why are you here?"

At that point, Jax let our big guy out of the back of the van. When he walked around the side, I thought Kat was going to melt. "Look at him! He's beautiful."

I smiled. "He's why we're here. How are the vets doing?"

"Pretty good. They're only giving fluids to two dogs. The rest are popping back pretty quick once they get in the air conditioning."

"Good! This guy was lying on a bed, stuck in a bedroom in the back of a house, and hasn't gotten up for a few days. So we thought letting him stand was a good idea."

"Why don't you take him to see the vets, and then we will let him lie outside."

"Would you like that, boy?" I asked the dog.

He looked up at Kat and kissed her hand.

"How about if I take him over?" she said. Jax handed her

the leash and off they went.

My cell phone rang. It was the firemen. They had a live dog—and he wasn't happy. They were a little further down the street where we had met them earlier.

"We're on our way to you," I said.

I went over and told Kat that we had to help the firemen, but we also had two more addresses. She asked for the list and said she would give it to Cindy and Anthony, who were on their way back with two rescues.

As Jax got our list from the van, Kat looked at me and said in a low voice, "I hear you are doing some interesting things."

"It seems I have some special helpers."

She laughed at that. "Go get the dog," she said and waved me off.

When we pulled up to the fire truck, I saw water in the street ahead of us, where there hadn't been any before. I wondered if it was the levees leaking again and how much more time we would have down here.

I got out of the van, went around the back, and walked toward a white house with a chain-link fence. The paint was peeling and I saw the water line was up to about 8 feet. Behind the house were two separate buildings that looked like small cottage-type houses. One was totally collapsed. The firemen had cut a hole in its roof so they could check for people inside.

One of the fireman walked up to me, pointed to the collapsed building, and said, "There is a nasty dog in there. We have to get him out, because it looks like there are a couple of people in there—and we need to have an accurate body count."

I asked Jax if she wanted to get this one. "I think it's your day," she said. "Besides, he says the dog is nasty. So he's all yours."

I got my catch pole and put on my gloves. There was no gate, so I had to climb over the fence to get in the backyard. There was a fireman on the roof, standing near the hole. Pointing to the back right corner, he said, "The dog is over there. It's like he is defending something."

"Would you mind keeping watch after I go in, and keep him from coming out?"

"Sure."

I peered into the hole. It was totally dark inside what was left of the house. I let my eyes adjust and looked around. Then I pulled my head out and yelled for Jax.

She popped around the corner and I asked her, "Is this yard fenced off all the way around? I can see it is to our right and in the back, but what about left side of the cottage over by you?"

She went to the left and yelled back, "This side is totally open, boss."

"Can you get to the back corner behind the cottage?"

"There's some water, but I think I can. Let me put on my mud boots. They're in the van. Be right back."

"Get your catch pole too."

I sat with the fireman and waited. I could see the dog was beginning to read my mind. "Hurry up, Jax. He's coming. You have to get in front of him to push him back my way."

I heard her yell, "I'm going as fast as I can." One of the other firemen told us she had gotten hung up in a fallen tree.

I looked down at the dog and saw he was a pit bull. *"Hey!"* I said.

He looked at me and started to growl. I said, *"What's up with that! I have good food and water. Let me take you out of here."*

"I'm guarding my mom and dad and brother."

"I can see that."

I saw a human arm and a leg. To the left, there was a deceased German shepherd. It looked like the pit bull had to eat off of them to stay alive.

"I see something I want you to do for me, ok?"

"What? Do for you?"

"Yes. I think if you get out and get some fresh air, then these men can see how your mom, dad, and brother are. Would that be ok?"

"Yes, but I have to guard."

"If you're out of the house, do you have to guard?"

"No, not my yard."

I thought so. *"It belongs to everyone, right?"*

"Yes. It's my play yard. For me and my brother."

I knew I couldn't wait much longer. As I looked at the pit, I yelled, "Jax, you better be over there!"

"She's still stuck in the tree," said a fireman.

"Ok. Well, we have to go now."

I looked at the pit. He was below me, to my right. To my left was another hole. I said, *"Do you see the light coming out of that hole? Can you get out of that hole?"*

"I tried. I don't think I can."

"Why don't you walk over this way and see what you can do here," I said, lowering my catch pole with the loop open.

As he started to walk toward me, I said, *"You know, I have this neat leash. I can connect you and me together so we can get you out of here. What do you think?"*

"I want out! I can't get out!"

"Walk this way and I'll help you. Go toward the light and I will connect us."

He came closer and closer. When he stood right below me, I looped the catch pole around his head and tightened it slightly. The pit backed up.

"Whoa! Hold on there. We have to go together now. Ok?"

"How am I going to get up there?"

I looked at the fireman, who was surprised that the snarling dog had just been looped. "How did you do that?"

"I talked to him."

He looked at me and smiled. "You did something, all right. Now how are we going to get him up here? Is he going to bite?"

"I'll ask him. Why?"

"If he'll be nice, I'll go down there, pick him up, and get him out."

I looked down at my pit. *"This nice man said he would come*

down there and lift you up to me. Will you be nice to him?"
The dog looked at me and then at the fireman, back and forth.
"I think that is the best way."
"Ok, but I get scared easy and I growl."
"I have heard you growl. It is very fierce. But if you growl at the fireman, he'll get scared. And he'll just want to leave you down there. So you have to be nice, ok?"
"Ok."

I told the fireman I would move the pit off to the left and he could get down to the right. Then I would pull the front of the dog my direction, keeping his face toward me.

I moved the catch pole to the left, asking my pit to make room for the fireman. He did, and the fireman jumped down into the hole. Another fireman handed me some nylon rope and I threw one end down to him. He said, "I'll put this around the front part and then I'll pick up the back of him."

"Wait a minute and let me tell the dog," I said. The fireman looked at me like I was nuts.

"The fireman is going to lay the rope down. I need you to walk over it, so we can make a loop that will go under your armpits. I will then pull up the front of you. The fireman will have to touch you to lift up your butt. And then you will be out of the hole. Ok?"

He looked at the fireman and put his head down a little, looking for the rope on the ground. I told the fireman what I had said. He looked at the dog and said to me, "He's waiting for me to put the rope down."

"Yes."

He smiled up at me. "You really are talking to him."

He put the rope down quickly so he could keep his distance, and the dog stepped over it. Then he took the end and tied it around the pit. I said to the fireman, "I'm going to pull and you push."

Another fireman came up behind me and said, "I'll pull too."

"Ok, thanks. Then I can just focus on the head."

I told the pit that we were going to lift him on the count of three. "One, two, threeeeeee."

We both pulled. The pit pushed off the fireman in the hole and up he came, onto the roof right next to me. I looked him in the eyes and said aloud, "Good boy! Let's get you out of here."

He walked to the edge of the roof and lay down. I could tell he was exhausted. I jumped off of the roof and told him to come to me. I used the catch pole to pull him in a bit. I put my left arm around his shoulders and my right arm around his butt. I lifted him up and got him off of the roof and away from some debris. Then I lowered him gently to the ground.

Jax came around the back of the house. She was glad to finally be free of the tree. I said, "Now you have to climb the fence and go get your bolt cutters to cut it. This pit is too tired to go any further than he has to."

"Ok, cool. Cutting!" she said and headed for the van.

The dog lay down for quite a while near the cottage. He needed water.

The firemen offered to help and Jax actually let them. She gave them the bolt cutters and went to get some water for our boy. We moved at the dog's pace. It was slow going. They cut the fence and got out of the way. My pit just looked at me. I said, *"You ready?"*

"Almost."

He looked back at the house and asked, *"Can you get my brother out?"*

"I think you know that your brother is already out, don't you? It looks to me like he is there beside you."

The pit looked to his right and said, *"Yes. I think you're right."*

The pit smiled and got to his feet—his brother's spirit was leading the way. We walked a little way along the side of the front house and he lay down again. Jax was right there with the water. He took a big drink and said, *"My brother says I can go with you. That you are safe."*

I smiled. *"I'm glad."*

Then I said aloud, "What you do think, big guy? Want to head to the van, go for a ride, and catch a bit of a breeze? We drive with the windows down. It will cool you off a little."

He stood up again and made it to the back of the van. Jax gave him some food and more water. Then we helped our boy into a kennel and lifted him into the van.

We thanked the firemen and told them to let us know if they found any more animals. When we got to the drop-off lot, the big rig was closed up and ready to go. The vet checked our new pit and said he'd be ok if we drove him in our van back to Lamar-Dixon. Cindy, Anthony, Sharon, and Glen were all out at the last two addresses on our list. Kat asked Jax and me to wait for them.

"You guys can come back together, but you need to be out of town by four o'clock. Hurricane Rita has worked back up to a big one—and it is headed directly for us," she said.

I called Cindy. She and the others were trying to catch a dog that had gotten out and was under the house. Thankfully, there was still a fence all the way around the property. She said she thought they could get him and be back in a half-hour. If not, she'd call us for some help.

While we waited, Jax and I talked about our new friend and how he had survived his time in the attic. I chatted with the pit, and we found out his brother had told him to eat him to stay alive. There was no water, though, so he did the best he could. We asked him if he had a name.

"Dog. That is what they called me."

I told Jax, who said, "We have to come up with something much better than that!"

I asked the pit, *"Is it ok if we come up with another name for you?"*

He smiled and wagged his tail. *"Really? I can have a new name?"*

"Yes, and you can help us choose it."

Jax could see how excited he was and started suggesting names, none of which seemed to fit him. So she said, "How about if we name him something about his experience? How about Flapjack? That's how the house looked, like it had flipped over."

I looked at Dog and there was no response. Then I said, "How about Pancake, because it was as flat as a pancake?"

I looked at Dog. He was wagging his tail. *"Do you like Pancake?"*

"That was something I ate, I think."

"You very well could have. They are round, thin things made in a skillet. They are kind of soft to chew."

"Yes! I have had them. I like food. My mom always gave me what was left over."

I smiled at him. I could see on his face that he just remembered his parents and brother had passed. I said, *"Then in her honor, why don't we call you Pancake?"*

He smiled and wagged his tail. *"Yes, yes, for mom."*

"Ok, Pancake it is!"

"Pancake. Like good food. Yum, yum. I have a good name now."

We heard vehicles coming and then saw the rest of our group pull in. The smiles on their faces told us they had caught the dog they were looking for. We ate some snacks as we swapped stories about our new rescues.

Soon two of the fire engines rolled by. The firemen yelled over to us, "We were called to get out. The hurricane is causing waves to go over the dam and the flooding is increasing."

I looked at our group and said, "Looks like our break is over. We are supposed to be in front of them."

Cindy asked me, "Does that mean the water is high and it's going to flood?"

"I think it means it is no longer safe to be down here. Let's head out."

Because we had a dog in the vehicle with no air conditioning,

I turned on my flashers on the interstate and drove a little faster to get him back to camp. The others did too, and we looked like an official rescue mini-convoy.

Every car and truck we came upon moved out of the way, and the people waved vigorously when they saw we were animal rescue. Some even honked their horns at us.

While Jax tried to nap on the way to Lamar-Dixon, Pancake and I had a nice conversation. I told him he'd see lots of dogs there to make friends with and that he would find someone new to take care of him.

I could see him smile in the rearview mirror. *"My mom and dad didn't let me out of the yard, so I couldn't make friends. Just my brother. I did talk to the poodle across the street."*

I looked up at him in the mirror. *"Is she alright? Did she get out?"* I was hoping we didn't leave a dog down there with more water on its way.

"Yes, she got out early. Someone came to get her."

"I'm sorry it took so long for us to come and get you."

"I'm still here!"

"Yes, you are. But I think you might need some fluids and some more food." Our boy was looking a little weak.

"What are fluids?"

I tried to explain that the vets would put a tube in his arm to put a cool liquid in his body—and it would make him feel really good.

"Ok. I thought you said they would give me food. I like food best."

"Yes, of course, they will."

Pancake was weak and I had noticed earlier that his stomach looked bloated. Debra had said their bodies start to bloat there from starvation. I knew our little Pancake had been through a tough time.

I looked at him in the mirror. *"Why don't you take a nap? We have a ways to go. I'll wake you when we get closer."*

"Ok."

I pushed a little harder on the gas pedal. The road was clear ahead.

When we arrived at camp, I saw the big white tent was gone and wondered what was going on. We pulled up at intake and were third in line behind our big rig. I knew it would take a while to unload the truck. We opened the doors of the van to let Pancake catch what little breeze there was. Jax went to help unload the big rig. There were plenty of volunteers already there, so I sat with Pancake and told him about our camp.

From the back of the van, all he could see was the growing line of vehicles with rescue animals in them and the human shelter on the other side of camp. We heard dogs barking and he sat up, excited for his turn to be processed—and then to get that food we had talked about.

As I sat with Pancake, Lois the shrink walked up. She was a sight. She had on a Hawaiian shirt with bright yellow flowers, beige shorts, and hiking boots. She was carrying a ukulele.

"You're a hard person to find," Lois said.

I smiled. "I just got back."

"Did you hear Eric's going to have a meeting at six-thirty? Another hurricane is coming—Rita."

"Yes, I heard that downtown. It's starting to flood again."

Lois came up close to me and whispered, "People have an easier time chatting to me dressed this way. So I'm incognito. If I don't tell them what I do right off the bat, it's easier for them to talk. And with another hurricane coming, people are scared. Volunteers are pulling out right and left."

"Gotcha. So what's the ukulele for?"

"I'm singing to the animals as they come in. Let me show you. Where did you get this fellow?"

Pancake smiled as I told Lois the story of how we found him. He looked at her with his head tilted to the side, in what I call a "curious puppy tilt." He said, *"She looks different from anyone I have ever seen."*

I told Lois what Pancake said and we both laughed.

Lois told Pancake, "I'm going to sing you a song about your adventure."

She started to strum her ukulele and made up a song about him. It ended with us being at the front gate and how his life would be happy from now on.

When she finished, Pancake said proudly, *"I'm famous now. People are singing about me."*

"Yes, you are famous now. Good job, Pancake! Good job, Lois!"

She laughed. "Let me give you a hug, Terri. There's a long line of cars for me to visit, so I best keep moving. I'll see you at the meeting."

The big rig started pulling out and Jax came back to the van. "There's a meeting in a little while. We have to take down our tents before it gets dark. They are expecting high winds to start. They could get up to 100 miles an hour."

We moved the van forward. When we reached check-in, Pancake got scared. I told the volunteers I would take him out of the kennel, just to be on the safe side. I wasn't sure how he would react. I gently opened the gate and looped a leash over his head. I backed up, and as I did, Pancake bolted out of the kennel. I thought, "Oh no! He's going to bite!"

He dashed right to me and jumped up, wrapping his paws around my waist. He buried his head in my waist and held on tight.

"You saved me! You saved me!" He was shouting from the top of his lungs. A loud "Wooooowwooooowooo" came out of him.

Everyone within earshot ran over and circled around us. He kept hanging on to my waist and I held him too. As we danced in a circle, I saw all the people around us, smiling and crying at the same time. Tears came to my eyes and I watched them land on his head. It seemed like we stayed that way for quite a while. Time was standing still for Pancake and me—together, holding each other. I will always remember it as an eternal moment.

When I popped back to real time, I wiped the tears from my eyes and told Pancake, *"That's my boy! You are going to be just fine."*

He tucked his head back down and hugged me again. *"I just want you to know, if it wasn't for you, I wouldn't be here."*

"Yes, you would. Yes, you are! Here! Right now. I think we should get you those fluids, though. Let's get you checked."

The vet walked up and said, "You're that animal communicator, aren't you? How does he feel to you?"

"I think he needs fluids. He's dehydrated."

"I think you're right. We're using some electrolytes in the water, because all of the animals coming in right now are in need of fluids. Why don't you get him set up in a kennel and he can just drink them up."

I told Pancake we were going to go see some dogs and get him set up for the night. He was thrilled with his kennel and his water. When we gave him a little food, he looked at me. I said, *"A little bit at a time. They are going to feed you several small meals, because they want you to keep the food in your stomach. You will find, because you haven't eaten much lately, that this amount will make you feel full. Ok?"*

"Ok," he said, looking a bit disappointed.

"We need to make sure you stay healthy."

"Yes, because I made it! Look at all my new friends!" He looked around at all the dogs and was delighted just to be with them, even though they were separated in their own kennels.

"Yes, you have lots of new friends to chat with and share stories. But I also want you to get some rest and make sure you drink quite a bit of water. There are several people here who will be taking care of you, so you be nice. And when the time comes, you get a good home, ok?"

"Ok. Will I see you again?"

"I will check on you every day while you're here. I know that big trucks are coming to take a lot of you to new places that are safe. So if you go before I get back, you be good and take care of yourself."

"Thank you."

"You, my dear boy, are very welcome. I'll check on you later."

As I walked away, Pancake lay down to take a nap. I was sure he was exhausted.

A group of people was assembling at the front, near the intake area. I saw Jax and walked over by her. She said, "I took care of the van. I emptied it out and washed it. It's behind us, so after the meeting, we can get out quick. I figure we can sleep in the van tonight, since we have to pack up our tents."

Eric Sakach drove up in a golf cart and pulled out his bullhorn. "Thank you all for being here. I want to make everyone aware of what's going on. We have another hurricane headed our way. It looks like it will hit us tomorrow or the next day. We don't know yet if it will be a direct hit or slide to the left and hit the Gulf Coast of Texas. Either way, we'll be in for a lot of water from rain.

"We are having buses come to take volunteers to different locations away from this area so you'll be safe. They'll be here within the hour. Those of you who feel scared or not comfortable with being here right now, I suggest you go get your gear, head to Barn One, and board a bus. Get out of here now. There is no need for you to stay for the rest of the meeting. Again, if you feel the slightest bit afraid or concerned, I want you on a bus so you can get to safety."

Several people left the meeting. Jax and I looked at each other. She asked, "Are you going?"

"No, not with them. If you feel like you need to leave, go ahead and go."

"No, I'm good."

Eric continued. "I need one hundred volunteers."

I raised my hand, as did Jax and several others. He looked at me, caught my eye, and smiled. "Thank you all, but you don't even know what you just volunteered for. Let me tell you, and then you can decide. I need one hundred volunteers to stay here at Lamar-Dixon to feed and water and walk the animals until the weather gets too bad. Then it will be just feed and water them. We don't want to lose any of them, after all they've been through. Now let me ask you again: who would like to stay behind to take care of the animals?"

I raised my hand, and then Jax raised hers. She looked at me and said, "Are you sure?"

"Yes, someone has to keep them calm. Someone has to explain that another flood might be coming and that we are here to try to keep them safe."

There were fewer hands in the air this time. "Thank you," Eric said. "Now I need volunteers who are licensed to drive large vehicles. If you have a Class A or B license, I need ten drivers."

I raised my hand and saw a few others go up.

"You are going to go get large trucks that we'll place around the ends of Barn Six and Barn One to enclose them and keep the weather off of the animals. It may be necessary to move some of the animals to the center of the barns to keep them safe."

Then Eric asked, "How many of you have motorhomes or trucks with fifth wheels?"

Several hands went up. "I need you to move your vehicles along the edge of the barns. We'll try our best to enclose all of the sides. If you have cars or vans, put them underneath the roof line and along the sides of Barns Two, Three, Four, and Five—like we are circling the wagons. The winds come from the back side of the barns, so I want to focus on enclosing those areas with all of the vehicles we have left."

Those of us with Class A and B licenses went to a Ryder truck-rental lot in Gonzales and returned in a banana-colored caravan of different-sized vehicles. When we arrived at Lamar-Dixon, I passed my little tent, still in the corner all by itself. I saw Jax's tent and the Texas fifth-wheels were still there. The big rig was already parked on the end of Barn Six.

We all pulled up at Barn One and parked snugly, front to back with bumpers touching. We handed in our keys and were told we could stay in the backs of our trucks if we wanted. I said I would sleep in my spay/neuter van and was instructed to park it under the eave between Barns Two and Three, alongside the horse barn.

I went to take my tent down and get my gear. I was almost at the front of Barn One when I saw people loading their bags on two Greyhound buses, getting ready to depart.

I had most of my gear packed as the winds picked up to a good breeze. It hadn't started to rain, and I said a small prayer, thanking the powers-that-be for allowing me to get my gear in dry wind.

Jax pulled up in the van. She had been in Gonzales too, getting us provisions. "Food mostly. Might be a couple of days. Who knows what we'll have to eat. So I made sure you and I are taken care of."

She gave me the keys to the van and I finished packing my gear, while she went to pack up her tent. I tossed my large duffle and my rolling suitcase into the van right behind the driver's seat. Jax tossed all her gear in the back of the van, shut the door, and said, "Let's go eat. I heard food was on the way when I came through the front gate."

I put the van into gear and we drove to the food truck. We picked up dinner and went to our new parking spot by the back of Barn Three. I parked so we could open the side door of the van and sit in the back, under the barn roof, to have our dinner.

The barn leader came over and greeted us, saw that we had dinner, and left to get some before it ran out. After we ate, we looked around our new home. We went to the center aisle and headed up through the horse stalls to see who was there.

There was one stall with cots and food in it. A woman, who was sitting on one of the cots, looked at us and said, "You aren't health board, are you?"

"No. Why?" I asked.

"They made us take this down—no food or humans sleeping with the horses."

"Really? Looks like nice digs to me."

Jax was so impressed that she decided to sleep there instead of our van. I told her to make herself at home while I took a shower and went to the laundromat in town.

I headed to the showers first, because there was no line and I wanted to get a hot one, just in case I wouldn't be able to take any more for a while. Next I went to the laundromat and caught up on my journal as I waited for my clothes to dry.

It was 11:50 p.m. as I pulled back into my spot at Barn Three. "Oh boy!" I thought. "I better get some sleep. We have a long day ahead of us tomorrow. We have to secure the barn so the wind doesn't blow things into the animals and hurt them."

I crawled into the back of the van, set my alarm, and laid out some clothes. Then I pulled a jacket over me and out I went.

CHAPTER ELEVEN

Friday, September 23, 2005

I woke up without my alarm. It was 5:00 a.m.—I had slept in.

It was still dark outside when I got up to check things out. As I walked to the restrooms, the camp was unusually quiet—the kind of silence that makes you aware of everything around you.

The lights were bright in the restroom. I looked in the mirror and saw my face was very tan from all the sun I had gotten the last few days, even with my hat on. As I studied my reflection, I got a strange sensation and thought, "Here we go—you better be ready."

Back outside, the sun had begun to lighten up the sky. The grounds were still quiet, and I realized that I was experiencing the calm before the storm. I looked around. A lot of people had left in preparation for the storm, but there were more volunteers here than I thought there would be.

The motorhomes were aligned around the back side of the barns, but the front sides were still pretty open. I went to the van to get some turkey jerky, which I figured would be my breakfast. Then I decided to work in Barns Two and Three for a while, wrapping up supplies to prevent them from being flying objects when the winds picked up.

Six other people were awake and had the same idea. One of them found some plastic sheeting and we started loading pallets and wrapping everything. We tried to keep like items together, so when the storm was over, we could easily find what we needed.

At 7:00 a.m., a light rain began. It was actually nice and warm. I got my rain gear and returned to the supply area to keep wrapping. The wind picked up around 8:00 a.m.—not too fast, just a breeze.

I walked over and joined Jax at a meeting at the incident command motorhome. Eric let everyone know that the storm was headed our direction. "We have to get ready and batten down the hatches. I want anything that looks like it could be a projectile tied down. Let's get the animals out and walked as early as we can today. Also we need some help moving kennels in Barn Five from the far side to the interior, so they are out of the main force of the wind and rain."

I remembered that Pancake was on that side of Barn Five, so I knew where I was going right after the meeting.

Eric continued, "We are going to get down to one hundred people today. If you're not in the one hundred volunteers we chose yesterday, I'd like for you to pack your things and leave camp as soon as possible. We will be working a skeleton crew the next few days. So those of you who are going can head out. You don't need to stay for the rest of this meeting."

Some people turned and started to walk away. Eric waited until they left. "We have a woman arriving about ten o'clock. She'll be taking all the bunnies and the birds being housed in the restrooms by Barn Three. Those animals won't make it through the storm."

He paused and looked into all of our faces. "Again, if you are having difficulty with any of this, you can leave the grounds with the others."

Ten more people left.

"The woman coming to pick up the bunnies and the birds will need help loading. How many of you here have been helping with those animals?"

Several hands shot up. "Good, the four of you will help her

load her motorhome. Let's just hope it's big enough to carry them all.

"Next on the agenda: food. We are working to get everyone meals. Those of you with vehicles might want to go to town and get provisions, just in case. The restaurants we're buying food from will close during the storm. We don't know how long it will take for Rita to go through. Of course, the storm might decide to stall right around us, so we could be here for a few days.

"We've been hearing about small tornadoes in the area." There were gasps in the crowd. "So if we get a warning, we'll blow a whistle and someone will go around in the golf cart to let you know to head to the restrooms—where the bunnies and the birds are now. When it's all clear, we'll tell you so you can resume work.

"Finally, thank you for being here. I know the animals are thanking you, especially for taking care of them during the storm. We'll have a meeting at noon to keep you updated. So now you can get to work, and we should have breakfast for you in about 30 minutes. Thank you!"

I looked at Jax and said, "We have to move Pancake. That side of Barn Five is exposed to the winds and the storm. Let's go."

He was awake when we arrived and tickled to see us. *"They fed me two times yesterday and they walked me before bedtime. I'm very spoiled here,"* he said, smiling.

"What a good boy you are! We're going to move you to the other side of this row and put you in the center of the barn. There's going to be another storm, and we want to make sure that you're safe."

There was a look of fear on his face. *"More water!"*

"Well, I hope it's just rain. But if it gets back near you, Jax and I will be here, and we will do everything we can to make sure all of you are ok. But right now, let's move you so you can meet even more friends and be safer than you are."

"Ok." Then he looked at a black pit bull to his right. *"Can*

my new friend come with me?"

"Sure. Let's you and I go for a potty break, and Jax can take your kennel around to the other side."

As we stood out on the field and looked at the sky, Pancake said, *"The wind is nice, but I can smell big rain. I'll be ok because you are here. I made it this far. I'll make it farther."* I kneeled down and gave him a big hug. *"That's my boy. Let's go get you and your friend set up, and I'll check on you later."*

Jax had his kennel cleaned when we returned, and volunteers had begun to move the other kennels. I asked one woman to keep Pancake and his buddy together.

"Sure," she said. "I'll put it on their paperwork too."

"Thanks, that's great! I'll be back to check on this one. So if you move him, just let me know. My name is Terri."

"I know who you are. You're the animal communicator. When the storm comes, can you come back and help keep the animals calm?"

"I sure can. That's why I'm here!"

We looked out of Barn Five and saw the food being delivered. The thought of a hot breakfast was just too tempting. The rain had let up to a drizzle, so we walked over and got a good meal in us.

Afterward we went back to Barn Three. Jax had offered to help feed and water the horses, so we parted ways. I re-joined the growing group that was trying to get everything buckled down.

At 10:30 a.m., the rain stopped. The golf cart rolled by and we heard a whistle blowing, our signal for a tornado. As I headed to the bunny bathroom, I looked around at the sky and could tell that there was no tornado coming. But I did want a break, so I kept going. The bunnies and birds were still in residence, and the restroom got pretty crowded once the humans all piled in.

We waited.

Turned out it was a false alarm—the first of several. Over the next hour and a half, the guy in the golf cart came through at least three more times. Some people headed to the restrooms, but I watched the sky carefully and kept working. After a while, the man's face was red from blowing the whistle and he looked like he was going to fall off the golf cart any minute. We wondered whether he was having a meltdown or was just nuts.

By noon, the rain was back, coming down harder than before. Just short of a downpour, it still felt like a nice summer rain.

Eric addressed the group. "All the dogs in Barn Five have been moved to the center of Barn Five or Barn Four. They are considered secured. The bunnies and the birds are just pulling out—the woman had trouble getting here because of some roadblocks. So I'm glad none of you are driving today. I would recommend you stay at camp, unless it is an emergency.

"The storm appears to be getting stronger and is still headed right for us. We must make sure everything that can fly around is secured. It's a big job, and I thank all of you for all your help. We'll be keeping the horses in their stalls for the remainder of the storm. We don't need any frightened animals taking off. You should be able to walk the dogs again this afternoon.

"And...the gentleman in the golf cart, who was blowing the whistle erroneously, has been retired and removed from camp."

Several of us started to giggle. Pretty soon, everyone was giggling.

"Ok, get it all out of your systems," Eric said. The giggling turned to real laughter.

He waited for us to get our composure back. "Now, serious business. There is still the threat of tornadoes. So if we have a real warning, I'll be going around in the golf car with my bullhorn, and then you can all head to the tornado shelters in the restrooms.

"They think the storm will hit us later this afternoon," he continued. Just then, there was a pretty good gust of wind. "It appears the wind has arrived! So let's get all battened down.

Our next meeting will be at five. We're going to try to have dinner delivered at that time. I'll see you then."

I headed back to Barn Three and saw that most of the supplies were secured. I decided to walk around and see where else I might be able to help out. The rain was picking up and the winds were making it slant. I had on my yellow rain pants and jacket—and I looked like a big banana. With my red boots, I thought I was making quite a fashion statement.

As I went through Barn Two, I saw a woman walking a black Rottweiler. Suddenly the dog backed out of his leash and bolted.

"Oh no!" I shouted. He ran toward the back of the barn, where there was a big open field. I knew he would be gone if I didn't catch him. I moved as quickly as I could, trying not to scare him. He saw me out of the corner of his eye. It was "game on."

I picked up my pace and started talking to him. *"What about the food here? Where will you go? I would like to meet you."*

I ran a little faster and was gaining on him. Then I turned on all the burners. I got next to him, grabbed him by his shoulders and waist, and stopped running as his shoulders came up into my arms.

"I've got you! Look at how handsome you are!"

He looked at me and turned his head. Realizing he was going to stay with me, the dog kissed my face. As I turned around to carry him back, the rain hit me directly in the face and I could taste it in my mouth.

"You are fast," I said.

He smiled. *"Yes, I like to run. You do too."*

"Yes, I guess so." I laughed.

Two women headed to us, one with a leash and the other with a catch pole. "Thank God," I thought. "He's getting heavy."

The woman with the catch pole put the loop around his neck and tightened it slightly, then I put him on the ground. She thanked me profusely for catching the Rott and said, "Man, you can run. I thought this guy was gone."

"I did too. I'm glad I got him."

I found the woman in charge of Barn Two and told her that we shouldn't be walking dogs anymore—the weather was too bad. We decided to get everyone together for a meeting.

It was a motley crew of volunteers that assembled to listen to me. "No one will be walking any dogs until this storm is over. If I see anyone walking a dog or taking a dog outside, you will be removed and taken off the grounds. You can take them out of their kennels to go to the bathroom, but make sure the stall door is locked so they don't go anywhere. Pick up the poop and just let them pee on the cement—we can hose that off later. Don't open a stall door unless all of the animals are in their kennels. Ok, I'm going to let you get back to your jobs. Thank you for your time and all that you're doing."

When they dispersed, I said to the barn manager, "You have to be strong with these people. If someone doesn't do what you ask, you let me know and I'll remove them."

"Thank you. I know I lost control of this barn, but I didn't know what to do. I'm so grateful that you caught that dog."

"Me too. I'll be back to check on you. So if you need anything, let me know. My van is parked next to Barn Three, and Jax in Barn Three usually knows where I am."

I went to the command motorhome and told Eric what I had done. I also said I thought we had some stowaways, people who hadn't left when they were told to go.

"That's good work. If that happens again, feel free to take over the barn. I've heard of other problems there. If you do need to send someone home, just come and get me and I'll help you escort them out. We don't have security anymore— apparently they are afraid of a little rain."

I thanked him for his support and headed over to Barn Three to help Jax feed and water the horses. On the way, I walked through Barn Two to make sure everyone knew I was still around. They all seemed to be doing what I asked. That made me happy.

When I got to Barn Three, I saw the horse people were very organized. Jax and I put in the hay and feed, then one person came behind us to put in the water, and another followed to clean up the stall.

At 5:00 p.m., we stopped and went to the meeting, which was being held in the middle of Barn Five to keep us out of the rain. Eric said, "Thank you for being here. As you can see by looking around, our numbers have shrunk once again. I truly thank all of you who are still here, still helping, and still willing to help with the animals during this time.

"The storm is kicking up a pretty good wind. I want you all to be safe. If you can, stay inside the interior of the barns and keep as dry as possible. Let's just hope this thing blows over. The food is being delivered up front here. So have dinner and batten down the hatches.

"Who needs a place to sleep tonight? There have been offers of space in some of the campers. Come see me after the meeting if you need a place. And finally, there will be no more walking of any animals until this storm is over. We almost lost one today. If an animal gets out in this storm, we'll never find it.

"Keep yourself safe as well. Pray that the storm shifts away from us. Right now, it looks like we're in the bull's eye. I'll see you all in the morning. If something happens tonight, stay safe. If necessary, I'll go from barn to barn to inform everyone of what we're doing. Again, thank you!"

Jax walked up beside me and asked, "What do you think?"

"I think we might be in for some more sideways rain. And if all hell breaks loose, hang on."

We ate dinner and talked to some of the other volunteers. They told us how the sky will change colors when the hurricane hits, turning red and then purple. One of them said, "If it gets to black, hang on to anything that can keep you here, because the wind will pick up and you could go flying. Be ready if the wind suddenly dies down and stops, because you're in the eye of the storm and it will start again in full force very shortly. So don't think it's over yet. If you do, you could go with the hurricane when the eye moves."

I looked at the sky and saw it was beginning to turn colors. Blue-black clouds were heading our way. It looked like nasty thunderstorms.

After our meal, Jax and I helped finish feeding the horses and made sure their stalls were secure. I went back to Barn Two and checked on the folks there. They were doing pretty well. I made sure all the dogs were inside their kennels and that the gate of each stall was latched.

Back at Barn Three, I found Jax and the horse gals playing cards to kill time. Jax asked to speak with me in private, and we went to the back of the barn. "What do you think about the storm?" she asked.

"I've been keeping an eye on the sky. It's turning pink now, so that means that red is coming and then..."

"Stop! I don't want to know! If it gets real bad, just check on me."

"Ok. If it gets bad, you hang on to the metal bars of a barn stall—no matter what. I need to stay in the van. The folks from Barn Two might need me, and that's where I told them I'll be. I also have a metal beam from the barn that I can grab, if need be."

"Ok. I'll see you in the morning." Then she looked me in the eyes. "I'm scared shitless! But don't tell anyone. Are you scared?"

"For some reason, I'm not. Maybe there's just too much to do. But it's totally ok that you are. If you need to talk, you know where to find me. Sleep well."

"You too," she said and headed back to the card game. As she rounded the corner to the horse stall, I saw her square her shoulders, trying to put up a good front for everyone. I smiled, then wondered why I wasn't scared.

I walked back to the van—I wanted to get it ready for the

night. The rain was coming sideways now. It had gone through most of the barn and some of the horses were wet. But it was still quite warm outside. I looked at my clothes, packed neatly in my bags, and decided I would just sleep on top of it all. I looked up at the sky again. It was bright red. The winds were still picking up. I hoped we had done a good job wrapping the supplies so things didn't start flying.

I climbed up in the van, lay down, and realized I was more tired than I thought. I looked at my watch. It was 10:30 p.m. I said a prayer for the animals—and for all of us who had stayed behind to help them.

I pulled out my journal and used my headlamp so I could write about what had happened today. I took one more look at the sky, and it was blacker still. I thought, "I should get some sleep before the hurricane hits. Who knows what we'll need to do then?"

I said another prayer, ending it with, "And thank you, God, for helping me catch the black Rotty today. I know you made him slow down."

I lay back in the van. The last thing I remembered was closing my eyes.

CHAPTER TWELVE

Saturday, September 24, 2005

I jumped awake and sat up straight. I looked around, startled. I thought, "Where am I? Oh yes, the van. The hurricane! Where is it?"

I looked out the van door and realized I left it open. It sounded like the winds had calmed. In fact, there was dead silence. I checked my watch. It was 4:30 a.m.

I got out and walked to the edge of the barn. It was still dark outside and there was a slight redness to the sky. I wondered, "Were we in the eye of the storm? Had it passed and I slept through it?" Then I realized, "It's going away!"

I thanked God and took a deep breath. It was raining lightly—a nice, warm rain. The storm was still too close, but I knew in my heart the worst had passed and that we were going to be ok. I took another deep breath. I felt very light, very happy, and wanted to share this moment with someone.

I already was. I looked around. There was a white horse on my left and a chestnut on my right.

"You two ok?" I asked.

"Yes," they both answered at the same time.

"Rain is nice now," said the white horse, and the chestnut nodded its head.

We smiled at each other. The three of us were sharing a very special private moment—the joy of being alive!

I turned and went back to the van. It was too early to feed

the horses, and no one else was up. So I thought I would lie down for a few more minutes.

The next time I awoke, it was 6:30 a.m. I walked to the edge of the barn and looked up. The red had almost faded away—the sky was becoming blue! We were safe, the animals were safe, and we could get back to work.

I heard a few people getting up and knew the feeding of the horses would begin soon. There was a meeting at 7:00 a.m., so I went over and woke Jax. Then I walked to Barn Two to make sure everyone was up and getting ready for the meeting.

People were assembling when I got to the center of Barn Five. We were all curious about where Hurricane Rita was.

"Yahoo! And good morning!" yelled Eric, beginning the meeting. "I have some good news: Hurricane Rita turned in the middle of the night and has hit land on the Texas-Louisiana border. It's been reduced to a tropical storm. There's still a lot of rain and flooding—some places in Texas were hit pretty hard. We do feel, though, that we are out of the danger zone."

"Hurray!" Everyone whooped and hollered, and I saw the relief on people's faces. The worst was over.

"Now here is how it stands. The rain should be clearing up around noon. Don't unwrap anything until after our noon meeting. I want to make sure the storm is gone before we unpack all of our good work. There were a few things flying around in Barn Six—they were on the worst side of the storm. Barn Five had a few things get loose, but the rest of the barns either haven't reported anything, or I don't know about it yet. So does Barn Three have anything to say?"

"We're good," said the leader.

"How about Barns One, Two, and Four?"

All reported they were good. Eric continued, "It appears all of the animals made it and are safe. Give yourselves a big round of applause for that!"

We clapped and there was more cheering.

"I want to be serious for a moment now. I personally—not

HSUS, but me personally—want to thank each and every one of you for staying with me during this 'disaster upon another disaster.' You people are the bravest I have ever known. I will remember all of you for the rest of my life. There are not a lot of people who would put their lives on the line with a full-on hurricane coming right at us. You're all heroes today. You stayed, even though you might be hurt or die, and you kept taking care of the animals. I don't know how to thank you, except to say from the bottom of my heart, and speaking for each and every animal here: THANK YOU!"

He raised his hands and began applauding all of us. We joined in and applauded him back. As I looked around at the people who were still here, I saw about twenty men and the rest were women. All of us were misty-eyed, even the men, and very glad that Rita had turned away from our animals.

Eric continued, "I know that The Humane Society of the United States is in your debt. We thank you as well.

"Now today's agenda. I have heard from the volunteers who were bused out that they will be returning around midday. So they'll hopefully be able to give all of you a well-deserved break. As long as the rain is light like this and the wind is gone, I think it is ok to resume walking the dogs, so they can get a little exercise and we can clean up their kennels. This will also mean that bathing can resume for any animals that need baths. If the wind kicks up, we'll stop walking them and we'll have a meeting so I can update you.

"I think breakfast will arrive around eight-thirty. So you can get back to work and break when it gets here. I'll see you all at noon."

I told Jax I was going to see Pancake. She was off to feed and water the horses and would catch up with me later. As I rounded the corner, I heard Pancake. He saw me coming and was dancing in his kennel. *I made it! I made it! I made it! The rain was going sideways. Did you see it? Did you see it?"*

"I did. I did. Would you like to go for a walk?"

"*Really? I can? I have to poop.*"

I giggled. "*I bet you do.*"

I saw Red, the volunteer I had met my first day at Lamar-Dixon, and told her I would take Pancake out. She smiled and said, "He's been looking for you since daylight! While you're gone, I'll clean his kennel."

"I'll fill out his paperwork when I get back."

I smiled at Pancake. "*Let's get your loop on, and we are out in the rain. Ok?*"

"*Still raining?*"

"*Yes, but it's a light rain. I think you might like it.*"

"*Ok, if you're going with me.*"

"*I am.*"

We headed out for a few minutes of freedom. When we got to the edge of the barn where he could see the rain, he asked me, "*It look ok to you?*"

"*I think so. Let me show you.*" I still had on my rain gear and stepped out from underneath the roof. He looked at me for a moment, then stepped into the rain too. He stood at the edge of the barn for a few moments and then decided he had to poop, rain or no rain.

After he was done, he stood in the rain and looked around. He took a deep breath and released it like he was letting go of something.

"*Are you ok?*" I asked.

"*Yes, I just miss my brother and my mom and dad.*"

I kneeled down by him, and he tucked his head in my chest. "*I'm sorry about your family. I know they would want you to have a good home to go to. And I know you will get a good home.*"

"*I hope so. I saw my brother last night. He came and lay down with me. He said he would keep coming until I didn't need him, or until I can go with him.*"

"*Well, that was very nice, wasn't it?*"

"*Yes, and he told me last night I would be ok and I would see you again. That's why I was looking for you. I knew you were coming.*"

I hugged him tightly. As I released him, he turned around and we both looked out at the field and the rain for quite a while.

"You two done hugging? I think it's my turn." It was Jax. She came out from Barn Five and over to us. I stood up and Pancake started dancing. *"It's Jax. It's Jax."*

I told her what he was saying. She kneeled down and Pancake kissed her face. Tears rolled down her cheeks—she was as happy to see him as he was her.

I handed her the leash and she gave him a big hug. I watched them for a few moments, then decided to let them have their own time. I reached down to pet Pancake goodbye. I smiled at him and said, *"Remember we can always talk telepathically, my friend, as long as you need me. But I'll see you later today. You be a good boy, ok?"*

He smiled. *"I will. I'm standing in the rain."*

"Yes, you are, my friend. Yes, you are."

I went back to his kennel and documented his walk with me. As I finished, Red walked over and asked, "Where is Pancake?"

"Jax has him and will bring him back in a bit."

"Ok. He doesn't have a home to go to, does he?"

"No, he doesn't. His mom and dad were in the house where we found him. His brother, a German shepherd, had passed too."

"I'm thinking of taking him home to Virginia, if they let me. You think he would like it?"

"I'm sure he would. Do you have any other pets?"

"I have a sweet German shepherd."

I could tell by her energy and connection to her shepherd that Pancake would fit right in. "Well, if anyone asks me, I'd say that would be a perfect place for him. Go talk to Eric Sakach about adopting him. You can also tell him that Terri Steuben agreed you should take him."

I went to see how the supply area had fared during the storm. Everything was still as it was when we wrapped it up. I thought maybe at noon we could begin unwrapping it.

After breakfast, Jax went back to cleaning the stalls and

bringing water to the horses. I helped her out for a while. At noon, we all had our meeting with Eric.

He told us the volunteers were on their way back and should be here soon. Rita was grinding down, but was continuing to drop a lot of water through Texas. We were in the clear.

Eric said, "We will resume search and rescue tomorrow. It's too wet to put up tents right now. So keep staying in the Ryder trucks and the campers until we can get the big tent back up. Right now, I'm not sure exactly when that will be, but I'll let you know. Those of you sleeping in the barns will probably have to look for other accommodations. The return of the volunteers also means the return of the Health Department, and they won't allow any humans or food to be kept in the barns.

"With the other volunteers coming back, those of you who have been doing search and rescue should get your vehicles ready to return to New Orleans tomorrow. Those of you with Kat's LASPCA group will have a meeting tonight at seven back where you usually do."

Eric thanked us again for staying to help HSUS. "Ok, you can get back to work. Our next meeting will be at five o'clock by Barn One. A lot of the volunteers will be returning and there's more room there. See you then."

As we turned to go, a bus pulled in and stopped in front of Barn One. The people inside waved out the windows and shouted, "We're back!"

Jax and I looked at each other. Camp was about to get very busy again. I was glad we'd be going downtown tomorrow.

I went back to the supply side of Barn Three and met the group that had wrapped everything. We started by opening up what we knew would be needed right away. After a short time, John and Ernie showed up! They had been on that first bus back. I introduced the "supply managers" to everyone. They thanked the crew and told us they could take over. "We'll be open for business within the hour," Ernie said.

I was glad to see them again. I said, "I'll come over later to get supplies for search and rescue. We'll be back at it tomorrow."

The returning volunteers got right to it. Unfortunately, not all of them were trained in dog handling. As I went to my van to get a Gatorade, I heard someone yell, "A dog is loose!"

I looked back at the field and saw a black Australian shepherd running toward Barn One. I got in the van and turned on the engine. I dropped the gear into drive and headed for him. I reached down, grabbing for my catch pole, and began chatting to the dog. *"You're on a good run, aren't you?"*

I saw the shepherd look over his shoulder and knew he could hear me. I kept driving toward him. All of a sudden, he turned to the left. I stopped the van, jumped out, and ran his direction. As I opened the loop, I said, *"Ok now, I think you have had your fun. Stop!"*

He stopped! I wasn't that far behind him, so the loop went right over his head and I was able to pull it closed. I had him. We looked at each other and he smiled.

"That was fun!" he said.

"You do that again and I will have to spank you!"

He put his head down. *"Ok. Sorry. I just wanted to run."*

"I know you did. So did you get it out of your system?"

"Yes, that was fun!"

"Let's walk to my van and I can get you back to your kennel, ok?"

"Ok. I like to eat."

"And where exactly were you running to?"

"Just running. I like to run."

"I see. So how about next time you take someone with you, ok?"

"Ok. You want to go running?"

I smiled. *"We just did."*

He smiled back. *"Yes, we did. I mean next time."*

"I'll find someone to run with you."

I looked back toward the barns and saw Jax coming over to us. She said, "Good catch. I didn't know you could run that fast. Looks like you're still doing rescue, even when you're not in New Orleans."

I had to laugh. "It would appear so. Do you know where this guy belongs?"

"He came out of Barn Four. I'll take him back so you can get the van."

"Good. He needs to be out. Tell someone to put on his paperwork that he likes to run."

"Ok. And they need your help over in Barn Two with a bunch of puppies."

I petted the shepherd on the head and said, *"Now you be good—and only run when you are with someone."*

They took off at a slow trot. I drove back and parked the van in my spot by Barn Three. When I got to Barn Two, the barn manager met me and said, "We need you to come talk to some puppies. They aren't moving. We're afraid they are going to die if they don't eat."

She led me to a horse stall where there were six pit bull puppies. Two didn't look very good and were not moving at all. It felt to me like their heads hurt, their stomachs were nauseous, and they just felt weak. The other four looked like they were doing better—they were moving around a little bit.

A woman named Carrie was sitting with them. She told me, "I've been watching them since they came in two days ago. I'm not sure if these guys are going to make it. I've taken care of puppies a lot, but I can't figure out these guys."

"Give me a minute. I'll chat with them and see what I can do."

I got in the stall, went down on my knees, and flattened myself. I looked right into the half-opened eyes of a little boy. I smiled and said to him, *"Hi, I'm Terri. Can I chat with you?"*

"Yes," he said.

"You look like you don't feel very good."

"What's the point? They're just going to kill me when I

grow up anyway."

"*What do you mean?*"

"*The guy at the house said we are going to be used for bait dogs because we aren't strong enough for him.*"

I knew what the problem was now. I looked around me and said, "*Do you see that man here?*"

"*No. I'm trying not to look. He scares me.*"

"*How about if I look with you. But I would have to pick you up. Would that be ok?*"

"*I suppose.*"

"*You would have to open your eyes to see if you see him. And if you do, you tell me, ok?*"

"*Ok.*"

I stood, gently picked up the puppy, and held him at eye level, facing out. I turned us slowly in a full circle. "*Do you see him?*"

His eyes were barely open, but he could see. "*No.*"

"*That's right! He's gone! Do you remember when people came and took you away from that place and brought you here?*"

"*Yes. But I thought it was just another place where they were going to put us in boxes so we couldn't move. I heard him talking about taking us someplace to get us ready. Then they would use us as bait, whatever that means. He said that we would be good for that, and then they'd be rid of us. We would serve a purpose for them, and then we would be dead.*"

"*I see. So right now do you even see any men here?*" I slowly turned around again.

His eyes opened a little more. "*No. I don't see any men.*"

"*That's right. Do you know these woman have been trying to help you?*"

"*I thought it was because they wanted us to get fat, so they could kill us.*"

"*No, my little friend. They have taken you away from the bad man to save you, so you can live a long, happy life with someone else. You can be someone's house dog, if you would like that?*"

"*Really?*"

"*Yes, really. These women are here to rescue all of you animals from the big hurricane, which was all the water and the wind and the rain. Do you remember that storm?*"

"*Last night? Or the one before?*"

"*The one before. That's the one I was talking about.*"

He turned his head to look at me and opened his eyes a little wider. "*You can hear me?*"

"*Yes, I can. And you can hear me, can't you?*"

"*Yes, I can.*"

"*The other women here have trouble hearing you, but they're doing the best they can.*"

I kneeled back down and turned him so we were face to face. I said, "*What do you think? Would you like to stay and maybe be someone's friend? Go to a nice house to live with your very own family?*"

He looked at me, then looked away. I turned my head and saw there were now eight women looking over the horse stall at us. I smiled and said to him, "*See, you have a lot of new friends who want to meet you.*"

"*Really? They're all nice?*"

"*Yes, they're all nice.*"

"*What about my brothers and my sister?*"

"*They can go to families too, just like you.*"

"*Really? They won't eat us or kill us or use us as that bait stuff?*"

"*No, you and your brothers and sister are going to be just fine.*"

He kissed me on the cheek. "*I like you!*"

"*I like you too. Here's what I need you to do: I need you and your brothers and your sister to start moving around more, so the muscles in your legs will hold you up. That way, you can walk around and play and jump and have fun. I also need you to eat food, drink water, and pee and poop. Can you do that?*"

"Yes, I can do that. My legs don't work very well right now, though."

"I know. But with practice, they will. I want you all to do this right now. Because if you continue to wait, they will get stuck that way. I'm going to put you back on the ground and let's just see what you can do."

I gently lowered him so his feet touched the dirt in the barn. He looked up at me and I asked him, *"How does that feel on your feet?"*

"It kind of tickles."

"That's because you're not used to it. In a day or two, you will be running around in here and playing with your brothers and sister. Now I'm going to let go of you for a moment."

He was a little wobbly, but the puppy stood on his own. Then he actually took a step and made his stance a little wider.

"Look at you! Very good to put your feet out so you can stand better. Good job! I want you to keep practicing. And remember, the food they feed you here is good."

"Yes, it is good. I just thought they were supposed to kill us."

"That, my little one, is over. You have a full life ahead—and so do your brothers and your sister."

I looked over my shoulder at the fence. The women all had tears in their eyes. I tried hard to keep my emotions in check because I knew I had a few more puppies to work with.

I looked at Carrie and said, "Here's what you need to do, and you need to say it exactly as I'm telling you. Tell them all they are going to a good home. Their lives will be as family pets, and they will have people who will love them and care for them. They need to eat the food and drink the water so they can get very healthy and get stronger. The man they knew before is gone, and all these people here want them to live long, happy lives. They also need to poop and pee so they can put more food in their tummies."

Carrie smiled. "Will they will understand me?"

"Yes. Talk to them like they are children and tell them what you want them to do. Talk in the positive. Let me chat with the rest to get them started."

I looked at the other boys and said, *"Do you see your brother moving over here? Look at me."*

Their eyes began to open. *"You are all going to be fine here. The man that is bad is gone. These people are here to help you. So here's what I need you to do. I need you to start using your feet and legs. Move around so you can strengthen your muscles. That will make you hungry. Then I need you to eat and drink water so you can poop and pee."*

One of them opened his eyes wide and looked at me. He said, *"I want to do that! It's ok now?"*

"Yes, it's ok now. You can move."

I could see their legs beginning to move. One tried to stand and Carrie helped him. He looked at her and kissed her hand. I told her, "He likes you. And he's thanking you for helping him. But I figure you already know that."

I looked at the little girl puppy and could tell she would need more help. She was on her side with her feet tucked in. I was still on my knees and I worked my way over to her. I put my face down to hers. I said, *"Can I pet you? You look very soft, and you are very pretty."*

"I am?"

"Yes, you are absolutely beautiful!"

Her energy shifted. I could tell no one had ever said anything nice to her. I lightly touched her head and gently pet her. As my hand moved down her spine, I saw her body moving and stretching with it.

"Is it true?" she asked. *"What you said to my brothers? We are all going to be ok?"*

"Yes, you're all going to be ok."

Her eyes smiled at me and she opened them wider. She took in a deep breath and sighed. Tears came out of her eyes and I caught them with my fingertips. I gently picked her up and could tell she was the most dehydrated of all the puppies.

"You're going to be ok," I repeated. *"I need you to drink lots of water and eat too."*

"I will try. I'm just so tired."

"It's going to be ok." I held her to my chest and snuggled her. As I touched her legs, I knew they had already begun to atrophy and she would need some help getting them to stretch out.

Carrie was watching us and I said to her, "This little girl is going to need your help. When I try to straighten her legs, they pull back. I need you to gently stretch her legs out a bit, like this, and then release them. And then do it again. See, this time her leg stretched further out."

Carrie's eyes lit up. "Puppy therapy! I can do that."

"Then I would also do with her like I did the little boy: help her to stand until she gets used to it. And she also might need some fluids—or cranberry juice diluted with water or sugar- or honey-water—to get her some electrolytes. All of the puppies probably could use a little to get them jump-started."

"I know where there's some honey. We've been using it in our tea."

I gently put the little girl back on the ground on her side. I didn't want her to feel disappointed because I knew she couldn't stand yet. Then I gently moved her legs and feet so she could lie on her stomach with her feet under her. She looked at me, smiling with her tongue out—she knew she had accomplished a very big thing.

I said, *"Look at you, my little girl. You are a big girl for lying that way on your feet. Look at you!"*

A twinkle appeared in her eyes, and I knew she was going to make it.

"They going to be ok?" the barn manager asked from over the stall.

I glanced up at the women. "I think so. Yes. They're all going to make it."

I looked at Carrie and said, "If you need me for more help, just let me know and I'll come back."

"Thanks. What was the problem?"

I went over and whispered in her ear. "They were not healthy enough to be fighting dogs, so they were going to be used as bait—as training dogs."

Tears immediately rolled down Carrie's cheeks. I said, "Don't talk about that. Just what's happening now."

"Thank you. I know what to do," she said wiping the tears from her cheeks.

"I'm glad I could help. Keep me posted."

As I turned to walk out of the stall, Carrie said to one of the other women, "I need a small water dish and some honey. Right away."

I looked at the group of women and they were still wiping tears from their eyes. Everyone thanked me and went back to what they were doing before. I walked away with the barn manager—out of the puppies' earshot—and explained what they had been through.

"A breeding farm for pit bulls! That pisses me off," she said. "I will keep you posted on them. Keep your phone handy in case I find something else. And thanks again."

"Tomorrow I'll be going back to New Orleans to do search and rescue."

"Ok. When you get back, we might have more animals for you to talk with."

I laughed. "Never a dull moment here."

I went back to the horse barn. It was feeding time. As I helped Jax roll the wheelbarrow of hay from stall to stall, I chatted briefly with a couple of horses. They all seemed calm and happy. Whenever a horse snorted or kicked the stall, Jax asked me what they were saying.

I told her the black stallion had said, *"I want to eat now. I always eat first at home."*

Jax laughed and said to him, "We're getting to you."

Then I told her, "The brown horse next to him says he's spoiled rotten."

Jax laughed again, looked at the brown horse, and said, "You're right about that!"

We continued down the stalls until all the horses were fed. Then we headed over to Barn Six, where the quarter horses and carriage horses were being kept, to help with the feeding and watering there. Shortly after we arrived, a beautiful white horse started kicking her stall. One of the women tried to calm the horse down, but wasn't having any luck.

I heard the horse yelling, *"My dad is here! My dad is here! I want to go home! I want to go home! Daddy! Daddy! I'm over here!"*

I looked at the woman and suggested she get out of the stall. I said, "Her dad is here. She wants to go home."

She got out of the stall and we looked around. There were no horse trailers or trucks in sight. But I knew her dad must be coming.

Pretty soon, a truck with a double horse trailer pulled up in front of the barn. Our white horse began kicking the stall again. *"I'm here, Daddy! I'm here! Down here!"*

I said to the woman, "That's her dad. You better bring him over here before she hurts herself or tears up the stall."

She ran and got the guy. He opened the stall and I closed the door behind him. The man and his horse both cried. The horse hugged him, with her head over his back, and pulled him toward her. He had both arms around her neck and sobbed with delight to have found his baby. He told us he didn't know which shelter they had taken her to and had been looking for his horse Lady since Katrina hit. He said he didn't think to look at Lamar-Dixon because he had heard it was mostly dogs.

Lady was not letting him go. There was not a dry eye in the area. The joy of her daddy finding her could be felt throughout the barn. I sensed from the other horses that they were also waiting for the same kind of reunions with their moms and dads.

After a few minutes, the barn manager came over and told the owner they needed documentation that this was his horse so they could let her go with him. There had been some people trying to steal horses, and HSUS was requiring proof before they would release any more.

The man looked disappointed. He had nothing to offer the barn manager. He had lost everything in the storm and had to borrow the truck and trailer to look for Lady.

Lady didn't want to let her daddy go and was still hugging him with her head. He looked at the barn manager and said, "I understand. I wouldn't want you to let her go with just anyone either. But I don't know how I'm going to prove to you that this is my horse."

I knew this was his horse—and so did everyone else in the barn. The barn manager looked at me. "I know it's his horse, but what about the rules?"

I said, "You have to do what you think is right."

She said to the man, "I'll need some kind of proof."

He hugged Lady again and cried. Then he told her he would find a way to get her out of here. Lady was obviously upset and started kicking around. He quieted her down and said, "Now Lady, it will be ok. They're taking good care of you here. I will find a way."

He stepped out of the stall and continued talking with the barn manager. As he started to walk toward his borrowed truck, Lady kicked the sides, the back, and the front of the stall. She had a major fit and was going to break out of her stall, no matter what. She yelled, *"Daddy! Daddy! You come get me! I'm going with you!"*

Lady then reared up to see if she could get out of the stall over the top. The barn manager ran toward the man, yelling at him to wait. He turned in his tracks.

They walked together back toward Lady. She began to calm down, but was still snorting and screaming, *"Daddy! Daddy!"*

She quit when he got back to her stall. The barn manager looked at him and said, "I think you should take her with you. Otherwise, we won't have a stall left when she gets through with it."

He smiled broadly. "You mean it?"

"Yes. We can't have a horse getting hurt on my watch. She's obviously yours."

He hugged her. "Thank you! Let me get my halter."

He went over to Lady and told her she was going home. Her tail went up, then her head went up. She was definitely a happy horse!

When he left to get the halter, Lady watched him leave— and again, she was not happy. "I'll be right back," he said.

I looked at Lady and said, *"Watch him go to the truck to get your halter. He'll be right back and take you home. Watch him."*

She put her head out of the stall and watched him walk all the way to the truck. She wasn't happy when he stopped to open the back of the horse trailer. She yelled and kicked the stall again.

When he returned, he unlatched the gate and got in the stall. He put the halter on her and Lady calmed right down, knowing she was going home with her dad. As he led her out of the stall, she was dancing like a happy child. She smiled and said, *"Look at me, everyone! I get to go home with my dad!"*

He loaded her into the horse trailer and drove away— reunited. We all looked around and smiled at each other. There was no doubt in our minds that one lucky girl was going back to her family!

It was time to head to the 5:00 p.m. meeting. When I arrived at the back of Barn One, I saw that our numbers were growing again. Eric informed us that Hurricane Rita was now a rainstorm heading up north of Texas.

He said, "The ground is still too wet to put tents down, so you'll have to find other accommodations. Rescue operations will begin again tomorrow, and we will start shipping animals to other shelters in different states.

"Lamar-Dixon is full to the brim, so we've had to come up with alternate locations. Animals will be going to our good friends in Texas. Also Colorado, Virginia, and California. Some animals are very lucky—they'll be flying out to California. Someone has donated an airplane flight to California. A whole load of animals will ride in the passenger section of the plane."

There was cheering all around when we heard that news.

"The vehicles will be coming tomorrow to load up and head out. The other shelters will keep the animals for three months in hopes of reuniting them with their families. We'll need volunteers to take the paperwork with the animals and help load them on to transport vehicles. If anyone is interested in helping, please see me after the meeting.

"Ok, that's it. Dinner will arrive shortly. You all have a good night. We'll see you in the morning at seven o'clock."

Eric looked at me and waved me over. He asked me about Red, the woman who wanted to adopt Pancake. I told him I thought it was a good fit.

"I got the same feeling. Have her come see me again and I'll get her the right paperwork to take him home."

I went to see Pancake to tell him the big news. His new mom was there, hanging out with him. As I watched them from a distance, I saw how happy they were together. Red was petting Pancake and he sat there, adoring her back.

I approached and they both looked up at me. I smiled at Red and said, "I have good news. Eric Sakach says you can take Pancake home with you. You need to see him again for some final paperwork, but then you're good to go."

She got tears in her eyes and thanked me.

Pancake tucked his head into her chest. *"Thank you! Thank God! I get a new home!"*

I kneeled down and he gave me a very big kiss on each cheek. Then he smiled and looked me in the eyes. *"Thank you! You were right. I can have a happy home now!"*

"Yes, you can."

I relayed what Pancake had told me. Red said, "I'll make sure that he has a very good home with Benny."

"I know you will."

I turned again to my pit. *"Pancake, let me give you one last hug. Because tomorrow I have to go into town and rescue more animals. I might miss you, so I want to give you a very big goodbye hug."*

Pancake stood up, came over to me, and rolled on his back so I could pet his tummy. When he got up, he tucked his head into my chest one more time and I gave him a last squeeze.

"Please take good care of him," I said to his mom as I headed off. I was thrilled because I knew one more animal had lived through this disaster and was getting a new home. At that moment, I felt like I was really doing some good.

I got back to Barn Three and met up with Jax. We decided to load up the van in the early morning, after I slept in it that night. Jax wanted to sleep in the horse barn one more time, before the stall was changed back to a feed stall.

We got dinner and then went to our meeting with Kat to see what was in order for tomorrow. The Texas folks were back with their campers, and the big rig was parked behind them. They were waiting in their lounge chairs for the meeting to begin.

They had spent the last two days in a hotel in town and were happy to be back at work. Rita had hit close to their homes, but everything seemed to be ok for them. Their animal shelter in Texas had taken in a lot of dogs from Katrina, and now some of the land was flooded. So those pets had to be transported to yet another shelter.

Kat arrived and looked rested—she and her group got two days off during the rainstorm. She said she caught up on some sleep, but still had a massive amount of paperwork to finish. She told us all to be ready to head out at 5:00 a.m. It was the shortest meeting we had since coming to Lamar-Dixon. Kat was headed off to another meeting, and a lot of us had things we needed to get done.

I dug around in my gear, got out a new set of clothes, and headed to the showers. Then I drove into Gonzales to do laundry. When the owner saw my HSUS t-shirt, she offered to wash my clothes for free while I did other errands.

"It's the least we can do for the people who come here and help us with the animals," she said.

I went to the grocery store and picked up some canned goods and snacks. When I got back, she handed me my clothes, all clean and folded. I thanked her and went back to camp.

I pulled up to my current home under the eave of Barn Three, opened the side door of the van, and got set up for my night's rest. I found Jax and told her I was going to check one more time on Pancake. She told me Red had taken Pancake with her to the hotel so she wouldn't have to come back tomorrow.

Jax explained, "Eric told her they were going to beef up security again tomorrow, and it would be easier for her to take Pancake tonight. She brought him by to say goodbye, but you were in town. So I gave him a hug for you."

I went out to the back of the barn and looked up at the stars and the moon. I got real quiet and said in my head, *"Pancake, you ok?"*

"YES! I'm sleeping inside—and I'm on the bed!"

"Good for you. I know you have picked a good home. You take care."

"I will."

I looked at the sky a little longer, then went to the back of the van for some sleep. I shut the door to the van because the lights were still on in the horse barn. I wrote in my journal and set my alarm for 4:15 a.m. It was 11:30 p.m. when I closed my eyes.

CHAPTER THIRTEEN

Sunday, September 25, 2005

When my alarm went off, it took me a minute to realize where I was. I didn't see my tent. It was totally dark. As I looked around, I made out the back of the driver's seat and remembered I had slept in the van again.

I opened the door and it was still warm outside. My headlamp was in my bag, so I reached for the clothes I had set out and got dressed in the dark. Then I headed to the restrooms to see how I looked. The lights were bright, and I closed my eyes halfway so I could see. I could tell I looked pretty good. I needed to find my hair brush, but other than that, I had done very well dressing myself in the dark.

I went to wake up Jax. I turned into the horse stall in Barn Three and saw three people lying on cots, with covers pulled over their heads. I picked the cot that Jax slept on before and woke up the wrong person. I immediately apologized and she pointed me to the right cot.

I woke up Jax, who looked like she was also having trouble remembering where she was. I told her I was going to load up the van.

"Let me get some things out of my bag first," she said.

She used my headlamp to dig around in her stuff. I don't think she found what she wanted, but she found what would work. She went back into to the barn to change.

I drove over to get supplies for New Orleans. I had to totally restock: bottled water, litter pans, flattened kennels, bags of dog food, and cans of dog and cat food. The van was fuller now. Because of our gear, we weren't able to carry as much. We would drop the supplies at our base so we would have room for any new friends we found today.

We met Kat's team and lined up our vehicles. We were headed to a new part of the city today, not far from the French Quarter. Other sections were still flooded from the Rita rainstorm and we couldn't get in them. We stopped at the gas station in Gonzales to pick up breakfast doughnuts and snacks. The interstate was quiet. Jax slept during the drive, and I enjoyed watching the sun come up on another beautiful day.

We followed Kat to our new drop site, the parking lot of a closed-up McDonald's at the intersection of Esplanade and St. Claude (the street signs were still there). Just looking at that building made us all hungry. She laughed when she saw our disappointed faces and told us she'd find an open McDonald's near Lamar-Dixon for tomorrow's meeting.

Kat began, "The big rig will be here shortly. Other people have been in this part of town before us, so some of the animals I have on these lists might already be rescued. Hopefully, they have marked the houses where the animals were taken and saved us some time. Here are your lists. Head out whenever you're ready."

Kat handed us a stack of papers. She said she had a number of new people to break in and figured Jax and I could handle things on our own. We dropped off our extra kennels and supplies, then took a look at the map and got going.

The neighborhood we drove into had nice, small homes. We pulled up in front of a two-story house, where we were supposed to get four cats. When we got to the front door, we saw the owners had left a note with "CATS" written on it. I unfolded the note and read: "The back sliding glass door is unlocked. Four cats are in rooms upstairs. Please keep the doors closed—we want to keep all of them together. Some of them are very good escape artists."

Jax and I got two carriers each and entered the house through the dining room. The interior was attractive, but the dark brown carpet was soaked with water. As we headed up the stairs, I saw the bedroom doors were closed and notes were attached to each door. The first one read: "White cat very friendly."

I said to Jax, "I'll go in first, shut the door behind me, and see where the cat is. Then I'll give you a heads up to come in with the carrier."

I slipped through the door and shut it quickly. I didn't see any movement as I looked around. The room was painted peach and there was an old vanity with a mirror that reminded me of one I had as a kid. It looked like the room was used for dressing and working—there was no bed, but it had a computer desk and bookcases. Everything was in order, because the flooding didn't get to the second floor. The damage was all downstairs.

Jax yelled through the door, "The cat's name is Cotton."

"Cotton, are you in here?" I said, not moving. I wanted to see if the cat would make an appearance for a stranger.

I looked on the floor and saw the owners had obviously known what they were doing. They had taken a large bag of cat food and dumped it on the floor. In the attached bathroom, they had filled the tub with water. We were going on four weeks and it was still half full. I assumed the other cats had the same setup and knew they were all probably ok.

When I came out of the bathroom, I saw Cotton, a long-hair white cat with a beautiful coat, sitting on top of a waist-high bookcase. I said, *"Hi there! Look at you. You are very pretty."*

"Hello. Have you come for me to take me to my mom? She said that if she couldn't come, I could go with the people who come to get me."

I smiled. *"You have a very smart mom."*

"Yes, I know. I have been careful with the food, like she said, because she wasn't sure how long it would be. I have been fine, but it gets hot in the day sometimes. So I just lie on the desk and soak it up. When it gets too hot, I go in the room (the closet). *It's dark in there and it stays cooler. Mom said I could. She calls it my favorite room. This whole room is my favorite room."*

"This is a beautiful room. Let me get something to carry you in, and then we can take you to your mom. Would that be ok?"

"Sure," Cotton said.

I yelled to Jax that I found one cat and needed a carrier. I didn't hear any answer. I cracked the door open and looked into an empty hall. There were carriers on the floor, so I figured she went out to the van to get something. I grabbed a carrier and set it on the desk.

"May I pick you up, Cotton?"

"Sure, I'm nice."

I gently picked him up and held him tightly to my chest. I petted his fur and he started purring. Next I placed him gently into the top-loading carrier. As we headed into to the hallway, Jax was coming out of the room at the end of the hall with a grey tabby in a carrier.

"Good job!" I said. "Since there's no gook on the floor, let's keep them up here and get the other two before we head out. Did you have any trouble with your cat?"

"I had to get him out from under the bed. That took a minute. But he's nice."

We both looked at the door to our next two cats. Jax read me the note: "There are two cats in here—one is black and one is black and white."

I went into the room first to make sure the cats were away from the door. Jax followed, handing me a carrier as she entered, and I closed the door behind her. We set the carriers on the floor and looked at a beautifully converted upstairs den with a large-screen TV, big leather sofa, coffee table, and bookcases filled with books and knickknacks. It also had a closet and a separate bathroom. Again, there was a large bag of cat food dropped on the carpet and the tub was still one-quarter full of water.

"Here kitty, kitty, kitty," said Jax.

I got quiet and said, *"I know there are two of you in here. Jax and I have your brothers in the hall in carriers, ready to go with us to find your mom and dad. I want to take you along. Would you come out so we can take you too?"*

I stood there, trying to get a fix on where it felt like they were. I said to Jax, "Check behind the bookcase under the TV."

"Bingo!" she said, then looked down at the black-and-white cat and said, "Let's take you to your mom. Ok?"

The cat didn't move, but she said to me, "I've got this one. See if you can find the other one."

I went back to my quietness and thought, "Where would I go if I wanted to hide?" I heard the black-and-white cat say, *"He's behind the sofa."*

I kneeled on the sofa and looked over the back. I saw the black cat and said, *"Hello. How are you? Can I take you with me to go get your mom and dad?"*

"They left us. They didn't mean to, but the people made them go."

"I'm sorry. Would you like to go with me so I can get you back to them?"

"No," the black cat said.

I looked at Jax and asked, "How's it going for you?"

At that moment, she reached down and pulled her cat out from behind the TV. She had her gloves on, but the cat wasn't making a fuss. She headed for a carrier, and as I opened the top for them, I told her, "Mine doesn't want to leave. I asked him if he wanted to go, and he said he doesn't."

"Well, how about if I take a couple of these guys out to the van?"

"Ok, and bring back a catch pole, just in case. I hate to use a catch pole with a cat, but we might need a small boost to get him in a carrier."

While she was gone, I took the last carrier, which wasn't a top-loader, and placed it on the end of the sofa. I hoped if the cat came out, he would walk right into it. I found a broom in the bathroom and decided to use it as a prodding stick.

By the time Jax returned, I had moved the black cat almost to the carrier. He was not happy with me. What I said to him didn't make any difference. He was staying put.

Jax came in with the catch pole. I asked her the cat's name.

"I don't know. How about we call him Shadow?"

"Ok, let me try that."

"Shadow, is it ok if I call you Shadow?"

"Sounds like a good name."

"Ok. Would you like to get in the kennel now?"

"No. I like it here."

"Well, I think you guys are getting low on water. And I think your mom and dad would like to see you soon. Wouldn't you like to see them?"

"Yes, I would like to see them. But they can come home. I'm here. I like it here!"

"Well, Shadow, your parents have been told to stay out of this area. They have sent us to come and get you. Can you get in the carrier so we can go?"

"No," he said again. He was wedged between the sofa and the wall, right at the edge of the carrier. All he had to do was take a couple of steps and we would have him. But he wasn't budging.

I looked at Jax and said, "He's not happy. Let me use the catch pole and get him looped. Then we can get him out and into the carrier."

I tried to loop him, but he wasn't moving. He was pushing his head hard into the floor. I told Jax, "I'm having trouble getting the loop under his chin."

"Be ready," she said.

Before I knew what she was doing, she pushed the other end of the sofa against the wall. It spooked both the black cat and me! Luckily, I got his head in the loop and was able to pull the cord back enough to catch him.

Instead of going into the carrier, Shadow jumped on top of it and tried to dart away. The catch pole stopped him and he hissed at me. I walked him across the room, and Jax got the carrier and brought it over to us. I tried to gently push him inside the carrier, but he was having none of it.

"Leave me alone! I'm staying here!"

I asked Jax to put the carrier on its end and leave the door open. With a quick swoop of the catch pole, I swung him up in the air, and down he went into the carrier. Jax closed the door as best she could on the catch pole. I opened the loop and slid the pole out of the carrier, and she latched the door shut.

"Fine. I'm in here. You happy?" said the cat.

I smiled at him. *"Thank you! Now we can take you to your mom."*

Jax was back in the hallway, where Cotton was still sitting in his carrier. She was looking again at the note and laughed.

"What's so funny?" I asked.

"I didn't read the whole note: 'The black-and-white cat's name is Fluffy and the black cat's name is Tornado. He is feral.' And look, it's even in big print: 'VERY MEAN!!!' There's three exclamation marks to make sure everyone knows."

"Well, I think we just had our tough one for the day. It's probably a good thing you didn't read that to me before."

Jax kept laughing as we left the house. We wrote on the door that we were taking the cats to Lamar-Dixon. We put the carriers in the van, then made sure our paperwork included the correct information, especially on Tornado. We noted that all of the cats were together, and we added the name of the owners, which I got from some mail I had seen on a table.

Our next stop, for another cat, was a half-block away. We parked on the side of the road in front of the house.

At that moment, a large brown car passed us and parked in front of the house we had just visited. A woman and a young girl got out and walked up to the front door. As I grabbed a carrier out of the back of the van, they walked over and the woman said to us, "Hello. Do you happen to have four cats from the house down the street?"

I looked at Jax, then back at the woman, and asked, "Four cats?"

"Yes. I live in the house down the street. I just got here and read a note about my cats. Then I saw your van. I'm hoping that you have them."

I looked her in the eyes. She seemed very sincere, but I wanted to make sure her name matched what I had found. "Do you have your driver's license with you?"

"Yes, let me go get my purse. I'll show you." She and the young girl, who looked to be her daughter, walked back to their car.

I closed the van door just to be on the safe side. The woman drove her car back, stopped behind our van, and got out. She pulled her license out of her wallet, handed it to me, and said, "I've been trying every day since Katrina to come down here and get my cats. They won't let us in. So today I found another way in—a back road."

I looked at her license. The name on it matched the name I had taken from the mail. She said, "I'm so worried. I'm just hoping that they're all still here and alive. Do you know where I can go get them?"

I looked at Jax and smiled. "Yes, I know exactly where you can get them. They're right here."

When I opened the van door, I thought the woman was going to pass out. Tears began to roll down her cheeks. "Are they all alive?" she asked.

"Yes, they're all alive. Although the black one is a little grouchy."

"You got the black one out? You got Tornado?"

"Yes. Although he didn't want to leave."

She smiled as the tears kept rolling down her cheeks. Her daughter started crying too.

Cotton howled from the van, *"My mom. My mom. My girl. There you are. I have waited so long to see you. There you are. Take me with you. Please, take me with you."*

I handed Cotton's carrier to his mom so he would calm down. He started rubbing on the side of it. The woman and her daughter continued to cry as they got reacquainted with their kids. She said, "I'm just so relieved they're all ok. I can't believe it."

"You did a good job leaving out the food and filling the tubs with water. Keeping them upstairs was very smart of you," I said.

She smiled. "Did they eat all the food?"

"About half of it."

"How does the house look?"

"There's damage downstairs, but the upstairs is fine."

She gave a big sigh of relief. Then she offered to go get their carriers and exchange them for ours.

"Let's keep these guys in the carriers they're in. We don't want to lose them now, after all of this," I said.

She smiled at Jax and me and said, "You two are the best. How can I thank you?"

"You already did. The looks on the cats' faces when they saw you was thanks enough for me. How about you, Jax?"

"Works for me," she said.

The mother and daughter left with Tornado and his buddies.

We went into our next house through a garage door that had been left open and found a black cat sitting on the sofa. I asked, *"Are you ready to go?"*

"Yes, please. This place is stinky!"

We saw that mold was beginning to grow up the walls, and I figured that this little guy must have a very sensitive nose. Jax put the carrier on the floor as the cat cried, *"Don't put that on the floor. It's dirty."*

I told Jax what he said. She immediately lifted it back

up and looked at me, surprised. "Do you think I have to get another carrier?"

I looked at the cat. He said, *"It just touched a little. I think it's ok. But put it up here."*

I asked Jax to put the carrier on the sofa. "I think this boy is ready to go."

Jax easily picked up the black cat and put him in the carrier. We loaded him onto the van and headed for our next house.

Our little black cat spent a few hours with us and was relieved to have someone to talk to. He liked that I could chat with him and told me about the rain that came after the water. He could see the other side of the street had water on it, but was glad that his side was up on a hill. He didn't like the water. He said his mom had left him food—and our timing was good, because he had just eaten the last of it. He liked being out in the fresh air, even though it was hot.

"As long as the sun is off of me, I'm good," he said. *"I get too hot because I'm black. I have to get in, and then out, of the sun. I like it, but I can get too hot. With not a lot of water, I had to stay out of the sun in the upstairs bedroom, because I didn't know how long I would be there. Had to conserve, you know."*

I smiled and kept listening to him chat. He talked about each day and how he would go from room to room to check to see if everything was ok. He got a little afraid when the second rainstorm came—the rain was hitting the windows sideways and it looked neat in the living room window. But he was concerned that the ground would flood again. Luckily, it just kept running down the street. He had watched it to make sure.

When he completed his whole story, he lay down, then curled up and went to sleep. He looked relieved that he could tell his experience to someone who would listen. Just like people, we all need to share and get things out.

Jax had no idea the black cat and I were chatting. I just let it go. She was in charge of the map, as we headed from one address to another to get pets.

We stopped in front of a cheery-looking white house, where our papers showed there was a dog. We saw a gate on the left and headed down the side to see if we could get in. When we came around the back of the house, we saw the glass from the sliding door was shattered all over the floor, as though something had hit it from the outside. The glass covered a dinette table and four brown-leather chairs with wheels.

As we looked around, we tried to get our bearings and see where the dog might be. We knew, because of the broken door, there was a possibility the dog was gone. As my eyes moved toward a hallway, I spotted a bloody paw print on the white tile. I pointed at it and said to Jax, "We have a problem. Look at that. Our dog is injured."

"Might make him angry."

"Or scared. Let me follow the trail and see what I find. You stay by the door, in case he decides to leave."

I began to walk down the hallway. The blood looked bright red, so the cut was new. "That's a good sign. We can get him help soon," I thought. I went around a corner and there were more bloody footprints on the floor, like the dog had been going back and forth, trying to figure out how to get out.

The walls looked like the building had shifted, which might have caused the glass to break. At the end of the hall was a living room. No dog there. I saw the front door and stairs to the second floor on my right. I called to Jax to come and join me. The dog had to be upstairs, and I figured she could more easily stop the dog at the top of the stairs than trying to block the whole sliding door downstairs.

We went upstairs. The hallway went both to the left and the right. I said, "I'll go to the left and you stay here."

I looked in the two rooms on the left and saw nothing hiding under the beds, in the closets, or anywhere. I was thorough. Then I went to the right and found our little dog in the master suite, sitting on the end of the bed. It was a black border collie whose right front paw was injured. He had put little red paw prints all over the white bedspread.

"Hi there. How are you?" I said.

Jax could tell I had found our guy and joined me at the bedroom door. The dog didn't respond. He just kept sitting there, looking at both of us. I paused at the door and said to her, "Why don't we both go in and shut the door."

As Jax closed it, I walked toward another doorway, thinking it must be the bathroom. I saw that the bathroom was open on both sides, with no doors, and that it went into the other bedroom. I was relieved we hadn't headed for the dog, because he could have escaped through the bathroom and into the whole house.

I told Jax that I had to block this door because it was open all the way through. I asked her to go around and close the other bedroom door, just in case he went that way. While she did that, I stood in the doorway, trying to talk with my friend. *"Hi. Can I look at your foot? We need to help you get that bandaged, so it can heal. Does it hurt?"*

"No. It doesn't hurt. No."

Jax came back and I told her this guy wasn't chatty. She stood in the bathroom doorway as I slowly headed toward him.

He stood up on the bed and said, *"Game?"*

I smiled. *"No, we are going to go to a special place. Ok?"*

"No. Game!"

He jumped off the bed and darted around my left side. As I stuck out my leg and arm to try to block him, he jumped through the gap and headed for Jax. The collie escaped past her too and went into the other bedroom. He was fast.

I looked at Jax and said, "He wants to play. He's calling this a game."

"Great! Now what?"

"Well, let's hope his foot is ok, because he is getting blood everywhere."

We both headed to the other bedroom. I went over to the far side and our border collie squealed with delight. The game was on! He hadn't had anyone to play with for almost four weeks. *"Have you eaten?"* I asked, thinking food might slow him down. He wasn't interested. He knew that we were here to catch him and take him somewhere safe—and that we had food. But right now, he wanted to play. I told Jax, "Let's just let him run a bit and see if either his foot hurts or he gets tired."

It was an hour before he was done. The collie jumped up on the foot of the bed, sat down, and said, *"Good play time! I'm ready to go now."*

I walked up, petted him, and then put the catch pole on him. When we got downstairs in the hallway, I picked him up to keep his feet safe. He licked my face all the way to the van, saying, *"You guys are good at playtime! Can we do this again?"*

I smiled. *"Well, maybe we can find someone for playtime. Hopefully it will be your parents."*

He smiled. *"I like that! Let's go get them."*

What a happy soul. He ate a good amount of food and drank a lot. He was very thirsty after his playtime. Then he lay down in the kennel and was asleep before we started the van.

We headed directly back to the drop-off site. It was almost noon, and I wanted to have his foot looked at. Most of our group was there, unloading their rescues.

The vet examined the collie's foot and wanted to take him into the back of the big rig to check that all of the glass was out. The dog smiled as he was carried away. Such a happy boy! He made everyone who saw him that day smile.

After lunch, we went back out to an address to check for a dog. He was supposed to be on the second floor of the four-plex. We went up the stairs and, luckily, the front door had an easy lock for Jax to open with an old credit card. We searched and searched. We saw a large, empty bird cage, so we figured someone must have come and taken the bird.

Finally I found our dog. He was on the balcony and the sliding glass door was closed. He was lying on his side and had passed. I looked at him—a little white Scotty—and said, *"May God be with you now, my little friend."* I heard him say, *"I'm fine. Tough as ever."* I looked at Jax to relay the message. "Don't tell me! I know you're talking to him. Stop it!" she said.

"It's a good thing," I assured her. Then we left, making sure we documented everything at this address.

We went to the next house and saw one side was missing. We headed down the side to the backyard. I climbed up on the back porch and saw the dog. He had passed and was lying in a birdbath that now was bone dry. It looked like the backyard had flooded, the dog got up to get a drink, and the water was probably bad.

As I looked over the porch and down at the dog, tears fell out of my eyes and landed on the dirt and brush below. He was a little dog—a Yorkie, I guessed, about 10 pounds. I pointed him out to Jax and she began to cry too. She went down to the yard and covered him up with a towel from the truck. We were both very sad when we left him.

The paperwork for our next address wasn't specific, so we didn't know what we might find. We pulled up to a small house. Jax stayed up front, while I walked down the side to check things out. When I rounded the corner, I realized the whole back of the house was missing. I saw the back bedroom and halfway through the house. It looked empty.

Then I looked to the left corner and spotted our rescue. It took her a little time to get up and on her feet. Once she did, she stood there and looked at me like, "Who are you?"

I said, *"Just a minute. I have a friend for you to meet. I'll be right back."*

I turned and went to where Jax was waiting. I smiled and said, "You can get this one. She's in the back of the house, just standing there."

Jax looked at me funny and headed toward the back of the house. I followed her to see what she was going to do.

She went around the corner, looked around, and said, "It looks empty."

The girl I saw had lain back down, but when she heard us chatting, she decided to stand up again. As she began to stir, Jax looked at me and said, "No f**king way!"

I doubled over laughing. Standing in front of us, on the back bedroom floor, was a pink pig—a 500-pound pink pig, to be more specific. She smiled at us, and as long as we kept our distance, she was ok.

I looked at her and asked, *"Are you ok?"*

"Yes. There was a lot of rain the other day. But now I'm better."

I smiled. *"Yes, there was a lot of rain. How did you get here?"*

"My mom and dad left me. They said they would be back."

"I see." I gathered that she was supposed to have been a small pig, and then grew very big.

When Jax started toward the pig, she darted at us. I said, "Let's give her some room," and Jax backed off.

The pig said, *"I have to pee."*

"Ok, where do you go?"

"Out in the backyard. Past you."

"Let me and Jax get out of your way and you can go."

Jax and I moved back and the pig walked to the edge of the house. She daintily used several boards lying there to get down and out of the house, which was on a cinder-block foundation. Her steps were very light and gentle for her size. When she stepped out of the house, it actually went up a bit.

She headed to what must have been her spot in the corner of the yard and went pee, then walked to the other side and pooped. She grunted a little bit and tossed some dirt around with her nose. She turned, went over to the house, and ever so gently, stepped back up to the bedroom.

The pig lay down and said, *"Good. I did good."*

"Yes. You did good."

I looked at Jax. "I don't think we can take her. She won't fit in the van, and I don't think the tires would hold her."

Jax smiled. "Well, that looks like her water dish. So I'll go get her some water."

While she was gone, I chatted with our pig. *"Where is your mom and dad?"*

"I don't know. They come every couple of days. But they have been gone for a long time now."

I wondered if we were going to have to call Kat and have someone with a big truck come here and take her to Lamar-Dixon.

Jax came back followed by a nice-looking couple in their 60s. The man was about 5 feet, 2 inches tall and dressed in black slacks and a short-sleeve shirt buttoned up the front. His wife was just a little shorter and also wearing dress slacks. She had a sleeveless shirt on and was holding a sweater.

As the woman came around the corner, she could no longer contain herself and started waving her arms in the air. "Is my Petunia ok? Oh my God, I don't know what I would do if she were hurt! Is she alive?"

I pointed in the pig's direction and the woman went up the make-shift steps to her girl.

Petunia got on her feet. *"Mommy! Daddy! You're back! Yay! Yay! You're back. I knew you'd be back. You said you would."*

The woman wrapped her arms around Petunia and gave her a big hug. The pig's feet even danced—she was so excited to have her mom home.

Then Petunia looked up and saw her dad. She quickly headed his way, down the boards into the backyard and out to papa. He hugged her, then started teasing her and they chased each other around the backyard. I'm sure Petunia had no idea how big she was. Right now, it didn't matter—it was obvious she was daddy's little girl.

The wife came over and said, "We've had trouble getting back into town with the storm and all. Petunia won't drink or eat unless we're here. She won't go to the bathroom either. She waits for us."

"Oh, she did go both pee and poop after we arrived. She went over there and over there," I said, pointing.

"Yes, those are her spots. Good. I hate for her to hold it that long. It's been two days. But now I know we can come back into town, so we should be ok."

"I'm sorry about your house." I saw that one of the storms had knocked it off its blocks and it tilted to the left.

"It's just a house. As long as Petunia is ok, I'm fine."

We gave them some water and the pig took a big long drink, then decided she had to pee again.

"What does she eat? All we have is dog and cat food."

"She can eat dog food."

"We'll leave you a couple of bags and also some water."

"Thank you! We don't know where to take her. We decided it was better to leave her here. People don't understand how much we love this pig."

"I think I understand. You got her when she was small, right?"

"Yes, she would fit in the palm of my hand. My husband is her best friend. We don't have many friends because of her. We're afraid people will call someone and take her away. That would break my heart."

"Let me call someone who can get her the right food."

I went to van, called Kat, and told her about Petunia. She took down the address and asked if we could take the pig to Lamar-Dixon. I said, "I don't think that's a good idea. The owners are coming down most days to be with her. They just need some food and more water until they can figure out what to do with her."

"Ok. She should really be eating the same food goats eat, like pellets. I can have some delivered and bring some water too. I'll just document that we need to feed in place."

I smiled. "I think that's a great idea. Petunia gets a little grouchy if you try to take her away from here. I don't think she would go nicely."

"I'll make sure she stays put. Tell the owners that I will

keep it low-key. We don't want the press, or anyone else, to get ahold of this."

I returned and saw the happy family still playing in the backyard. I asked the man what Petunia weighed.

"The last time we weighed her, she was about 350 pounds," he said. "But she's gotten much bigger since then. We really can't take her out anywhere. So we just play with her in the backyard. She's our daughter. Our sweet girl. You see, she is delightful."

Petunia was definitely glad her parents were home. They couldn't live in the house in its current condition, so they were staying at a friend's home and visiting their girl daily.

I told him what Kat had said, and he was relieved. "Yes, keeping this quiet is good," he agreed.

"But we'll need to mark the front of your house so they will leave Petunia here. The only thing I have is spray paint."

"It's ok, spray away. Just as long as she can stay here, then we can see her and we will all be happy. It will be a while before anyone can do anything about our house. We are healthy, happy, and we all have each other. The rest is replaceable."

I smiled. "Ok, I'll make sure that your house is marked with her to stay."

I looked at Jax, our spray-paint wizard. She grinned and got right to the task.

As we got in the van, I saw she had put really big lettering on the front of the house: "PIG IN BACK YARD LEAVE HERE!!! OWNERS COME DAILY!!!"

I smiled. "Jax, Rembrandt would be proud."

"I'm proud of Petunia. She's such a good girl to have weathered both storms all by herself. I'm surprised a dog pack didn't try to eat her."

"I'm pretty sure there is a bad side to that pig. If I was a dog, I wouldn't mess with her."

"Me either."

We headed back toward the drop-off site. I turned a corner and stopped the van in the middle of the street. I pointed to a townhouse with cement stairs. On the side of the stairs, there was a message in orange spray paint: "THANK YOU!!! HSUS FOR SAVING MY CATS!!!"

Jax looked at the sign and said, "That's nice."

Emotion welled up and tears came to my eyes. "Perry and I saved their cats. That's the house I told you about, where Perry took the cats back to the people."

I sat there for a moment, letting it sink in that I was being thanked for helping the cats get back to their family. My heart sang!

I didn't think I would ever hear from any of the people we helped. I just knew we were there to help the animals. Those words painted on the cement made me very proud of the work I was doing. I looked at Jax and said, "We better go. More to do."

Kat called and told us the big rig was full, so she wanted everyone to head back to the drop-off site. When we got there, she came over and handed me a piece of paper with an address on it. "This is where you and Jax are staying tonight. It's the house where all of the people I work with are sleeping. It will only be a spot on the floor, but you'll be inside for a change. And you won't have to put up your tent again. You can stay with us until you leave on Tuesday, and I can take you to the airport."

I smiled and looked at Jax. "We have a house to sleep in tonight."

"Sweet," Jax said.

"We have to go to Lamar-Dixon first and unload, and I'm sure you two have things to do," Kat said. "But I've talked with everyone else and we are going to meet at the steakhouse for dinner. You're welcome to join us. A lot of people are leaving at the same time, so it will be a thank-you dinner—and our seven o'clock meeting. I'll see you there."

Our ride back to Lamar-Dixon was nice and peaceful, but unloading the truck was a bit of an event. Kat's group had brought in one hundred animals that day and we had a lot to do to check them in.

As we finished up, the manager of Barn Two arrived and asked me to come and look at the puppies again. "You have to see them. It's truly amazing," she said.

When we walked into the barn, Carrie was waiting for me. I looked in the stall and saw the six puppies. They were all moving, and four were playing like regular puppies. I smiled and said, "They have really popped out of their shells."

Carrie gestured to me. "Come on in. Look at them. It's a miracle! Those four are going to be just fine, and these two are on their way. A little behind the rest, but they are going to be ok too, I think."

I kneeled down to get eye-level with the boy I had spoken to before. He recognized me and slowly stood all on his own. He walked over to me, still a little wobbly.

"I'm walking! Look at me!" he said, with a big smile on his face. Then he licked my cheek.

"Look at you is right! You're doing really well."

"I'm going to walk even better tomorrow. I'm helping my sister too."

I looked at his sister, who was now trying to stand by herself. She was wobbly and shaking, unused to lifting her own weight. But she did it. Her head came up and she looked at me and smiled.

"Made it!" she said.

"I see you did."

Carrie said, "That's the first time she has gotten up by herself."

"Wow," I said.

I picked up both puppies. *"Now look at you two. You are both going to be just fine."*

The brother looked at his sister and said, *"I hope we can go together. Our brothers are ok, but I would like to take care of my sister. She has had a hard time.*"

I looked from face to face and could see the bond these two had. I looked at Carrie and told her what the brother had just said. She looked up from the other puppies. "I think that can be arranged. I'm leaving tomorrow and I have permission to take them all with me to continue helping them. I will adopt out the brothers to good homes. I was thinking about keeping those two, because they might need special care, if you know what I mean."

I looked at Carrie and said, "I think I do."

I looked at each of the puppies in my arms and asked them if they would like to live with Carrie for their whole lives. You could feel their response in the air.

"*YES!*" they both said at the same time.

"*Wow, someone has heard us!*" said the boy.

"*We are getting our wish!*" said the girl.

Then they both looked at Carrie with the biggest smiles that puppies can make. Carrie melted, as the tears flowed down her cheeks, and said, "I guess they are ok with that?"

"Yes, they both like that idea a lot."

"I have a black Lab that will just love these two."

I handed the pups back to Carrie, and then went to the incident command motorhome to check on where to leave Christie's spay/neuter van when I left for California. Eric was outside and smiled as I came up.

"How's it going?" he asked.

"Good. I'm headed home on Tuesday, so I need to know what you want me to do with the van."

"Are you still doing search and rescue?"

"Yes."

"Do you have a partner?"

"Yes. Her name is Jax."

"Let me check about the van. We'll probably be able to get Jax a new partner, and she can use it to continue doing search and rescue."

On the way back to the van, I found Jax with the horses in the center of Barn Three. We loaded up supplies, and then hit the showers before going to dinner.

We had a great meal. Kat's meeting consisted of telling us where the open McDonald's was for our morning meeting. She told us to have our breakfast and be ready at 6:30 a.m. It was nice to see everyone in street clothes—I didn't even recognize several of them without their hats!

It was dark when we arrived at the house Kat and the others had rented. We went inside and Jax chose a spot on the living room floor. I was shown to the master bedroom and given a spot off to the side of the room where I could lay my sleeping bag on the carpet. There were four other women sharing the room, and they were all happy to see me. I was surprised, because they didn't know me and I was intruding on their space. But they were glad to have me and swap stories.

Two gals were sharing the bed and had a big pillow between them. Another was on the floor on the other side of the bed, like me. The fourth had the walk-in closet all to herself. They had been living there for about two weeks. Kat had set it up, because some of her coworkers were without homes and were still working, even though they had lost everything.

The girls told me that Kat was sharing a room with some women down the hall and that the three guys had the other room. They offered the shower. I told them I took my shower at Lamar-Dixon earlier, but would take them up on it tomorrow night after being in New Orleans.

The girls got into a full-blown conversation about their boyfriends, so I was able to pull out my sleeping bag, unroll it, and put my clothes on the floor. I wrote in my journal for a while, then set my alarm and put in my ear plugs. Off to sleep I went.

CHAPTER FOURTEEN

Monday, September 26, 2005

I slept well on the floor and didn't know anything until my alarm went off. It took me a minute to remember where I was. The other women didn't move—luckily, I hadn't disturbed them. I grabbed my clothes, went to the bathroom, and got ready to go. It felt great to get a good night's sleep.

I headed to the living room and saw that two of the men were just waking up Jax. I told her I would be out in the van when she was ready. I didn't want to disturb anyone else, especially those who had the day off.

We went to a McDonald's in Gonzales, ordered our breakfast, and finished eating by the time Kat's meeting began. She gave a short briefing, then paired us up. Jax and I were assigned to work with Gary and Richard.

As we drove down the interstate to our staging area in New Orleans at the closed McDonald's, we talked about our new partners. We knew Richard was a bit high strung, but Gary seemed like he'd be fine to work with.

"I think we're in for it today," I said.

"No. I'm in for it. You're leaving tomorrow."

Our intuition was right. We spent most of the day trying to calm the guys down and moved slowly rescuing the animals. We found that Gary was ok, until it was time to capture a dog or a cat. Then he turned into a crazed version of Gary with an "I've got to get this animal, no matter what" attitude.

At one of our first addresses, they scared a dog away and we couldn't find it. They were wasting our time and energy, so I decided to give them a taste of their own medicine.

I ran straight at Richard and Gary and started screaming at them, just like they had approached the dog. They didn't realize what I was doing, and I had both of them running down the street. Richard was the better runner of the two and he moved away fast, thinking I had lost my mind.

When I stopped, Jax smiled at me. Gary, then Richard, walked back to their van and she said to them, "Terri was just showing you what you looked like to that dog. Why don't you two take a break and stay in your van. If you come back out before we catch this dog, you'll see ME all crazy—and that's way worse than Terri."

I looked at Jax and said, "Let's go."

She went to the left of the house and I went to the right. Sitting in the back yard was our dog, a Rottweiler.

I said, *"Boy, those guys are gone. How about you go with us before they get back?"*

He stood up and walked my direction. He said, *"Are they coming back? They want to hurt me."*

"They're just anxious. They want you to go with them."

"Are you kidding? They sure didn't seem like they liked me, the way they were chasing me around."

"Sorry about that."

Jax rounded the corner on other side of the house and stopped to wait while I talked to the dog.

"Good time to get out of here. Want to go with me?"

He lifted his leg to pee. *"Sure, you seem nice. What do I have to do?"*

"Just let me get us connected with this necklace so we can walk together."

He stood there and let me ease the loop of the catch pole around his head and tighten it just enough so we could stay together. When I looked over at Jax, she was gone. I headed the dog toward the front, where she had the kennel out.

Gary and Richard couldn't believe it. They had tried for 45 minutes to catch our Rott, and Jax and I did it in about two minutes. They decided, of course, that they had worn the dog down. Jax just shook her head and got in the van.

The dog said he was glad to be with us. He also told me that he liked to ride in cars. I gave that bit of information to Jax, and she began to give him a blow-by-blow description of where we were going.

We drove up to the next address and saw an SUV parked outside. Jax and I looked at each other. We wondered if the owners were back and then saw Janis, who worked for HSUS, come out of the house with a cat.

I pulled over to the side and we marked the address off of our list. We asked Janis if they needed help and she told us they were good.

I looked at her and said, "Did you check the whole house?"

"They only have a cat."

I wondered if that meant she checked all over, remembering the dog on the balcony who had passed.

She was getting ready to head out. I asked, "Aren't you going to mark the house that you got the cat, just in case it ends up on someone else's list?"

"We don't have any paint," said Janis.

Richard hopped to and got her the spray paint he had.

Jax and I went inside and checked the whole house. It was empty. When we came out, I asked Richard to mark the house, but he had given his only can of paint to Janis. Jax rolled her eyes, got our spray paint from the van, and marked the house: "1 CAT TAKEN HSUS/ LAMAR-DIXON."

When we got back in the van, I looked at Jax and said, "I think it's a good thing I'm going home."

"I might go home soon myself," she replied, as we watched Gary and Richard pulling out in front of us, not knowing where they were going. They went to the corner and turned right, then had to make a U-turn when they saw us go left. I stopped and we waited for them to figure it out and catch up.

Jax said, "I have six more cans of paint, but I'm not going to give any of it to Richard until tomorrow. He'd just give it all away to the next pretty girl that came his way."

We both laughed.

After lunch, we were sent to Lakeview again, the area that smelled of toxic fumes. It still smelled and we had to wear our face masks, but at least our eyes didn't burn this time.

The roads still needed clearing and we had to navigate around downed trees and electrical lines. We pulled over at an intersection. When I got out of the van, I saw three animals—a stuffed bunny, a stuffed monkey, and a stuffed dog—on the side of the road. Amazingly, they were clean and in good condition.

I looked at Jax and said, "Do we have any cat carriers?"

"Yes. Why?"

"I need three of them."

She got out and went to the back of the van as I picked up the stuffed animals. I said, "Let's put these in carriers and see what they say back at the big rig."

"This should be funny."

"Can you see the look on Kat's face when we tell her we have a monkey?"

Jax smiled. "She might send you home, you know."

"I leave tomorrow anyway," I said, and we laughed.

We checked the rest of the addresses we had in Lakeview, and the animals had either gotten out or been rescued earlier. I was glad, because the air in this neighborhood would have killed any living thing if it stayed there too long.

We went back to the staging area, where Kat was standing outside the big rig.

I yelled over to her, "Hey, Kat, we have a monkey!"

She looked at me curiously and headed to our van. "I like monkeys," she said.

Jax opened the back of the van and pulled out the carrier.

"Cute little fellow," Kat said, and then realized it was a stuffed doll. She smiled, turned an embarrassed shade of red, and started laughing hard. "Thanks, you guys, I needed that!" I said, "That's not all. We also have a bunny and a little dog."

"Real or stuffed?"

"Stuffed, of course."

"Take it to the big rig. Linda over there likes bunnies. I think we can get her, just like you got me with the monkey."

We pulled the van over as if we were going to unload. Kat held the carrier so the others could only see the back of it. She said in a loud voice so Linda would hear her, "Wow, look at this! A monkey. And you also said you have a bunny?"

Linda came running. "A bunny? Where?"

I pointed to Jax, who was in the back of the van with the carrier. The back was pointed out so Linda couldn't see the bunny.

She reached for the carrier and said, "Give that to me. Now you, little bunny, I have you now. You're going to be all right."

We watched to see what Linda would do. She walked to the back of her truck, set the carrier down inside, and opened the door. Realizing her bunny was stuffed, she pulled it out, looked at everyone, and said, "I think rigor mortis has set in."

We all broke out in laughter.

Linda gave an evil eye to Kat and continued, "But that's ok, because I'm going to keep it for a souvenir."

I looked at Linda and said, "We also have a dog."

"A real one?"

"No, a stuffed animal, like you have."

Nick, a new volunteer, got out of the back of the rig and said, "I'll take that one."

Jax tossed him the carrier. He took out his prize and gave it a big hug.

"Ok, you guys," Kat said. "Back to work."

We finished the day and headed back to Lamar-Dixon to unload another big number of rescues: ninety-five animals. It amazed me that, in the fourth week after Katrina, we were still getting out live animals. "What survivors they are," I thought.

As I walked around camp one last time, I said my goodbyes to all of the friends I had made. I took Jax to meet Eric and see if he wanted her to keep the van. He spoke with her for a few minutes and then told her he would let her know later that night.

Eric asked me to come over. He gave me a big hug and whispered in my ear, "Since Jax is working with Kat, she can continue to use the van. Tell her when she is done, to bring it back to incident command. Now, you be safe—and thanks again."

"Thanks, Eric. Be safe yourself," I said as we hugged goodbye.

When Jax and I arrived at the house, someone had ordered pizza. We all pitched in money and enjoyed a warm meal—two nights in a row. I felt uptown.

I took a nice hot shower and headed for my spot on the floor. I laid out jeans and a t-shirt for my trip.

Then I wrote in my journal and smiled when I was done. Tomorrow I would be headed back to California.

CHAPTER FIFTEEN

Tuesday, September 27, 2005

I woke before the alarm and lay there with my ear plugs in, looking at the ceiling and thinking to myself, "I'm going home today."

I got up, grabbed my clothes, and headed to the bathroom to get dressed. I pulled my two bags into the living room, where the guys were waking up Jax.

I said, "Hey, Jax!"

"Yeah!" she said, not yet awake.

I tossed her the keys to the van. "Here ya go."

She lit up like a lightbulb. "Really? I get to have the van?"

"You can have the van," I said, and relayed the instructions from Eric.

Kat asked me to ride with Jax and the rest of the team to breakfast. Then after the meeting, we would transfer my bags to her truck and she would take me to the airport.

"Ok," Jax handed me the keys. "You're still the boss, until you leave—and then it's my turn."

I smiled. "Let's go eat."

We got our breakfast and Kat had her meeting. She got everyone started and headed off to New Orleans.

I gave Jax a hug, thanked her for all of her help, and told her to be safe. We both started to get misty-eyed.

Jax said, "I better go, before I cry. I hate to cry. And just so you know, I'm still holding you responsible for turning things back on in me."

I laughed and held up my hands in defense. "Ok, Ok."

Jax's partner was a new volunteer, just in from the Midwest. I wished them both well as Jax helped me put my bags in Kat's truck.

Kat was on her phone or the radio most of the way to the airport. When we arrived, she helped me get my bags. We hugged, then she looked at me and said, "If you decide you want to come back, just let me know. You're one of our best! Thank you!"

"Thank you, Kat. I hope you get a break pretty soon. It's been a lot on your shoulders."

Her phone rang again. "Never a dull moment," she said and got back in the truck. We waved at each other as she pulled away from the curb.

I stood there for a moment and looked around. The airport seemed peaceful and quiet. I placed my bag on top of the rolling duffle and headed into the terminal.

The people behind the counter were very pleasant and asked if I was there to help with relief.

"Yes. And now I am headed home," I said.

I handed them my bags but kept my small backpack. I passed through security and headed to get a snack and water, just in case I would need them.

I found my seat on the plane, pulled out my book, and noticed that the flight attendants were also very nice to me.

My flight was routed to Los Angeles with a stop in Atlanta. The plane began to taxi out and I heard an attendant give the usual instructions about the safety features of the airplane. Then she said…

"And we here at Delta would also like to thank those volunteers from The Humane Society of the United States for all of their help with the relief effort in New Orleans. They have saved so many animals. We are all very thankful for each and every one of you."

I looked down and saw my t-shirt. I hadn't noticed I had put on my HSUS shirt for the trip home. I smiled to myself and thought, "Oh boy, everyone is going to know it's me."

I had looked around a little when I boarded and didn't notice anyone else from HSUS, but some of them could be on the plane too.

The announcement was very nice, I thought. But when the applause began and carried on for a long time, I had to look out the window so that no one could see the tears in my eyes. I wiped them away as they began to roll down my cheeks.

The man sitting next to me tapped me on the shoulder. I wiped more tears away and turned to him.

"I just want to personally thank you," he said and he offered his hand. I shook it.

"My Labrador would never forgive me if I didn't thank you in person when I had the chance."

I smiled back at him. "Thank you. Give your Lab a big hug from me."

"I will," he said.

I looked back out the window as the applause continued. I was going home!

EPILOGUE

When I got home from Louisiana, it was not "life as usual" for me. I hadn't realized how tired I was. I slept a lot more—until 3:00 p.m. the first day, noon the second day, and 11:00 a.m. the third day. I now understood why these deployments are limited to two weeks: it takes a while to readjust. I had been operating on an adrenaline rush, and I needed a chance to recover.

For the first couple of weeks, when I heard a dog bark, I sometimes thought, "I have to go save that dog!" Whether I was getting in the car, walking to the mailbox, going to a client's house, or carrying bags out of the grocery store, it triggered the reaction I had in New Orleans. Then I remembered I was home, and I would smile and laugh out loud, knowing the dog was all right.

Looking back on my experience, I am impressed by the strength and intelligence of the animals. They taught me a number of lessons on courage, determination, and resourcefulness that have stayed with me. When I remember their smiles and wagging tails, I am reminded of the joy pets bring to us and how important they are to our happiness and well-being.

I will never know what happened to most of the animals I helped, but I have been able to talk telepathically to a few of my rescues. Whenever I checked on them, they told me they were doing fine.

Dr. Debra Campbell adopted the red puppy we worked on, named him D.J., and took him home with her to Massachusetts. You can still see the burn marks on his feet and tail, but he's one happy dog!

I consulted with a couple of responders who had adopted and brought traumatized animals home with them from their Katrina deployment. One woman had a pair of kittens—she named them Lamar and Dixon!—that got up on the roof the first time it rained and were afraid to come down, because they thought they'd be safe from the water up there. I had to explain to them that this rain was different than the flood.

Another gal had a dog who had issues when he got wet by some sprinklers in her backyard. So I spent a couple of hours playing with him and showing him how they could turn on and off—nothing to be afraid of.

As I was finishing this book in spring 2015, I chatted with Jasmine, who had survived by eating Pop-Tarts. She told me she's still a healthy and fat cat, but has a few aches and pains these days. Her family didn't return to New Orleans. Their new home (somewhere in the Carolinas) has a window where she loves to lie in the sun.

I have also talked through my experiences with other responders from Southern California who I met while in Louisiana. I made some wonderful friends, and it has helped us all to share on a personal level what happened to us in that disaster zone.

My Katrina deployment made me an even more determined animal advocate. A month after my return, I was invited to the state capital in Sacramento to work on getting a law passed that would provide for the evacuation of pets with their owners in a natural disaster. California Assembly Bill 450 was adopted and my state became one of the first in the nation that requires disaster preparedness agencies consider household pets, service animals, equines, and livestock in emergency evacuation planning.

In October 2006, the federal Pets Evacuation and Transportation Standards (PETS) Act became law, mandating rescue, care, shelter, and essential needs for individuals with household pets and service animals, and for the household pets and animals themselves, following a major disaster or emergency.

The PETS Act created a scramble for every town and municipality to add animals to their evacuation plans, and people were eager to learn what they could do to prepare for the next disaster. I was called on to speak about my Katrina experience and was one of the responders asked to help Los Angeles and Orange counties set up their animal response and evacuation plans. I spoke to community groups and consulted with my clients about disaster preparation and response. I also included advice for pet owners in my how-to book on animal communication. I urged everyone to get ready to take their pets with them in an evacuation—and told them specifically what to do if they had to leave their animals for the rescuers.

My classes with the Surf City Animal Response Team became a lot more realistic in teaching responders how to react to emergency situations and set up shelters. Having lived through it, I could explain all the ins and outs of what might actually happen when a disaster plan is activated.

In addition to my volunteer work with SCART and HSUS, I became a member of the Equestrian Training Institute, the Humane Animal Response Team, and other groups. I wanted to do all I could help make sure that animals are taken care of before, during, and after an emergency.

I continued to respond to disasters closer to home, including wildfires in San Diego and Orange counties, where I got experience in saving large numbers of animals in a short period of time. I also have worked with law enforcement officials and served with other HSUS volunteers on hoarding, fighting, and animal abuse cases in California and Hawaii.

Hurricane Katrina proved to be a turning point for the animals—fortunately, much good has come from their suffering. With every year that passes, I believe we are becoming more prepared to keep our pets safe from harm.

I pray that this is so, because I don't ever want to hear another traumatized animal say, *"Why did Mommy and Daddy have to leave me?"*

PHOTO GALLERY
Lamar-Dixon Shelter

PHOTO-1   HSUS used six of the eight 20,000-square-foot barns at the Lamar-Dixon Expo Center in Gonzales, Louisiana, for its temporary animal shelter. Barn 5 was where pets were checked in and examined by a veterinarian.

PHOTO-2   On the left is my little, two-person pup tent, which served me very well during my deployment. Inga Gibson's tent is on the right. We pitched them at the far corner of the site where it was quiet.

PHOTO-3   The supply areas along Barns 2 and 3 give you an idea of the space we needed for the pet food and other donations that were being brought in daily.

PHOTO-4   Lucky came through surgery like a champ and recovered in a kennel big enough for us to get in and sit with him. He was operated on in the middle of the night in the back of an ambulance, where I held up a flashlight so the vet could see what she was doing.

PHOTO-5   Wayne Pacelle, HSUS president and chief executive officer, gets on the bullhorn to address the responders at one of our daily briefings.

PHOTO-6   The stalls in the barns held horses or kennels with all shapes and sizes of rescued dogs, cats, snakes, and other pets. Bunnies and birds were kept in the women's restroom.

PHOTO - 1

PHOTO - 2

PHOTO - 3

PHOTO - 4

PHOTO - 5

PHOTO - 6

PHOTO GALLERY
New Orleans Drop-off

PHOTO - 7   My first search-and-rescue partner, Perry Nelson, is at the deserted gas station and convenience store in the Lower Ninth Ward of New Orleans. We used it as a drop-off site for the animals we found on the streets and got out of homes.

PHOTO - 8   A little pit bull happily waits at the gas station to be taken to safety.

PHOTO - 9   Our teams used pick-up trucks, SUVs, and vans to get animals to the drop-off site. Then they were moved to larger vehicles for the one-hour ride to the shelter in Gonzales.

PHOTO - 10   Dogs and other animals rested in the shade until we could take them all back to Lamar-Dixon at the end of the day.

PHOTO - 11   We left food and water on the streets so animals like this dog could survive until we had the chance to rescue them. Our initial focus was taking in only those pets that were injured, sick, or in immediate danger.

PHOTO - 12   Most of the pets I spoke to were fine after I explained to them that they were being taken to a safe place where their moms and dads could find them.

PHOTO - 7

PHOTO - 8

PHOTO - 9

PHOTO - 10

PHOTO - 11

PHOTO - 12

PHOTO GALLERY
Searching and Rescuing

PHOTO - 13 I explain to Brownie that she needs to eat and drink water before running off with a snack. I didn't know she was taking the food back to a buddy.

PHOTO - 14 Brownie runs off with a big dog biscuit in her mouth for her friend Penny, a four-pound Yorkie who wouldn't have been safe on the streets. I later told Brownie that she was the best protector ever!

PHOTO - 15 By the third week after Hurricane Katrina, we were rescuing severely dehydrated and starved animals. This dog was one of the more severe cases, but fortunately, he bounced back after we got him fluids, food, and water.

PHOTO - 16 Marking houses was one way that all of the different response crews could communicate with one another. Federal agents, local officials, military personnel, and our animal rescue teams relied on this information to get our jobs done.

PHOTO - 17 The pews in this little church were moved around by the flood, and there was mud everywhere when Perry and I stopped to feed three dogs that had been left upstairs.

PHOTO - 13

PHOTO - 14

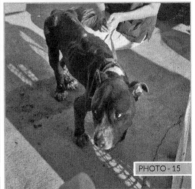

PHOTO - 15

PHOTO - 16

PHOTO - 17

PHOTO GALLERY
The Streets of New Orleans

PHOTO - 18   The National Guard not only kept the peace, but troops helped us save the animals. Many dogs roamed the streets and formed packs to hunt for food.

PHOTO - 19   This is the road where I sensed a dog, and then spotted him in a puddle of water trying to stay cool. The three Guardsmen, Jax, and I were all crying as I carried him to our van.

PHOTO - 20   There was lots of activity at the base camp we used the days we worked with the National Guard. The big, air-conditioned Texas SPCA truck is in the background. The trailer had a room where a vet could examine and treat our rescues, and there were straps in the back to secure the kennels for transport.

PHOTO - 18

PHOTO - 19

PHOTO - 20

{ 313 }

PHOTO GALLERY
Working as a Team

PHOTO-21   I was asked to help with a litter of pit bull puppies who had been abused by their owner and had no will to live. Once I explained to them that they were safe and the bad man was gone, they began eating, drinking, and trying to stand again.

PHOTO-22   After the volunteers nursed the puppies back to health, one of the boys shows off how well he's doing and how happy he is to be going to a new home.

PHOTO-23   Psychologist Lois Abrams played a ukulele and sang to the animals. She was a great comfort to the pets and rescuers alike.

PHOTO-24   This is the last of the three chows we rescued, after feeding them on the street for several days. He eluded Perry and me, but Cindy and Anthony finally were able to bring him in and reunite him with his two siblings already at Lamar-Dixon.

PHOTO-25   Kat Destreza of the Louisiana Society for the Prevention of Cruelty to Animals led the effort to rescue the animals from New Orleans.

PHOTO-26   Horses were kept in two of the barns, and the volunteers who fed, watered, and exercised them were a well-organized group.

PHOTO - 21

PHOTO - 22

PHOTO - 23

PHOTO - 24

PHOTO - 25

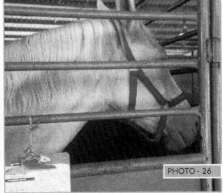

PHOTO - 26

PHOTO GALLERY
Pancake Gets to Safety

PHOTO-27   Rescuers cut a hole in the roof (see arrow) to get Pancake out of his collapsed home. He was the only one in his family—animal or human—who survived.

PHOTO-28   Pancake and I wait by the house while Jax and the firemen cut down a chain-link fence so we can get him out of his yard and into our van. The dog was very weak, so we moved at his pace.

PHOTO-29   The spray-painted sign "LIVE DOG TO REAR" alerted everyone that there was a pet to be saved. Once we got Pancake out, we added "1 DOG TAKEN TO LASPCA 9/22" to tell all of the other teams that the dog had been rescued.

PHOTO-30   Back at Lamar-Dixon, Pancake shows everyone how happy he is to be free. See how bloated his belly is from starvation.

Photographs courtesy of Dr. Lois Abrams, Dr. Debra Campbell, Susan Keyes, Perry Nelson, and Patti Williams. There are additional photos and videos on Terri Steuben's website and YouTube site. Visit www.TerriSteuben.com.

PHOTO - 27

PHOTO - 28

PHOTO - 29

PHOTO - 30

ACKNOWLEDGEMENTS

There are many individuals who helped me put this project together. As with all books, it takes the right people coming in to help at the right time to turn a concept into a reality. I am grateful that, when I put the word out for assistance, everyone pitched in where they could.

My Katrina journal wouldn't have become a book without Diana and Dave Eastman. Diana encouraged me to write my stories, then took on the huge job of editing and coordinating the book production. Dave was a diligent editor, removing unnecessary extras and making the text more clear for readers. I am very thankful to have both Diana and Dave in my life—all because a friend referred them to me when they needed help with two rescue kittens, Rocket and Sparkey. These lovely cats contributed to both of my books, helping us humans "get it right."

Thanks to the rest of the team that enabled me to make this book the best it could be: Stacey Francis, Terry LaMotte, Melinda Oldfield, Therese Quesada, and Adrienne Sweetser.

I was able to make it through my two-week journey to Katrina and the writing of this book because of Pamela Keller. She helped me prepare for my trip and offered me support throughout my deployment. With her military background, she was a genius when it came to getting me packed effectively, making sure I took extra socks, a small pup tent I wouldn't have to share, and a lightweight duffle and rolling bag to hold all of my gear. Pamela is always there for me, by my side, cheering me on with my animal adventures.

Also, thank you to my "best girls" Aspen (now in doggie heaven), Maggie, and Olivia, who said, *"Mom, you have to go!"* The three of them chatted telepathically with me in the early mornings, while I drove from Lamar-Dixon to New Orleans. My new addition NoElle was a puppy when I wrote this book. She watched my mind's eye as the events unfolded and became very afraid at certain points. I told her it all happened before she was born and she should look at it as a story. She would say, *"Ok, but I don't like this part."*

I was one of a huge number of trained volunteer responders, officials, and caring citizens who went to help out along the Gulf Coast after Hurricane Katrina. I am proud to have deployed with such a talented group of people. Their dedication to saving the pets and their triumphs in the face of adversity are reflected in every page of this book.

Thank you to the animal advocacy organizations that I've worked with and the responders whom I deeply respect, including: Inga Gibson, Wayne Pacelle, Dave Pauli, Melissa Rubin, Eric Sakach, and Christine Wolf of The Humane Society of the United States; Kathryn Destreza of the American Society for the Prevention of Cruelty to Animals; Perry Nelson of the Louisiana Search and Rescue Dog Team; Debra Campbell, D.V.M., of the Pet Haven Animal Hospital; Lois Abrams, Ph.D., and Susan Keyes of the Surf City Animal Response Team; Joy Falk of the City of Laguna Beach Animal Control; Brynne Van Putten of Critter Catchers; Mindy Miller of Miss Kitty's Rescue; agriculture educator Patti Williams; HSUS volunteer Karen Thoms; Valerie Schomberg of the City of Newport Beach Police Department Animal Control; Debi Geary, Debbie Kelly, and Jeff Kelly of the Equestrian Training Institute; and Jeff Kermode of the Irvine Police Department.

In particular, I want to give a shout-out to a special group of those responders: Joy, Brynne, Mindy, Karen, Patti, and Valerie. These amazing women supported me as I wrote this book and shared their memories and photos of Katrina. I am grateful for their friendship and thankful that our chats over dinner about our adventures in response are largely in the past—and that now we can all just talk about our everyday lives!

Finally, let me acknowledge the pet owners in New Orleans and across the country whose lives were impacted by Hurricanes Katrina and Rita. To those who lost their animals in this tragedy, who were reunited with their pets, and who adopted displaced animals: you have a special place in my heart. Thank you for the love and protection you provide to the cats, dogs, birds, horses, rabbits, and all of the other animals that we are lucky to have and share this world with us.

THE HUMANE SOCIETY
OF THE UNITED STATES

The Humane Society of the United States
offers information on how to keep your pets safe
in natural disasters and everyday emergencies.
The organization's website contains checklists and tips for
protecting pets, horses, and farm animals. It also offers
information for those interested in becoming a trained
HSUS Animal Rescue Volunteer and what individuals
can do to help spot and report animal abuse.

Go to *www.HumaneSociety.org.*

ABOUT THE AUTHOR

Terri Steuben gives animals a voice. Terri is an animal communicator who has counseled thousands of pet owners for 25 years. Using her psychic abilities and practical experience, she helps people better understand their animals and solve behavior problems. Terri also has the special gift of medical intuition that allows her to feel where animals are experiencing pain or discomfort; her insight enables pet owners and veterinarians to pinpoint health issues and provide the appropriate care. She is a Reiki master and uses this alternative therapy with animals to address a range of health concerns.

In addition, Terri is a trained volunteer who serves on disaster response teams to keep animals safe in emergencies. She has been deployed with The Humane Society of the United States National Disaster Animal Response Team, the United Animal Nations Emergency Animal Rescue Service, and the Mounted Assistance Unit Equestrian Training Institute. She is called in to work alongside law enforcement officials in search-and-seizure operations involving animal hoarding and abuse.

Terri is a public speaker and trainer, who presents on animal communication techniques, holistic health approaches, and emergency preparedness.

Terri's first book, *Secrets of a Pet Whisperer: Stop Telling Your Animals to Misbehave*, is a how-to communication guide for pet owners that also contains information and checklists on preparing for emergencies.

To learn more about Terri Steuben, go to her website at *www.TerriSteuben.com.*